SOURCES IN EUROPEAN POLITICAL HISTORY
Volume 2: DIPLOMACY AND INTERNATIONAL AFFAIRS

Also by Chris Cook

*SOURCES IN EUROPEAN POLITICAL HISTORY, Volume 1: THE
  EUROPEAN LEFT *(with Geoff Pugh)*
*SOURCES IN EUROPEAN POLITICAL HISTORY, Volume 3: WAR
  AND RESISTANCE *(forthcoming, with Tim Kirk and Bob Moore)*
*SOURCES IN BRITISH POLITICAL HISTORY, 1900–1951 (6 vols)
  (with Philip Jones, Josephine Sinclair and Jeffrey Weeks)
*THE AGE OF ALIGNMENT: Electoral Politics in Britain, 1922–29
*A SHORT HISTORY OF THE LIBERAL PARTY, 1900–88
 THE SLUMP *(with John Stevenson)*
*BY-ELECTIONS IN BRITISH POLITICS *(with John Ramsden)*
*BRITISH HISTORICAL FACTS, 1760–1830 *(with John Stevenson)*
*EUROPEAN POLITICAL FACTS, 1789–1848 *(with John Paxton)*
*EUROPEAN POLITICAL FACTS, 1848–1918 *(with John Paxton)*
*EUROPEAN POLITICAL FACTS, 1918–1984 *(with John Paxton)*
 THE LONGMAN ATLAS OF MODERN BRITISH HISTORY,
  1700–1970 *(with John Stevenson)*
*THE POLITICS OF REAPPRAISAL, 1918–39 *(with Gillian Peele)*
*THE DECADE OF DISILLUSION *(ed. with David McKie)*
*CRISIS AND CONTROVERSY: Essays in Honour of A. J. P. Taylor
  (with Alan Sked)
 POST-WAR BRITAIN: A Political History *(with Alan Sked)*
 THE LONGMAN HANDBOOK OF MODERN BRITISH HISTORY,
  1714–1987 *(with John Stevenson)*
 THE LABOUR PARTY *(ed. with Ian Taylor)*
 TRADE UNIONS IN BRITISH POLITICS *(ed. with Ben Pimlott)*

Also by Bob Moore

REFUGEES FROM NAZI GERMANY IN THE NETHERLANDS,
  1933–40

Also published by Macmillan

SOURCES IN EUROPEAN POLITICAL HISTORY

Volume 2
Diplomacy and International Affairs

Chris Cook
Head of Department in the Faculty of Humanities,
Polytechnic of North London

with

Tim Kirk
Lecturer in History, University of Warwick

and

Bob Moore
Lecturer in History, Bristol Polytechnic

MACMILLAN

First published 1989

Published by
THE MACMILLAN PRESS LTD
Houndmills, Basingstoke, Hampshire RG21 2XS
and London
Companies and representatives
throughout the world

Typeset by Latimer Trend & Company Ltd, Plymouth

Printed in Hong Kong

British Library Cataloguing in Publication Data
Sources in European political history.
Vol. 2: Diplomacy and international
affairs.
1. Europe. Political events, 1848–1985.
Historical sources: Archives—Lists
I. Cook, Chris, 1945–   II. Kirk, Tim, 1958
III. Moore, Bob, 1954–
016.9402′8
ISBN 0–333–27775–9

CONTENTS

PREFACE AND ACKNOWLEDGEMENTS

A very large number of people helped in the preparation of this volume. Whilst it would be impossible to thank all by name, certain special acknowledgements must be made. An extremely deep debt of gratitude is due to the many scores of archivists and librarians who responded so readily and so helpfully to the letters and questionnaires sent out during the compilation of this volume.

The compilation of the first two volumes in the *Sources in European Political History* series has taken the compilers to archive centres in many parts of Europe. Particular thanks must be given to our colleagues in Vienna, namely Dr Elizabeth Springer of the *Haus-Hof- und Staatsarchiv*; Dr Elizabeth Klamper and Dr Siegwald Ganglmeier; Dr Eva Irblich and Dr Gerhard Renner of the Austrian National Library; the staff of the *Verein für Geschichte der Arbeiterbewegung*; and Dr Mikoletzky of the *Allgemeines Verwaltungsarchiv*. At the *Bundesarchiv*, Koblenz, the project's thanks are due to the Director and his staff, in particular to Dr Werner Krause, who gave most generously of his time and made available unpublished material on the holdings of the archive. For her work on the project in Brussels, grateful thanks go to Ms Marie Bittlestone. The staff of the League of Nations Archive in Geneva gave generously of their time. Professor Paul Preston gave very useful information on archives in Spain. In London, particular thanks are due to the staff of the German Historical Institute and the Sikorski Institute and Polish Museum. Among personal friends and colleagues who have given practical assistance thanks are due to Chris Lee, Angela Raspin, Julia Sheppard and Richard Storey.

A very major debt is due to the Polytechnic of North London for facilitating the production of this volume. The initial research assistance was made available by the allocation of funds by the Polytechnic. The granting of a one-year secondment from my normal duties during the 1986–87 academic year by the Director of the Polytechnic made the early work on this volume possible. I must record my thanks for the support of the subsequent Director, Leslie Wagner, and the Dean, Sandra Ashman, for their help seeing this volume through to completion.

A wide variety of sources, published and unpublished, have been used in the compilation of this volume. A more detailed listing is given in the Select Bibliographical Note (Appendix I). A very special mention must be made, however, of the absolutely invaluable guide for Germany produced by Professor Mommsen. No words of praise can do justice to the value of this monumental work. Although this volume includes known additions and changes to that of Professor Mommsen, its debt to that pioneering volume remains very high. Similarly, the guide on the papers of French politicians has been invaluable.

The paucity of existing published guides to European archives only serves to re-emphasise the debt owed to the scores of archivists who so readily cooperated in the production of this volume.

Finally, three remaining acknowledgements are needed. In London, my thanks are due to my publishing editor Tim Farmiloe for his help and support in seeing this volume through to publication. In Amsterdam, where the original idea for this series was born, my debt is a wider one. It is to all those friends and colleagues who made successive visits to that delightful city so pleasant. And, to my co-authors Tim Kirk and Bob Moore, my very deep thanks for the many hours of labour, as well as good company, that went into this volume.

Polytechnic of North London

CHRIS COOK

INTRODUCTION

This is the second volume in the planned series of *Sources in European Political History*. The first volume aimed to provide an outline guide to the surviving personal papers of over 1000 individuals active in the socialist, labour, radical and revolutionary movements in Europe.[1] The period covered was broadly from 1870 through to the end of the Second World War in 1945. This second volume aims to provide a similar guide to the private papers of a further 1000 individuals active in European diplomacy and international affairs over a similar chronological period. The scope of the volume embraces not only statesmen and ministers, but diplomats, ambassadors and the many others involved in the formulation and implementation of foreign policy.

It is hoped that within this volume the historian and researcher will find material on the major themes of European diplomatic history and international relations. This volume, however, is concerned only with private papers. The official and governmental archives for the diplomatic historian are the subject of the invaluable guide produced by D. H. Thomas and L. Case.[2]

There are, of course, enormous difficulties in attempting to assemble information on private papers. The compilers of this volume are only too aware of the limitations of producing a guide such as this. Most entries were compiled from questionnaires sent to record offices. The entries in this volume in no way imply that the papers cited are necessarily available. In all cases research students should write to the institution concerned to check availability and access. In many cases, record repositories may be able to provide the researcher with unpublished finding aids and fuller details of collections of papers in addition to the necessarily often sparse information outlined in this volume.

There are very major gaps in the private papers available for the diplomatic historian during this period. The turbulent history of Europe during the last century, with such events as the Russian Revolution and the Nazi dictatorship, have meant that papers have either not been kept or have been lost. Police raids, prosecution, exile and banishment have led to the loss of invaluable material for the historian. This problem is particularly acute, not just for those countries suffering fascist dictatorship, but also for the countries of Eastern Europe.

This gap is partly compensated for by the rich holdings of Russian and Eastern European material in archive centres both in Western Europe and North America. Particular mention must be made of the holdings in North America at both the Hoover Institution on War, Revolution and Peace at Stanford University, California, and also at Columbia University Library.

Finally, the compilers would appeal to historians and archivists to inform them of any known additions and changes to the information cited here for use in future editions. Correspondence should be addressed to Dr Chris Cook, c/o International Archives Survey, Polytechnic of North London, Prince of Wales Road, Kentish Town, London NW5 3LB.

Notes
1. Chris Cook and Geoff Pugh, *Sources in European Political History: Vol I: The European Left* (Macmillan, 1987)
2. D. H. Thomas and L. Case, *The New Guide to the Diplomatic Archives of Western Europe.*

LIST OF ABBREVIATIONS

ABA   *Arbeijderbevaegelsens Bibliotek og Arkiv*
(Labour Movement Library and Archive, Copenhagen)

AdsD   *Archiv der sozialen Demokratie*
(Social Democratic Archive)

AMSAB   *Archief en Museum van de Socialistische Arbeidersbeweging*
(Socialist and Labour Movement Archive, Ghent)

AN   *Archives Nationales*
(National Archives, Paris)

ARAB   *Arbetarrörelsens arkiv och bibliotek*
(Archive and Library of the Swedish Labour Movement,
Stockholm)

AVA   *Allgemeines Verwaltungsarchiv*
(General Administration Archive, Vienna)

BA   *Bundesarchiv*
(West German Federal Archive, Koblenz)

BA/MA   *Bundesarchiv/Militärarchiv*
(West German Federal Military Archive, Freiburg im Breisgau)

CDU   *Christlichdemokratische Union*
Christian Democratic Union, West Germany

DÖW   *Dokumentionsarchiv des öestericichischen Widerstande*
Documentation Archives of the Austrian Resistance

FDP   *Freidemokrastische Partei*
(Free Democratic Party, West Germany)

FNSP   *Fondation National des Sciences Politiques*
(National Foundation of Political Science)

NSDAP   *Nationalsozialistische Deutsche Arbeiterpartei*
(National Socialist German Workers (Nazi) Party)

OURS   *Office Universitaire de Recherche Socialiste*

PA/AA   *Politisches Archiv des Auswärtigen Amtes*
(Political Archive, West Geman Foreign Office)

VGA   *Verein für Geschichte der Arbeiterbewegung*
(Association for the History of the Labour Movement)

WSLA   *Wiener Stadt- und Landesarchiv*
(Vienna City/State Archive)

NOTE ON SOURCES CITED

As mentioned in the Preface and Acknowledgements, certain existing published guides have been of invaluable help in the compilation of this volume. These are constantly referred to in the text. They are:

Cassels, A.	*Italian Foreign Policy 1918–1945* (Wilmington, Delaware, 1981).
Kimmich, C. M.	*German Foreign Policy 1918–1945* (Wilmington, Delaware, 1981).
Milewski, A. *et al.*	*Guide to the Archives of the Polish Institute and Sikorski Museum* (London, 1985).
Mommsen, Wolfgang A.	*Die Nachlässe in den deutschen Archiven* (*Mit Ergänzungen aus anderen Beständen*) *Teil I* (Boppard am Rhein 1981).
	Die Nachlässe in den deutschen Archiven (*Mit Ergänzungen aus anderen Beständen*) *Teil II* (Boppard am Rhein, 1983).
Toustier Bonazzi, Chantal de, and Pourcelet, François (eds)	*Guide des Papiers des Ministres et secrétaires d'état de 1871 a 1974* (Paris, 1978).
Young, Robert J.	*French Foreign Policy 1918–1945* (Wilmington, Delaware, 1981).

A

ACKER, Achille van (b. 1895)

Belgian socialist politician. Prime Minister, February 1945 to January 1946, March–July 1946 and 1954–58.

The *Archives Générales du Royaume*, Brussels, has van Acker's archive but this has not yet been classified and is for this reason inaccessible. The AMSB, Ghent, possesses a *Fonds* van Acker, consisting of twenty-four boxes of papers including correspondence, notes and reports, covering van Acker's career 1944–58. Permission is needed for consultation. The *Archief en Museum voor het Vlaamse Cultuurleven*, Antwerp, has a collection (ref. A.1835) which includes documents, letters and manuscripts. The extent of the collection is unknown.

ADENAUER, Konrad (1876–1967)

German politician. Mayor of Cologne and later leader of the Christian Democratic Union. First Federal Chancellor of post-war Germany 1949–63.

His personal papers are at the *Stiftung Bundeskanzler Adenauerhaus* in Rhöndorf am Rhein, where further information is available.

ADLERCREUTZ, Axel Gustaf (1821–80)

Swedish Government Minister 1870–74.

A collection of Adlercreutz's personal papers is in private hands.

AEGIDI, Ludwig (1825–1901)

German academic and public servant. Professor of Law at the University of Berlin. Counsellor to the German Foreign Office.

A small collection (0.06m) of his papers covering the years 1842–85 is at the *Geheimes Staatsarchiv* in Berlin. It consists of personal papers, printed material and newspapers. Other papers have been destroyed. (Source: Mommsen, *op. cit.*)

AEHRENTHAL, Count Alois Lexa von (1854–1912)

Austrian diplomat and politician. Austro-Hungarian Ambassador in St Petersburg 1899–1906; Prime Minister and Foreign Minister of Austria–Hungary 1906–12.

The *Haus-, Hof- und Staatsarchiv*, Vienna, has five boxes of his papers, including correspondence with Berchtold, Burián, Fürstenberg, Goluchowski, Kálnoky, Macchio, Mensdorff-Pouilly and Szécsen. The collection also contains press cuttings and excerpts from reports from St Petersburg. There is also an Aehrenthal family archive in the Žitenice branch of the state archive in Litoměřice, Czechoslovakia. In addition, a one-volume typescript of memoirs on relations between Austria–Hungary and Russia 1872–94 (in German) is in the Hoover Institution, Stanford University, California.

AGHNIDES, Thanassis (fl. 1920s)

Greek diplomat and international public servant. Under-Secretary General of the League of Nations; Greek Ambassador in London; Greek delegate to the United Nations.

The League of Nations Archive in Geneva is in the process of acquiring his papers.

AHLEFELD-LAURVIGEN, Carl William (1860–1923)

Danish diplomat and Foreign Minister 1908–09 and 1910–13.

The *Rigsarkiv*, Copenhagen, has one packet of his papers. The collection, covering the years 1890–1927, includes individual letters and political memoranda.

AHRENS, Georg (1890–1967)

German diplomat attached to the German embassy in Washington 1914–17. He held various consular posts in the 1950s.

A small collection (0.05m) of his papers is held at the Political Archive of the Federal German Foreign Office in Bonn. It includes a speech on Walther Rathenau 1947, and correspondence (1917–47) with diplomats and Foreign Office officials. (Source: Mommsen, *op. cit.*)

ÅKERHIELM af MARGRETELUND frih. Johan Gustaf Nils Samuel

Swedish Foreign Minister 1889 and Minister of State 1889–91.

A collection of Åkerhielm af Margretelund's papers is in private hands.

ALDROVANDI MARESCOTTI, Luigi (b. 1876)

Italian diplomat. Secretary-General of the Italian delegation to the Paris Peace Conference 1919; Italian minister, Sofia 1920–23 and Cairo 1923–24; Ambassador, Buenos Aires 1924–26 and Berlin 1926–29; Italian delegate to the League of Nations 1935–36.

A collection of his papers is held at the Historical Archive of the Italian Ministry of Foreign Affairs. In addition, one folder of his memoirs is available at the Hoover Institution, Stanford University, California.

ALFIERI, Edoardo Dino (1866–1966)

Italian politician and diplomat. Under-Secretary of State 1929–32, 1935–36; Ambassador to the Holy See 1939–40. Ambassador to Berlin 1940–43.

The *Archivio Centrale dello Stato*, Rome, has thirteen files of papers including material relevant to relations with Germany during the Second World War. The collection covers the period 1915 to 1960. (Source: *Guida Generale*.)

ALLARD de CHATEAUNEUF, (fl. 1914–18)

French diplomat. Embassy counsellor, Berne.

The *Archives Départementales de l'Isère*, has a collection of papers relating to public opinion in Germany and Austria–Hungary during the First World War (ref. 1 J 195 [1–6]).

ALPHAND, Charles (b. 1879)

French diplomat. Delegate to the Hague Conference 1923; Consul-General, The Hague 1924; delegate to the disarmament conference; Minister to Dublin 1930; Ambassador, Moscow 1933–36 and Berne 1936.

A collection of his papers is held at the Archive of the Ministry of Foreign Affairs, Quai d'Orsay, Paris, in the Collection *Papiers d'Agents* (6). The collection comprises one box of documents covering the years 1904–35 (Cote 227). (Source: Young, *op. cit.*)

AMEGLIO, Giovanni (1854–1921)

Italian general and colonial administrator. Served in Italian campaigns of 1887, 1893 and 1895–97; Far Eastern campaign 1902–05; Governor of Cirenaica for five years following the Turkish-Italian war 1913–18.

The material held by the *Archivio Centrale dello Stato*, Rome, covers the period 1894–1918, but relates primarily to the period 1915–18, when Ameglio was Governor of Tripolitania and Cirenaica. The collection consists of twenty-one files with a catalogue. (Source: *Guida Generale*.)

ANDRÁSSY, Gyula (Julius) (1823–90)

Hungarian aristocrat and follower of Kossuth. Exiled in London and Paris, he returned in 1857 and was eventually appointed Hungarian Prime Minister and Minister of Defence on the establishment of the Dual Monarchy in 1867. Appointed Foreign Minister of Austria–Hungary in 1871 and represented his country at the Congress of Berlin before resigning soon afterwards.

The Hungarian National Archives, Budapest, have a small collection of papers (0.02m) which cover the period 1867–71.

ANXIONNAZ, Paul (b. 1902)

French politician. Member of the consultative Provisional Assembly, Algiers and Paris 1944–45; Secretary of State for the Armed Forces (Navy) 1956–57; air attaché, Copenhagen 1939, Budapest 1940; Representative of Free France in Hungary 1940; Commander-in-Chief of Free French Air Force in the Middle East 1942.

The *Archives Nationales*, Paris, has one file containing official letters written by Anxionnaz as Secretary of State for the Armed Forces (Navy). (Provisional ref. *Entrée* 2658.) (Source: AN, *Guide des Papiers*.)

APPONYI, Count Albert (b. 1846)

Hungarian statesman.

A collection of letters concerning Croatian Home Rule, mainly 1893, is in the British Library (ref. Add. Mss. 43688G).

ARAQUISTAIN, Quevedo Luis (1886–1959)

Spanish diplomat. Ambassador to Paris.

The papers have been placed in the *Archivo Histórico Nacional*, Madrid. No further details available.

ARAX, Tevik Rustu (fl. 1914–18)

Turkish diplomat.

Two volumes (in French) of his typescript memoirs '*La Tragédie de la Paix*' are in the Hoover Institution, Stanford University, California.

ARCISZEWSKI, Tomasz (1877–1955)

Polish socialist politician. Extensive ministerial experience. Prime Minister 1944–47. From 1949, Chairman of the Political Council in London. From 1954, member of the Council of Three.

An extensive collection of papers (33 ft, covering the period 1944–55) is in the Polish Institute and Sikorski Museum, London. The material includes correspondence as Prime Minister 1944–47, as leader of the Polish Socialist Party 1944–54, and material on the crisis following the death of President Raczkiewicz.

ARENDT, L. (fl. 1885–1916)

Belgian public servant. Director-General, Ministry of Foreign Affairs.

The *Archives Générales du Royaume*, Brussels, has a very small collection of his papers, consisting of notes and press cuttings covering the period 1885–1916. These concern the history of the Congo, military questions and Belgian foreign policy, in particular the policy of neutrality.

ARMFELT, Alexander (1794–1876)

Finnish nobleman and State Secretary.

The *Valtionsarkisto*, Helsinki, has a collection of fifty-three files related to Alexander Armfelt which form part of the Armfelt family archive. The files include biographical material, notes and memoirs as well as letters related to his career as State Secretary. There is also correspondence with R.H. Rehbinders, L.G. von Hartmans, Constantin Fischer, Governor-General Menschikoff and A.E. Palmfelt. There are some restrictions on access to this collection.

ARMFELT, Carl Alexander (1850–1925)

Finnish nobleman and State Secretary.

The *Valtionsarkisto*, Helsinki, has a collection of twenty files which relate to Carl Armfelt, and which form part of the Armfelt family archive. The files include correspondence from the years 1859 to 1925 as well as other manuscripts and documents. There are some restrictions on access to this collection.

ARNIM, Harry (fl. 1870s)

German diplomat. Ambassador to Paris to 1874.

The FDH, Frankfurt, has a family archive (ref. G19).

ARNING, Wilhelm (1865–1943)

German doctor and colonial politician.

A collection of sixteen cases of his manuscripts, diaries and lectures is held at the *Niedersächsische Staats- und Universitätsbibliothek* (Göttingen). (Source: Mommsen, *op. cit.*)

ARTII (TEGSTRÖM), Pontus Kaarlo (1878–1936)

Finnish ambassador and diplomat. Ambassador in Moscow and Rome.

The *Valtionsarkisto*, Helsinki, has a collection of eleven boxes which contain letters and documents related to Artii's career as Finnish ambassador in Moscow and Rome, covering the years 1927 to 1936.

ASMIS, Rudolf (1879–1945)

German diplomat, public servant and colonial administrator. Consul in the Belgian Congo 1912–14; member of the German civil administration in Belgium 1914–18; Director of Foreign Trade Department, Foreign Office 1921; Ambassador to Bangkok 1925; Consul General, Sydney 1932; Foreign Office official 1939–44.

A collection of his papers is held at the Political Archive of the Federal German Foreign Office in Bonn. It includes manuscripts of speeches and publications on colonial politics and business, documents, correspondence, printed material, and photographs. There is also material on the native law and economy of Togo, where he was an administrator before the First World War, and on Germany's policy on Belgium. There is also some material on the Far East. (Source: Mommsen, *op. cit.*)

ASSER, Tobias Michael Carel (1838–1913)

International lawyer and prime mover in the Hague Conferences on Private International Law. Chairman of the Netherlands Central Council for Internationalism.

The *Algemeen Rijksarchief*, The Hague, has an Asser family archive (5.2m) which includes material on T.M.C. Asser (Inventory 2.21.14: Coll. 238). Other papers can be found in the Asser family archive, Amsterdam; the *Gemeentearchief*, Rotterdam; and letters to Asser (1899–1913) in the *Abraham Kuyperstichting*, Free University, Amsterdam.

AUBARET, Louis (fl. 1860s–70s)

French diplomat. Consul in Bangkok 1864–68.

One box of papers is in the archive of the French Foreign Ministry, Paris.

AUERSPERG, Adolf Prince (1821–85)

Austrian politician. Minister-President of Austria 1871–79.

There is an Auersperg family archive deposited at the *Haus-, Hof- und Staatsarchiv*, Vienna. However, the collection is privately owned, and permission is required to use it.

AUERSPERG, Karl Prince (1814–90)

Austrian politician. Minister-President of Austria 1867.

Auersperg's papers are in the Auersperg family archive at the *Haus-, Hof- und Staatsarchiv*, Vienna. The archive is privately owned and permission is required to use it.

AURIOL, Vincent (1884–1966)

French politician. Minister of State 1945–46; President of the Republic 1947–54.

The FNSP holds about 150 boxes of documents relating to his life and political career, divided into four volumes. The first volume covers Auriol's early career up to 1937, and includes material relating to the problem of interallied debts and his trip to the United States in connection with this matter. The second volume falls into two parts. The first part covers his period of office at the Finance Ministry (1936–37); the second contains material relating to the Spanish Civil War, the administrations of Blum, Daladier and Chautemps, and the beginning of the Second World War. The third volume also falls into two parts. The first of these contains material relating to his arrest and imprisonment; correspondence from the years 1941–43; his activity in Algeria 1943–44. The second part covers the period between the end of the war and his presidency 1944–46, and contains material on the Toulouse region after the liberation; relations between the Socialist Party and the Communist Party; Auriol's presidency of the Foreign Affairs Commission of the Consultative Assembly in Paris, and international problems; the Constituent Assembly and de Gaulle's government; and Auriol's election as president of the National Assembly. The fourth volume covers Auriol's presidency and includes files relating to state visits and international relations.

B

BAARNHIELM, Axel Henning Ambjörn (1868–1920)

Swedish diplomat and consul in Baku.

The *Krigsarkiv*, Stockholm, has a small collection of diary notes for the year 1918 (copies).

BADEN, Max Prinz von (1867–1929)

German politician. Appointed last Chancellor of Imperial Germany in October 1918. He was succeeded in November by Friedrich Ebert following the German revolution.

His papers are held at the Archive of the Margraves of Baden at Schloss Salem in Baden. A collection of his papers is held on microfilm at the Political Archive of the Federal German Foreign Office in Bonn. It includes speeches from October and November 1918.

BADOGLIO, Pietro (1871–1956)

Italian politician, soldier and colonial administrator. Chief of General Staff 1925–40; Governor of Tripolitania and Cirenaica 1929–33; High Commissioner for Colonies in East Africa 1935–36; Viceroy of Ethiopia, May–June 1936; President of the National Research Council (*Consiglio nazionale delle ricerche*) 1937–41; Head of Government 1943–44; Foreign Minister and Minister for Italian Africa 1944.

The *Archivio Centrale dello Stato*, Rome, has twenty-four files and ten boxes of papers covering the period 1925 to 1946. The material relates to the government of Tripolitania and war preparations in East Africa. (Source: *Guida Generale*.)

BAHNSON, Jesper Jespersen (1827–1909)

Danish officer and War Minister.

The *Rigsarkiv*, Copenhagen, holds a collection of his papers, along with those of his second wife Anne Christine *née* Lundsteen. The material covers the years 1844–1911, and includes manuscripts, letters and personal papers.

BAKHMETEFF, Boris Aleksandrovič (1880–1951)

Russian diplomat. Ambassador of the Provisional Government to the United States.

Over eighty-four boxes (about 32 000 items) are held at the Bakhmeteff Archive, Columbia University, New York. The collection contains official documents and materials of the Russian embassy in Washington, correspondence, items relating to the *Natsional'nyi Fond* and to the Humanities Fund, Inc., along with printed material. There are restrictions on access.

BAKHRAT, V.P. (fl. 1910s)

Russian diplomat. Last Tsarist Ambassador to Switzerland.

See under KOLEMIN, I.A.

BANASÍNSKI, Eugeniusz (b. 1886)

Polish consular official. Served in Tokyo, Moscow and Bombay.

A small amount of material is in the Polish Institute and Sikorski Museum, London.

BÁNFFY, Baron Dezsö (1843–1911)

Hungarian Prime Minister 1895–99.

The Hungarian National Archives, Budapest, have a collection of papers (0.88m) covering the period of his ministry 1895–99.

BANNING, Emile (1836–98)

Civil servant. Archivist and ultimately Director-General of the Belgian Ministry of Foreign Affairs; a prolific writer on Belgian foreign policy (neutrality, territorial claims) and colonial policy, in particular. Adviser to Leopold II. Was involved in his geographical conference on Africa, Brussels 1876, and in the African conferences in Berlin 1884–85, the Brussels conference 1889–90, and generally in the negotiations over the international status of the *Etat Indépendant du Congo*.

The *Archives Générales du Royaume*, Brussels, has Banning's papers. They cover his entire career, spanning the second half of the nineteenth century. They consist of notes and memoirs, including those pertaining to the Congo and the international conferences; historical, political and philosophical studies, speeches and articles, also correspondence with, among others: Leopold II (1876–92); Baron Greindl (1877–91); Strauch (1879–88); Baron Beyens (1882–85); Comte de Borchgrave (1871–92); Baron Lambermont (1890–95), and Frère-Orban (1879–94). A further collection is held at the Ministry of Foreign Affairs, Brussels.

BARANDON, Paul (1881–1971)

German diplomat and public servant. German representative at the Anglo-German Court of Arbitration in London 1920–27; Secretariat at the League of Nations, Geneva; Legation Secretary, German Foreign Office 1933–37; Consul-General in Chile 1937–42; Foreign Office delegate to the Reich Plenipotentiary in Denmark 1942–44; Foreign Office representative on Army General Staff 1945. Barandon took up an academic career at Hamburg University after the end of the Second World War.

A collection of his papers is held at the Political Archive of the Federal German Foreign Office in Bonn. It includes reports from Valparaiso, statements as evidence on German policy in Denmark, and notes on National Socialism (0.15m). (Source: Mommsen, *op. cit.*)

BÁRDOSSY, László (1890–1946)

Hungarian diplomat and right-wing politician. Legation Counsellor in London 1932–34; Ambassador in Bucharest 1934–41 and appointed Foreign Minister in February 1941, a post he held until 1944. He also served as Prime Minister from April 1941 to March 1942.

The Hungarian National Archives, Bucharest, have a small collection of Bárdossy papers (0.14m) relating to the year 1942.

BARGEN, Werner von (1898–1975)

German diplomat. Foreign Office representative to the military commander in Belgium 1940–44. Ambassador to Baghdad 1961–63.

A very small collection of his papers (0.01m) is held at the Political Archive of the Federal German Foreign Office in Bonn. It contains personal papers and material on Belgium. (Source: Mommsen, *op. cit.*)

BARRÈRE, Camille (1851–1940)

French diplomat. Embassy secretary, Stockholm and Munich in the early 1880s; delegate to the International Commission on the Suez Canal 1885; ambassador to Berne 1894 and Rome 1897.

A collection of seven volumes and two cartons of his papers is held at the Archive of the Ministry of Foreign Affairs, Quai d'Orsay, Paris, in the Collection *Papiers d'Agents (6) (Cote 8)*. (Source: Young, *op. cit.*)

BASILY, Nicholas Alexandrovič de (1883–1963)

Russian diplomat and statesman. Deputy Director, Chancellery of Foreign Affairs 1911–14; Council of Ministry of Foreign Affairs 1917.

A large collection of papers (twenty-five boxes) covering the period 1881 to 1956 is in the Hoover Institution, Stanford University, California. The collection includes correspondence, memoranda and notes on Russian politics and diplomacy, including Russian conduct in the First World War and the abdication of the Tsar.

BATTENBERG, Alexander, Prinz von, Graf von Hartenau (1854–93)

Prince of Bulgaria 1879–86.

There are two collections of Battenberg's papers. The first is in the Mountbatten Archive, Broadlands, England. The second is in private ownership. (Source: Mommsen, *op. cit.*, II, 4379.)

BAUDOUIN, Paul-Louis-Arthur (1894–1964)

Under-Secretary to the Prime Minister, Secretary of the War Cabinet and War Committee 1940; Under-Secretary of State for Foreign Affairs 5–16 June 1940; Minister of Foreign Affairs 16 June to 12 July 1940; Minister-Secretary of State for Foreign Affairs 12 July to 28 October 1940; Minister-Secretary of State to the Prime Minister 1940–41.

The archive of the Ministry of Foreign Affairs has five boxes of papers (ref. *Papiers* 40, *Inventaire* n. 296), donated by Baudouin's family in 1964. The contents relate to the armistices with Germany and Italy; Franco-British relations; relations between France and the United States, Spain and the Levant; the Syrian question; propaganda; the Japanese ultimatum; the Indo-China question; press and censorship. The collection covers the period December 1939 to October 1940. Access will be possible when the series 1939–45 is released. (Source: AN, *Guide des Papiers*.)

BEAUFORT, jhr. J.A.A.H. de (1880–1960)

Counsellor at the Dutch Ministry of Foreign Affairs.

The *Algemeen Rijksarchief*, The Hague, has an extensive collection of papers (22.5m) related to the de Beaufort family (Inventory 2.21.183: Coll. 343). Other papers can be found at the *Rijksarchief*, Utrecht, in the de Beaufort family archive.

BEAUFORT, Willem Hendrik de (1845–1918)

Dutch Foreign Minister 1897–1901.

The *Algemeen Rijksarchief*, The Hague, has an extensive collection of papers (22.5m) related to the de Beaufort family (Inventory 2.21.183; Coll. 343). Other papers can be found at the *Rijksarchief*, Utrecht, in the de Beaufort family archive.

BECK, Józef (1894–1944)

Polish Foreign Minister 1932–39.

Three folders of papers are in the Pilsudski Institute of America, New York. The collection includes correspondence, minutes of conversations and interviews and press cuttings, including material on his planned escape from Romania and the manuscript of his book, *The Last Report*.

BECK, Max Wladimir von (1854–1943)

Austrian public servant and politician. Minister-President of Austria 1906–08.

The AVA, Vienna, has a substantial collection (thirty-nine boxes) of his papers, covering the years 1887–1907. The holding contains material on the occupation and annexation of Bosnia–Herzegovina, relations with Hungary, the First World War, and nationality problems. There is also a collection of his correspondence (ref. 27/5).

BECK-FRILS, frh. Hans Joachim (b. 1861)

Swedish diplomat and head of the Political Department of the Swedish Foreign Ministry 1895–99.

The Swedish Foreign Ministry Archives, (*handarkiv*) housed at the *Riksarkiv*, Stockholm, have a small collection of his papers from the year 1899.

BEELAERTS van BLOKLAND, Frans (1872–1956)

Dutch Ambassador to Peking 1909–19, Foreign Minister 1927–33, and adviser to Queen Wilhelmina in London during the Second World War.

The *Algemeen Rijksarchief*, The Hague, has a collection of papers (0.8m) covering the period 1941–44 (Inventory 2.21.183: Coll. 229). For other papers, reference should be made to the archives of the Dutch Ministry of Foreign Affairs.

BEELAERTS van BLOKLAND, jhr. G.H.Th. (d. 1897)

Diplomatic representative in Europe for the Kruger regime 1883–97, and adviser to Paul Kruger at the 1883 Conference in London.

Papers and documents concerning Beelaerts van Blokland can be found in a number of archives. For further details, contact should be made with the Central Register of Private Archives, The Hague.

BELL, Johannes (1868–1949)

German politician. Colonies Minister 1929.

A collection of his papers is held at the *Bundesarchiv*, Koblenz. It contains memoirs, speeches, publications and memoranda relating to the Treaty of Versailles (0.30m). (Source: Mommsen, *op. cit.*)

BELOW, Otto von (1857–1944)

German infantry colonel. Commander-in-Chief, Eight Army. Candidate for the Reich presidency 1925.

The German Federal Military Archive, Freiburg im Breisgau, has a holding of von Below's papers covering the period 1857–1935. The collection includes material related to preparations and campaigns in the First World War in the East, Macedonia, Italy and France; memoirs; and private and service correspondence.
   Additional material on the period after 1918, which until recently was in private ownership, is now in the *Bundesarchiv*, Koblenz. This collection includes material on the *Heimatschutz* (home guard) for 1918; documents on the Eighth Army in Danzig 1919 and on his candidature for the Reich presidency 1925; and manuscripts and publications on historical themes. (0.30m) (Source: Mommsen, *op. cit.*, I, 249; II, 4442.)

BENE, Otto (fl. 1939–45)

German diplomat. Ambassador to Italy 1941.

The *Bundesarchiv*, Koblenz, has a small collection of material related to the resettlement of German nationals from the South Tyrol (0.15m). (Source: Mommsen, *op. cit.*)

BENNIGSEN, Alexander Graf von (1809–93)

German politician. Minister President and Foreign Minister of Hanover.

The *Gräfliches [1] Bennigsen'sches Archiv I, Banteln Kr. Alfeld/Leine*, has a collection of his papers, including his memoirs from the years 1848 to 1853, and his diaries from the years 1843, 1845 and 1850–90 relating to his career in Hanover (0.70m). (Source: Mommsen, *op. cit.*)

BENOIST, Charles (fl. 1920s)

French diplomat.

A collection of papers is housed at the *Institut de France*.

BERCHTOLD, Leopold Count (1863–1942)

Austrian diplomat and politician. Ambassador, St Petersburg 1906–11; Prime Minister and Foreign Minister of Austria–Hungary 1912–15.

The *Haus-, Hof- und Staatsarchiv*, Vienna, has ten boxes of his papers. The first three contain typescripts of his memoirs for the years 1909–14. Box four contains political letters from Archduke Franz Ferdinand and others, and copies of diplomatic letters from Windisch-Graetz, Aehrenthal, Czernin, Hebenlohe and Macchio. The fifth box contains typescript excerpts from his diary, and the rest contain miscellaneous documents and correspondence.

BERGAMASCO Eugenio (fl. 1910s)

Italian politician. Under-Secretary of State for the Navy in the Luzzatti administration 1910–11, and in the Giolitti administration 1911–14.

The *Archivio Centrale dello Stato*, Rome, has nine boxes of correspondence and miscellaneous documents on naval questions. The collection covers the period 1909–24. (Source: *Guida Generale*.)

BERGEN, Karl Ludwig Diego von (1872–1944)

German diplomat. Joined Foreign Service 1895, Political Division 1919. Ambassador, Holy See 1920–43.

The Political Archive, Federal German Foreign Office, Bonn, has copies of papers in a private archive. These include notes and correspondence on German-Vatican relations, Vatican problems and German Catholicism. The collection covers the period 1922–39 (0.02m). (Source: Mommsen, *op. cit.*)

BERGERY, Gaston (1892–1974)

French lawyer, diplomat and politician. General Secretary of Inter-Allied Reparations Commission 1918–24; Director of Cabinet, French Foreign Office 1924–25; Ambassador to USSR 1941.

The Hoover Institution, Stanford University, California has thirty-eight manuscript boxes of papers, including correspondence, telegrams and speeches on the domestic and foreign politics of France during the Second World War. The collection covers the period 1924–73.

BERGSTRÖM, David Kristian (1858–1946)

Swedish diplomat and statesman.

The University Library, Uppsala, has a collection of Bergström's papers which includes forty-six volumes of diaries for the years 1890–1940, and ten files of material related to his government service. There are also other files related to his political career and personal matters.

BERINKEY, Dénes (1871–1948)

Hungarian lawyer and Minister of Justice in the Mihaly Karolyi government. Served as Prime Minister from January to March 1919 before retiring from politics.

The Hungarian National Archives, Budapest, have a small collection of Berinkey papers (0.01m), which relate to the year 1919.

BERLIN, Pavel Abramovič (fl. 1920s)

Russian public servant. Head of the economic department of the Soviet Trade Mission in Germany, France and Britain 1925–1930.

Two boxes of his papers are held by the Bakhmeteff Archive, Columbia University, New York. They comprise reports collected during his work for the Soviet Trade Mission.

BERNHOFT, Hermann Anker (1869–1958)

Danish diplomat.

A collection of four volumes and eight packets of his papers is held at the *Rigsarkiv*, Copenhagen.

BERTHELOT, Philippe (1866–1934)

French public servant and son of Marcelin Berthelot (q.v), French Foreign Minister 1895–96. From 1914 Deputy Director, and later (1919) Director of Political and Commercial Affairs at the Foreign Office. Secretary General in the Foreign Office 1920–22 and 1925–33.

A collection of his papers is held at the Archive of the Ministry of Foreign Affairs, Quai d'Orsay, Paris, in the Collection *Papiers d'Agents (6)*. It comprises twenty-two volumes containing material from the years 1914–34 (Cote 10). (Source: Young, *op. cit.*)

BERTHELOT, Pierre-Eugène-Marcelin (1827–1907)

French politician. Minister of Foreign Affairs 1895–96.

M. Daniel Langlois-Berthelot, Paris, has thirty-three boxes of papers relating to Berthelot's academic, scientific and political interests. An inventory is being prepared. (Source: AN, *Guide des Papiers*.)

BERTHEMY, Jules (fl. 1870s)

French diplomat. Minister to Peking 1862–66.

One box and two volumes of papers covering the period 1863–75 are in the archive of the French Foreign Ministry, Paris.

BERTONE, Giovanni Battista (1874–1969)

Italian politician. President of the Italian delegation for Franco-Italian customs union; Minister of Foreign Trade 1949–50.

The *Archivio Centrale dello Stato*, Rome, holds thirty files and twenty-four boxes of papers from the years 1929 to 1966. The collection includes material on European integration. (Source: *Guida Generale*.)

BETHLEN, Count István (1874–1947)

Transylvanian landowner and politician. Leader of the counter-revolution which attempted to overthrow the Hungarian Soviet Republic in 1919. Served as Hungarian Prime Minister from April 1921 to August 1931 and remained influential in Hungarian politics until his death.

The Hungarian National Archives, Budapest, have a collection of Bethlen papers (2.53m) covering the period of his ministry, 1921–31.

BETHMANN-HOLLWEG Theobald von (1856–1921)

German politician. Interior Minister, 1907–09 and Reich Chancellor, 1909–17.

Most of his papers have been lost, but a collection is held at the *Bundesarchiv* Koblenz. The holding consists mainly of political material from the years 1915–18, including documents on submarine warfare (0.05m). There are extant collections of other relevant papers, including those of the Interior Ministry during his tenure of office there, which are at the *Deutsches Zentralarchiv* in Berlin. A collection of papers under Bethmann's name is held at the Political Archive of the Federal German Foreign Office in Bonn, and contains material on pre-1914 foreign policy.

BEUST, Friedrich Ferdinand Graf von (1809–86)

German politician. Foreign Minister, Saxony. Later Chancellor of Austria–Hungary.

The Austrian State Archive (*Haus-, Hof- und Staatsarchiv*), Vienna, has one carton of private correspondence covering the years 1863 to 1871.

BEYENS, Baron Eugène (1855–1934)

Belgian diplomat.

The *Archief en Museum voor het Vlaamse Cultuurleven*, Antwerp, has a collection on Beyens (B. 5385) which includes letters. The extent of the collection is not known. Permission is needed for consultation.

BEYERLE, Konrad (1872–1933)

German politician. Member of the political section of the General-Government of Belgium. Professor of Law at the University of Munich.

The *Deutsches Zentralarchiv*, Potsdam, has a collection of political and academic papers with details of his activity with the General-Government of Belgium, covering the years 1910–29. In addition both the *Stadtarchiv*, Konstanz and the *Rechtsgeschichtliches Institut* of the University of Freiburg im Breisgau have further collections relating mainly to Beyerle's academic activity.

BIANCHI, Leonardo (fl.1914–18)

Italian politician. Minister without Portfolio in the Boselli administration, 1916–17.

The *Archivio Centrale dello Stato*, Rome, holds twenty-four files covering the years 1916 and 1917, and including documents on military sanitaria. (Source: *Guida Generale*.)

BIEGELEBEN, Maximilian Feiherr von (1859–1945)

Ambassador of Hesse in Berlin.

Biegeleben's papers are in the possession of Gräfin Agnes von und zu Hoensbroech, Schloss Turnich, Cologne. The collection comprises personal papers and diaries for the years from 1896 to his death, and includes material on his candidature for the mayoralty of Cologne; reports as ambassador in Berlin between 1913 and 1927; German domestic politics 1913 to 1941; and material on his opposition to the *Schwarzes Korps* 1937–39. There are also some manuscripts and essays.

BIERING, Erik (1876–1964)

Danish businessman and diplomat.

Forty packets of his papers are held at the *Rigsarkiv*, Copenhagen. The material covers the period 1882–1964.

BILDT, Carl Nils Daniel (b. 1850)

Swedish Cabinet Secretary 1886–89.

A collection of his papers can be found at the *Riksarkiv*, Stockholm. Additional material is available at the Swedish Academy, also in Stockholm.

BILDT, Didrik Anders Gillis frh. (1820–94)

Swedish Minister of State 1888–89.

A collection of Bildt's personal papers is still held in private hands.

BILLOT, Albert (fl. 1880s)

French diplomat. Political Director, Ministry of Foreign Affairs 1882–84.

A collection of papers is available in the archive of the French Foreign Ministry, Paris.

BILLY, Robert de (fl. 1922–46)

French diplomat. Ambassador to Tokyo 1926–29.

Thirteen cartons of papers, covering the period 1922–46 are in the archive of the French Foreign Ministry at the Quai d'Orsay, Paris.

BISMARCK, Herbert von (1849–1904)

German politician. Secretary of State at the Foreign Office and Prussian State Minister.

His papers are in the Bismarck family archive. (See under Otto von Bismarck.) (Source: Mommsen, *op. cit.*)

BISMARCK-SCHÖNHAUSEN, Prince Otto von (1815–98)

German politician. Prussian Minister President and Minister for Foreign Affairs 1862–90; Federal Chancellor of the North German League 1867–71; Chancellor of the German Reich.

There are several collections of Bismarck's private papers. Bismarck's *Nachlass* is deposited at the Bismarck family archive at Friedrichsruh, Hamburg. The *Bundesarchiv*, Koblenz, has a collection of 116 reels of microfilm of the political part of the original archive, including the personal *Nachlässe* of Otto and Herbert Bismarck. This collection is described in detail in Lamar Cecil, 'The Bismarck Papers', *Journal of Modern History*, XLVII, no. 3 (September 1975), pp. 505–11. The third collection consists of documents from the 1840s, transcripts of dictation by his son Herbert, and official and personal documents of the young Otto. This collection is also at the *Bundesarchiv*, Koblenz (0.10m). In addition there are a few items in private ownership. (Sources: Mommsen, *op. cit.*, II, 4511; L. Cecil: *The German Diplomatic Service 1871–1914*.)

BIZAUSKAS, K. (fl. 1920s)

Lithuanian diplomat. Minister to the United States of America.

The Hoover Institution, Stanford University, California has one folder from 1924 containing memos on cooperation with the Lithuanian government.

BJÖRNSTJERNA, Oscar Magnus Fredrik (1819–1905)

Swedish Foreign Minister 1872–80.

There is a collection of Björnstjerna's personal papers in the *Riksarkiv*, Stockholm.

BLAU, Otto (1828–79)

German diplomat. Prussian Consul in Trebizond, Turkey and Sarajevo, Serbia 1858–64; Consul General, Sarajevo 1870; Consul General, Odessa 1872–79.

The Political Archive of the German Foreign Office, Bonn, has a holding of Blau's private papers. The collection contains personal papers; material on Persia; reports and travel reports from the period 1858–64; material on his service in Turkey, and as Prussian member of the European Commission for Bosnia–Herzegovina in 1861; and material on Bosnia, Herzegovina and Montenegro, 1861–72. There is also a great deal of private correspondence (0.30m). In addition the US National Archives, Washington, has a microfilm of four packets of documents relating to Blau's diplomatic service, and correspondence from the years 1852–77.

BLEHR, Otto Albert (1847–1927)

Norwegian Minister in Stockholm 1891–93 and 1898–1902. Prime Minister 1902–03 and 1921–23. Later Norwegian delegate to the League of Nations.

The *Riksarkiv*, Oslo, has a collection of documents (16.0m) consisting of correspondence, political and personal papers, and papers on the peace movement and the League of Nations. The whole collection covers the years 1891–1927 (Pa. 233).

BLODNIEKS, Adolfs (1889–1962)

Prime Minister of Latvia 1933.

His memoirs on Latvian politics and the 1934 *coup d'état* are in the Hoover Institution, Stanford University, California.

BLÜCHER, Adolf (1883–1968)

German diplomat. Chancellor of the German embassy in Bucharest 1925–42. German Consul, Bucharest 1942–44.

Blücher's papers are in private ownership, but the Political Archive of the German Foreign Office, Bonn, has copies. The material includes notes from his memoirs relating to his service in Bucharest, 1914–18 and 1925–44, and from his time as a Soviet prisoner of war from 1944.

16

BLÜCHER, Wipert von (1883–1963)

German Ambassador in Tehran and Helsinki.

A small collection (0.25m) of his papers is held at the Political Archive of the Federal German Foreign Office in Bonn. It contains his memoirs (1918–44), diaries (1931–35) and reports from Iran and Finland. (Source: Mommsen, *op. cit.*)

BLUM, Léon (1872–1950)

French politician. Prime Minister 1937; Deputy Prime Minister 1938; Prime Minister and Treasury Minister 1938; President of the Provisional Government and Foreign Minister, December 1946 to January 1947; Deputy Prime Minister 1948.

Blum's papers were deposited at the FNSP by Mme Léon Blum and M. Robert Blum in 1971 and 1976. The collection comprises 145 files including material on his literary and journalistic activity; the formation of the Popular Front government; and the Riom trials. The archive is divided into seven parts. The first part covers the years 1880 to 1933, and is subdivided into three sections dealing with his literary, political and journalistic activity respectively. The second of these sections includes material on his early years in politics, his speeches – including those in the Chamber – from 1920 to 1936, material relating to national and international socialist congresses, together with notes and correspondence. The second part covers the years 1934 to 1940, and consists mainly of material relating to the popular front and the Blum administration. The third part (1940–45) covers the Second World War, Blum's imprisonment and the Riom trials. The material includes his memoirs of 1940, documents relating to his imprisonment, correspondence, and documents relating to the Riom trials, including Blum's notes of his own defence. The fifth part (1945–50) covers his mission to the United States and the third Blum administration. This part of the collection includes his activities in connection with UNESCO, Indo-China, Palestine, and European problems. The collection is supplemented by press reports and obituaries after his death in 1950; articles, speeches, and other secondary material; and photographs, tapes, records, films and slides.

BLYTGEN-PETERSEN, Emil (b. 1905)

Danish diplomat.

A collection of six packets of his papers is held at the *Rigsarkiv*, Copenhagen. Covering the years 1940–78, the material relates to the Danish Council in London 1940–45, and talks for the BBC. There is film from Nuremberg 1947, and there are manuscripts of his articles.

BØDTKER, Bernt Anton (1831–1916)

Norwegian Consul-General in Alexandria 1871, Leith 1882 and Hamburg 1891.

The *Riksarkiv*, Oslo, has a collection of papers (0.02m) consisting of manuscripts and printed consular reports related to his diplomatic service (Pa. 122).

BØGGILD, Johannes Erhardt (1878–1929)

Danish diplomat.

A collection of four packets of Bøggild's papers, along with those of his wife are held at the *Rigsarkiv*, Copenhagen. Covering the years 1884–1953, the material includes correspondence, personal papers and manuscripts.

BOHLE, Ernst Wilhelm (b. 1903)

German politician. National Socialist. Foreign Department of NSDAP 1931; *Gau* Inspector, *Gau Ausland* 1932; Head of the Nazi Party's Foreign Organisation (*Auslandsorganisation, AO*) 1933–45; *Gauleiter, Gau Ausland* 1934; Head of the *AO* in the German Foreign Office (with the title of State Secretary, 1937–41).

His private papers are held by the Political Archive of the German Foreign Office in Bonn.

BÖHM, Vilmos (1880–1949)

Hungarian socialist. Minister of Defence in Bela Kun's Soviet Government. After 1945 Hungarian ambassador to Austria, Czechoslovakia and then Sweden.

Seven boxes of Böhm's papers, including letters and annotated books, are in the ARAB, Stockholm. Permission from Böhm's family must be obtained in order to consult this collection.

BÖHME, Georg (b. 1907)

German diplomat. Consul in Odense, Denmark.

Two packets of his papers are held at the *Rigsarkiv*, Copenhagen. The material includes family letters, personal papers and speeches.

BOLLATI, Riccardo (1858–1939)

Italian diplomat.

The *Archivio Centrale dello Stato*, Rome, has one box containing six letters on Italian foreign policy from the years 1915 and 1916. (Source: *Guida Generale*.)

BONIN, Joseph (fl. 1890s–1914)

French diplomat. Served in various posts in Indo-China, 1892–1904.

A collection of papers is in the archive of the French Foreign Ministry, Paris. The papers (35 volumes, covering the period 1901–14) concern China, Indo-China, Tibet and Central Asia. A list is available.

BONN, Moritz Julius (1873–1965)

German public servant. Director of the Commercial High School in Munich and member of the German delegation at Versailles 1919.

The *Bundesarchiv*, Koblenz, has a collection of manuscripts, documents, memoranda and newspaper articles from his whole career. There is also correspondence 1920–35, and 1961–64, and material on his activity in Versailles and on the reparations question.

BONNET, George-Étienne (1889–1973)

French politician and diplomat. Under-Secretary of State to the Prime Minister 1925. French Ambassador to the United States 1936–37. Minister of Foreign Affairs 1938–39.

The Archives of the Ministry of Foreign Affairs has six boxes of papers containing material on Germany and the Danzig question, the Spanish Civil War, the Franco-Italian dispute, Czechoslovakia, the *Petite Entente*, Franco-Russian relations, Anglo-French-Soviet negotiations on Russia, the Balkans, and the Baltic countries. The collection covers the period 1935–42 (ref. Papiers 40, Inventaire no. 299). Access will be possible when the series 1930–39 and 1939–45 are released. (Source: AN, *Guide des Papiers*.)

BONS D'ANTY, Pierre (fl. 1889–1906)

French diplomat. Consular service in China, 1889–98.

Seven volumes and two cartons of papers, covering the period 1889–1906, are available in the archives of the French Foreign Ministry, Paris.

BOON, Dr N.H. (1911–   )

Dutch Foreign Ministry Attaché, Minister and Ambassador who served in Spain, Italy and Venezuela as well as being a Dutch representative to NATO. Most postings are post-1945.

The *Algemeen Rijksarchief*, The Hague, has a collection of papers (1.5m) relating to the post-1945 period (Summary Inventory 2.21.205).

BORCH, Herbert von (1876–1961)

German diplomat. Chargé d'affaires, Peking 1925; director of Far Eastern Section, Foreign Office 1928–31. Ambassador to Peking.

Most of Borch's papers were destroyed in 1944, but the Political Archive of the German Foreign Office in Bonn has a very small collection of material from the years 1920–21 and 1928–30, concerning German-Chinese relations, customs negotiations, and conditions in China. (Source: Mommsen, *op. cit.*)

BORMANN, Martin (b. 1900)

German politician. Chief of Cabinet in the office of Deputy Führer, Rudolf Hess 1933–41; Head of NSDAP Party Chancellery, 1941–45; private secretary to Hitler.

The majority of Bormann's personal papers are privately owned by François Genoud. The Departmental Records Branch, Alexandria, Virginia, USA, has his personal and service correspondence.

BOSBOOM, N. (1855–1937)

Dutch Minister for War 1913–17.

The *Algemeen Rijksarchief*, The Hague, has a collection of papers (0.3m) related to Bosboom's ministerial career 1913–17 (Inventory 2.21.27: Coll. 111). Other papers can be found at the *Gemeentearchief*, The Hague, and reference should also be made to his published work; N. Bosboom, *In Moelijke Omstandigheden, August 1914–Mei 1917* (Gorinchem 1933).

BOSELLI, Paolo (1838–1932)

Italian politician. Prime Minister 1916–17.

The *Archivio Centrale dello Stato*, Rome, has sixteen boxes of material relevant to Boselli's Prime Ministership. (Source: *Guida Generale*.)

BOSSY, Raoul (fl. 1905–69)

Romanian diplomat.

His diaries and memoirs, *c*. 1905–69, have been acquired by the British Library (ref. Add. Mss. 63730–63741).

BOSTRÖM, Erik Gustaf Bernhard (1842–1907)

Swedish Minister of State 1891–1900 and 1902–05.

There is a collection of Boström's personal papers at the *Riksarkiv*, Stockholm.

BOTHNER, Harald (1850–1924)

Norwegian government minister 1905–07.

The *Riksarkiv*, Oslo, has a collection of diaries (0.06m) relating to the year 1905 (Pa. 130).

BOUÉ DE LAPEYRÈRE, Auguste (1852–1924)

French vice-admiral and Navy Minister 1909–11.

The *Service historique de la Marine*, Vincennes, has one box of private papers (ref. GG259). This contains material on the Franco-Chinese commission on the Sino-Annamite border of 1885–87 and 1888. It also contains copies of letters sent by Boué de Lapeyrère between 1891 and 1906, and telegrams sent and received in his capacity as Commander-in-Chief of the Mediterranean naval force in 1914. (Source: AN, *Guide des Papiers*.)

BOURGEOIS, Léon (1851–1925)

French politician. Prime Minister and Minister of the Interior 1895–96. Prime Minister and Minister of Foreign Affairs March–April 1896; Minister of Foreign Affairs March–October 1906 and June 1914; Minister of State 1915–16 and September–November 1917; President of the League of Nations 1920–23.

The Departmental Archives in Marne have seventeen boxes of material, including letters received by Bourgeois (J1109 to 1120, 1451 to 1455). The Archive of the French Ministry of Foreign Affairs at the Quai d'Orsay, Paris, has fifteen boxes of papers concerning international law, the peace treaty, and material relating to the League of Nations. (Source: AN, *Guide des Papiers*.)

BOUVIER, Emile (1886–1973)

French diplomat. Delgate to the League of Nations 1936–37.

The *Archives Départementales de L'Aude*, Carcassonne, has a collection of his papers.

BRANDT, Max von (1835–1920)

German diplomat. Ambassador in Peking 1875–93.

The Political Archive of the West German Foreign Office in Bonn has a small collection of his personal papers, including correspondence with Li Hung Chang and other Chinese dignitaries between 1880 and 1883, and with Foreign Office personnel 1894–99, including Friedrich von Holstein. (Source: Mommsen, *op. cit.*)

BRANDT, Willy (b. 1913)

German statesman. Berlin representative in the Bundestag 1949–57; Mayor of Berlin 1957–66; SPD Chairman 1963. Vice-Chancellor and Foreign Minister 1966–69; Federal Chancellor 1969–74; President of the Socialist International and of the North-South Commission.

Brandt's papers from 1932 on have been deposited in the AdsD, Bonn. As well as personal papers, these comprise correspondence, notes, manuscripts and collections of material concerning his journalistic activity, exile (1933–46; including the SAP), Berlin (1947–66), the SPD Executive, SPD organisation at every level and Bundestag elections, as well as his activity as Foreign Minister and Chancellor. These papers may be consulted only with Brandt's personal permission.

BRANTING, Karl Hjalmar (1860–1925)

Swedish Minister of State 1920 and 1921–23; Foreign Minister 1921–23.

The *Riksarkiv*, Stockholm, has a collection of Branting's personal papers. Also housed at the *Riksarkiv* are the archives of the Swedish Foreign Ministry which has an extensive collection of Branting's personal and administrative papers (thirty-seven volumes). This covers the years 1918–25 and includes correspondence on political and foreign policy issues. Other papers can be found at the *Arbetarrörelsens Arkiv*, Stockholm.

BRATLIE, Jens Kristian Meinich (1856–1939)

Norwegian General and Prime Minister 1912–13.

The *Riksarkiv*, Oslo, has a collection of documents (0.1m) consisting of letter-books from the years 1898 to 1926.

BRAUER, Artur von (1845–1926)

German diplomat and politician. Consul in St Petersburg 1875–81; Consul-General in Cairo 1888–90; Baden's Ambassador in Berlin; Foreign Minister, Baden 1893; Minister-President of Baden 1901.

The *Generallandesarchiv*, Karlsruhe, has a collection of private correspondence from the years 1889–1903, and political material 1897–1904. (Source: Mommsen, *op. cit.*)

BRÄUER, Kurt (1889–1969)

German diplomat. Counsellor of Embassy, Paris 1937–39; Ambassador, Oslo 1939–40; plenipotentiary of the German Reich in Norway, April–May 1940.

The Political Archive of the West German Foreign Office in Bonn has a small collection of his papers, including material relating to Germany's Norwegian policy in the Second World War and the occupation of Norway (0.20m).

BRAUN, Adolf Freiherr von (d. 1904)

Austrian politician. Director of the Imperial and Royal Cabinet 1865–99.

His papers, containing material relating to the war of 1866, were deposited in the Austrian State Archives by the Cabinet Chancellery in 1918 (one bundle).

BRÄUTIGAM, Otto (b. 1895)

German diplomat. Secretary to the Moscow Embassy 1928–30; Embassy counsellor, Paris 1936–39; Consul-General in Baku 1940–41; Deputy and then Director of the political section in the Reich Ministry of the East; civil servant in the Foreign Office 1930–36 and from 1953; junior assistant secretary 1955; and Consul-General in Hong Kong 1958–60.

The *Bundesarchiv*, Koblenz, has a very small collection of notes relating to his activity in the Foreign Office, in the Ministry of the East, and on the General Staff of the army. There is also correspondence with Herbert von Dirksen. Bräutigam's diary for the years 1941–43 is in the Manuscript Division of the Library of Congress, Washington, DC. (Source: Mommsen, *op. cit.*)

BRAY-STEINBURG, Otto Count von (1807–99)

German diplomat and politician. Bavarian Minister of Foreign Affairs 1846–49 and 1870–71; Bavarian Ambassador to St Petersburg, Berlin and Vienna 1866–70 and 1871–95.

The *Hauptstaatsarchiv*, Munich, has a collection which was erroneously classified as private papers, but has now been incorporated into the Bavarian Foreign Office collection. The documents are official papers related to the German Question of 1870–71, plans for a buffer state in Lorraine, and correspondence with the Austrian Chancellor von Beust. (Source: Mommsen, *op. cit.*)

BREISKY, Walter (1871–1944)

Austrian politician. Vice-Chancellor in the administrations of Mayr and Schober. Federal Chancellor, 26–27 January 1922.

The *Allgemeines Verwaltungsarchiv*, Vienna, has a collection of his papers relating to the period before the First World War, including material on the language question in Bohemia, Bosnia–Herzegovina, the Ukrainian question in Galicia, and relations with Hungary (*Ausgleich*) 1908.

BRICH-REICHENWALD, Peter (1843–98)

Norwegian government minister 1889–95.

The *Riksarkiv*, Oslo, has a collection of papers (0.4m) consisting of Brich-Reichenwald's personal and political papers, 1852–98 (Pa. 137).

BRIN, Benedetto (1833–98)

Italian politician. Navy Minister in the administrations of Depretis 1876–77 and 1877–78; in the Cairoli administration 1878; in the Depretis administrations 1884–85 and 1885–87; and in the Crispi administration 1887–89.

The *Archivio Centrale dello Stato*, Rome, has three boxes of documents from the period 1866 to 1888, of particular relevance to the Battle of Lissa and other naval matters. (Source: *Guida Generale*.)

BROCKDORF-RANTZAU, Ulrich von (b. 1869)

German diplomat. Minister, Copenhagen 1912–18; Foreign Secretary, December 1918 to February 1919; Foreign Minister, February to June 1919; Ambassador, Moscow 1922–28.

His papers are in the Political Archive of the West German Foreign Office in Bonn. They include correspondence, notes and official papers from the years 1899–1928 (nineteen packets). This material, together with his speeches, is on microfilm at the US National Archives, Washington, DC.

BRORSEN, Søren (1875–1961)

Danish Defence Minister.

There are five packets of his papers at the *Rigsarkiv*, Copenhagen. The collection, which covers the years 1875–1961, contains memoirs, military and political material, and reports of ministerial meetings.

BROTHERUS, Karl Henrik (Heikki) (1909–)

Finnish legation counsellor, diplomat and journalist.

There is a collection of Brotherus' diaries in the *Valtionsarkisto*, Helsinki which relate to the years 1943 to 1946. In addition, there is also a description of events leading up to the Anti-Comintern pact of 1941. The archive comprises one box and access is restricted.

BRUINS, G.W.J. (1883–1948)

League of Nations Commissioner for currency at the Reichsbank in Berlin.

The *Algemeen Rijksarchief*, The Hague, has a collection of papers (12.5m) which cover Bruins' entire career (1895–1948) in education, banking and economic affairs (Inventory 2.21.191: Coll. 341). (See also published inventory, V. van den Bergh and P.R. de Kievit, *Inventaris van het archief van prof. dr. G.W.J. Bruins*, The Hague, 1981.)

BRÜNING, Heinrich (1885–1970)

German Chancellor 1930–32.

Brüning's papers from the period before 1934, when he emigrated to the United States, have been lost. Those from after 1934 are in the possession of his secretary Claire Nix, Norwich, Vermont, USA. (Source: Mommsen, *op. cit.*)

BRUSEWITZ, Per Emil (1887–1974)

Swedish social democrat. Diplomatic service in Petrograd and Moscow, 1917–18.

Seventy boxes of Brusewitz's papers for the years 1917–72 are in the ARAB, Stockholm. These include personal documents, correspondence, manuscripts, transcripts and reports, together with printed and other material concerning his political activity.

BUCHER, Lothar (fl. 1850–85)

German diplomat.

The Political Archive of the German Foreign Office, Bonn, has three packets of material concerning English problems of the time, 1850–85, and the *Deutsches Zentralarchiv*, Potsdam, has one file and thirteen books containing shorthand notes of some of Bismarck's ideas and suggestions. The material from the Political Archive is also on microfilm at the US National Archives, Washington, DC.

BUCKHKA, Gerhard von (1851–1935)

Director of the Colonial Section of the Imperial German Foreign Office.

The *Deutsches Zentralarchiv*, Potsdam, has one dossier of letters from Johann Albrecht, Duke of Mecklenburg, from the years 1898 and 1899.

BÜHLMANN, Fritz Ernst (b. 1848)

Swiss politician and officer. President of Grand Council 1884 and 1888; National Counsellor 1875–1919; President 1900; Division Colonel 1895; Commander of IV Army Corps 1902–10.

Bühlmann's papers are at the Federal Military Library in Berne. The material includes personal papers, correspondence, and documents.

BULL, Edvard Hagerup (b. 1855)

Norwegian lawyer, financier and politician. Cabinet Minister 1905–06 and 1920–21.

The Manuscript Collection, Oslo University Library, has a collection of diaries for the year 1905. More of Bull's papers can be found in the *Riksarkiv*, Oslo.

BÜLOW, Prince Bernhard von (1849–1929)

German Chancellor 1900–09 and Prussian Minister-President.

The *Bundesarchiv*, Koblenz, has a substantial collection of papers in two parts. The first part, covering the years 1849–1929, includes personal and family papers, diplomatic reports, speeches, material on the Moltke–Harden trial 1907–09 and on the *Daily Telegraph* affair 1908–09, correspondence, and notebooks (4.50m). The second part is much smaller (0.40m). In addition the US National Archives, Washington, DC, has microfilm copies of three packets of telegrams and other written material; material relating to his time as Chancellor, and parliamentary speeches.

BÜLOW, Bernhard Ernst von (1815–79)

German Secretary of State at the Foreign Office and Prussian Minister of State.

The Political Archive of the West German Foreign Office, Bonn, has thirteen files of papers, including correspondence with his family from the years 1833–79, political correspondence relating to Mecklenburg and Denmark, and diaries. This material is available on microfilm at the US National Archives, Washington, DC.

BÜLOW, Bernhard Wilhelm von (b. 1885)

German diplomat. Present at Brest Litovsk and Versailles 1918 and 1919; chief, *Sonderreferat Völkerbund* 1923–28; Deputy Director of Section II of Foreign Office and specialist on Western Europe 1925–30; State Secretary 1930–36.

The Political Archive of the West German Foreign Office, Bonn, has one packet of personal correspondence from the years 1915–25. This is available on microfilm at the US National Archives, Washington, DC.

BURCKHARDT, Carl Jacob (1891–1974)

Swiss diplomat. Service in Vienna 1918; High Commissioner of League of Nations, Danzig 1939; President of the International Red Cross 1944–48; Ambassador to Paris 1945–49.

Burckhardt's private papers are available at the *Öffentliche Bibliothek der Universität* Basel. The collection includes biographical and autobiographical documents; material relating to Burckhardt's diplomatic activity in Vienna, Danzig and Paris, and with the Red Cross; and a larger collection of material relating to Burckhardt's literary and academic activity.

BUSCH, Klemens (1834–95)

German diplomat. Served in St Petersburg, Constantinople and Budapest, where he was Consul General in 1879; Ambassador to Bucharest 1885, Stockholm 1886, and Berne 1892. He also worked at the Foreign Office in Berlin, where he was head of the Far Eastern section.

The Political Archive, Federal German Foreign Office, Bonn, has a collection of his correspondence covering the years 1871–95 (0.15m). His papers, described by L. Cecil as 'voluminous, but insignificant', are also available on microfilm at the National Archives, Washington, DC.

BUSCH, Moritz (1821–99)

German publicist and Foreign Office civil servant.

The *Deutsches Zentralarchiv*, Merseburg, has a collection of his papers covering the years 1841–99, including diaries, notes, manuscripts, proof-sheets with Bismarck's corrections and correspondence. Other papers have been lost. (Source: Mommsen, *op. cit.*)

C

CAETANI, Gelassio (1877–1934)

Italian nationalist politician and diplomat. Delegate to the Paris Peace Conference 1919. Ambassador to Washington 1922–25.

There are two collections of his papers. The Caetani Foundation in Rome has a collection of the Caetani family papers; these contain little of relevance to his diplomatic activity. The second collection, comprising three boxes of miscellaneous papers from the years 1906–34, is at the Hoover Institution at Stanford University, California. (Source: Cassels, *op. cit.*)

CAILLAUX, Joseph (1863–1944)

French politician. Prime Minister, Interior Minister, and Minister of Culture 1911–12.

Twelve boxes of Caillaux's papers are deposited at the FNSP, Paris. Material includes documents on Agadir, manuscripts, memoirs, and correspondence. In addition the *Archives Départementales de la Sarthe*, Le Mans, has 2m of unclassified material relating to his administrative and political career between 1898 and 1914.

CAJANUS, Werner (1878–1919)

Finnish legation secretary and diplomat.

The *Valtionsarkisto*, Helsinki, has a small collection of letters and documents, comprising two boxes, which relate to Cajanus' career with the Finnish mission in Stockholm 1917–19.

CAMBON, Jules (1845–1935)

French diplomat. Ambassador to Washington 1897–1902; Madrid 1902–07; Berlin 1907–14; Secretary General in the Foreign Office 1915–17; delegate to the Paris Peace Conference 1919.

A collection of his papers is held at the Archive of the Ministry of Foreign Affairs, Quai d'Orsay, Paris, in the Collection *Papiers d'Agents* (6). The holding comprises twenty-seven boxes of documents from the years 1863–1934. (Source: Young, *op. cit.*)

CAMBON, Paul (1843–1924)

French diplomat. Served in Tunisia as Minister in Residence 1882 and Minister-General 1885; Ambassador in Madrid 1896, Constantinople 1898 and London 1898.

A collection of his papers is held at the Archive of the Ministry of Foreign Affairs, Quai d'Orsay, Paris, in the Collection *Papiers d'Agents* (6). It comprises nineteen volumes covering the years 1882–1920 (Cote 42). (Source: Young, *op. cit.*)

CAMPENON, Jean-Baptiste (1819–91)

French general and politician. Minister of War, November 1881 to January 1882 and October 1883 to December 1885.

The *Service historique de l'Armée de la Terre*, Vincennes, has four boxes of papers. These include notes, fragments of a diary and agendas from the period 1853–91; material on the mission in Tunisia; documents on the military laws voted between 1880 and 1890; and the Boulanger affair. (Source: AN, *Guide des Papiers*.)

CAPRIVI, Leo Count (1831–99)

German officer and politician. Chief of General Staff of 10th Army Corps 1870–71; Chief of the Admiralty 1883; Minister President of Prussia 1892; Chancellor of Germany 1890–94.

The *Bundesarchiv*, Koblenz, has a collection of personal correspondence and family papers (0.25m). In addition the US National Archives, Washington, has microfilm copies of papers relating to his appointment as Chancellor and Foreign Minister, and of his speeches.

CARANFIL, Nicolae George (1893–1978)

Romanian politician. Minister of Air and Navy 1935–37.

A collection of papers (eight boxes), covering the period 1914 to 1970 is in the Hoover Institution, Stanford University, California. The collection includes correspondence, diaries and reports relating to Romania during the First and Second World Wars. Boxes five to eight of the collection are closed until 1993.

CARLESON, Eduard Henrik (1820–84)

Swedish Minister of State 1874–75.

There is a collection of Carleson's papers in the University Library, Uppsala.

CARNOT, Marie-François-Sadi (1837–94)

French politician. President of the Republic 1887–94.

M. Pierre-Sadi Carnot has about forty boxes of material. Details of the contents are not available. The *Bibliothèque de l'École polytechnique*, Paris, has one box of material relating to Carnot's scientific and technical interests. Access to the latter collection is subject to the written authorisation of the *École*. (Source: AN, *Guide des Papiers*.)

CARTON DE WIART, Henry (1869–1951)

Belgian Christian-Democratic politician. Minister of Justice 1911–18, head of government and Minister of the Interior 1920–21, Minister of Colonies March 1924 to November 1926. Permanent representative to the League of Nations 1934–39.

The *Archives Générales du Royaume*, Brussels, has Carton de Wiart's archive, covering the period 1891–1950. It includes extensive correspondence and dossiers relating to his career including papers concerning the League of Nations but not, apparently, his position as Minister of Colonies. Access is free except for the cabinet minutes 1920–21, which are closed. An inventory has been published: A.-M. Pagnoul, *Inventaire des papiers Carton de Wiart* (Brussels: AGR, 1981), 235 pp. The *Archief en Museum voor het Vlaamse Cultuurleven*, Antwerp, apparently also has some documents and letters (ref. C.175). The extent and nature of the collection is not known. Permission is needed for consultation.

CASATI, Alessandro (1881–1955)

Italian politician. War Minister in the Bonomi administration 1944, and 1944–45.

The holding of the *Archivio Centrale dello Stato*, Rome, comprises five boxes from the period 1920 to 1951, including material relating to his term as War Minister. (Source: *Guida Generale*.)

CASTELL-RÜDENHAUSEN, Siegfried Erbgraf zu (1860–1903)

German diplomat. Ambassador in Santiago.

A collection of Castell-Rüdenhausen's papers is held at the Archive of the Castell Princes, Castell, Lower Franconia. It runs to 1m and contains material relating to his diplomatic activity in New York, Tehran, Rome, Tangiers and Santiago. (Source: Mommsen, *op. cit.*)

CASTRÉN, Kaarlo (1860–1938)

Finnish Prime Minister, April–August 1919.

The *Valtionsarkisto*, Helsinki, has an extensive collection of Castrén's papers comprising thirty-seven boxes. This collection includes correspondence and documents on his career as a senator and Minister of State.

CATROUX, Georges (1877–1969)

French politician and diplomat; general. Minister of State 1944–45; resident Minister in Algeria, 1–7 February 1956. Governor of Indo-China 1939–40; Commander-in-Chief, Levant 1941; Commissioner for the Coordination of Moslem affairs, Algiers 1943; General Commissioner Delegate for North Africa 1944; French Ambassador to Moscow 1945–48.

The *Service historique de l'Armée de Terre* has seven files containing material on the international history of Europe, North Africa and Indo-China 1919–69; the report of the commission of inquiry on Dien-Bien-Phu; personal correspondence. An inventory is being prepared. Access is by written authorisation of Mme Catroux, who donated the material in 1970, and the head of the *Service historique de l'Armée de Terre*. (Source: AN, *Guide des Papiers*.)

CHARLES-ROUX, François (b. 1879)

French diplomat. Before the First World War he served in St Petersburg, Constantinople, Cairo and London and from 1916 to 1924 in Rome. Minister, Prague 1927–32 and Ambassador to the Vatican 1932–40; Secretary-General in the Foreign Office, 1940.

A collection of his papers is held at the Archive of the Ministry of Foreign Affairs, Quai d'Orsay, Paris, in the Collection *Papiers d'Agents* (6). There are four boxes of documents from the years 1900–32 (Cote 37). (Source: Young, *op. cit.*)

CHAZAL, Baron Pierre-Emmanuel-Felix (1808–92)

Baron Chazal fought in the Belgian Revolution, was given a post in the war office and became *aide-de-camp* to Leopold I. He was twice Minister of War, 1847–50 and 1859–66. From 15 July 1870 to 20 September 1870 he commanded the Belgian *armée d'observation* and then the second territorial division. He retired to Pau in 1875, but maintained correspondence with various Belgian politicians and diplomats.

The *Musée Royal de l'Armée et d'Histoire Militaire*, Brussels, possesses a Fonds Chazal. The collection is very fragmentary and contains nothing on Chazal's periods as Minister of War, but does have a great deal on national defence, including a section on the Belgian mobilisation in 1870, and important correspondence from, among others, Leopold I, Leopold II and Brialmont. Details are available in M.-A. Paridaens, *Inventaire du fonds d'archive 'P-E-F Chazal'* (Brussels: MRAHM, 1980), 59 pp.

CHODACKI, Marian (1898–1975)

Polish diplomat.

A collection of papers (four folders) was given by his widow to the Pilsudski Institute of America, New York. The collection of correspondence, reports and memoranda concerns Polish inter-war diplomacy, in particular the Danzig question.

CHRISTEN, Sigurd (fl. 1903–37)

Danish diplomat.

A substantial collection of his papers, supplemented by those of his wife, is held at the *Rigsarkiv*, Copenhagen (*c.* 6m).

CHRISTMAS MØLLER, Guido Leo John (1894–1948)

Danish Foreign Minister.

A collection of his papers, supplemented by those of his wife, is held at the *Rigsarkiv*, Copenhagen. The collection which comprises seventy-five packets and covers the years 1908–48, contains letters, diaries, memoranda, political documents relating to his time in Sweden and England, and material on the occupation.

CIANO, Galeazzo (1903–44)

Italian diplomat and politician. Legation secretary, Peking 1927–28 and Consul-General, Shanghai 1929–31; Chargé d'Affaires and later Minister, Peking 1932–33; Minister for Press and Propaganda 1933–36; Foreign Minister 1936–43; Ambassador to the Vatican 1943.

A typescript of his diary (1939–43) is at the Hoover Institution, Stanford University, California. The so-called Rose Garden Papers are available on microfilm (ref. T-120, reel 4597) at the US National Archives, Washington, DC. Photocopies of the latter collection are available at the Foreign Office Library, Cornwall House, London. (Source: Cassels, *op. cit.*)

CIECHANOWSKI, Jan (1887–1973)

Polish diplomat. Secretary to Paderewski. Chargé d'Affaires, then Counsellor, London; Minister, Washington 1925–29; Ambassador in Washington 1941–45.

An extensive collection of papers, including correspondence, reports and other documentation is in the Polish Institute, London. There is much material on the Polish Embassy in Washington and the collection is particularly rich for the period when Ciechanowski was at the Polish Legation in London 1918–21. The Hoover Institution, Stanford University, California also possesses 118 boxes of papers from the Polish Embassy in America, 1918–56.

CIELENS, Felix (1888–1964)

Latvian politician and diplomat. Minister of Foreign Affairs 1926–28; Ambassador to France 1933–40.

A collection of his memoirs and writings, with some correspondence, is available in the Hoover Institution, Stanford University, California. The collection, in Latvian and English, covers the period 1913 to 1945.

CLEINOW, Georg (1873–1936)

Founder of the *Deutsche Vereinigung* in Posen and West Prussia.

The *Deutsches Zentralarchiv*, Merseburg, has a substantial holding of material on German eastern policy, 1914–35, with copies from the papers of Alfred von Kiderlen-Wächter. The collection covers the period 1914–15 (4.8m).

CLEMENCEAU, Georges (1841–1929)

French politician. Prime Minister and Minister of the Interior 1906–09; Prime Minister and Minister of War 1917–20.

The *Service historique de l'Armée de Terre*, Vincennes, has fifty-nine boxes of material, assembled by General Mordacq, head of Clemenceau's military cabinet (ref. 6 N 53 to 111). The collection includes the personal papers of the Prime Minister and the Minister of War; documents relating to the armistice, the peace conference and the peace treaty; post-war international affairs 1920–23; material on prisoners of war, and on the military government of Paris 1915–18. (v. J.-C. Devos, J. Nicot, Ph. Schillinger, P. Waskman and J. Ficat: *Sommaire des archives de la Guerre, Série N, 1872–1919*, Troyes 1974 (*Ministère d'état chargé de la Défense nationale, État-major de l'Armée de Terre, Service historique*). The archive of the Ministry of Foreign Affairs holds two volumes containing minutes of letters to Robert Cecil, Léon Bourgeois, Paul Doumer, Alexandre Millerand, relating to the provisioning of the war, the League of Nations, and the peace treaty, and covering the period 1914–20 (ref. *Fonds nominatif*, no. 198). The manuscripts department of the *Bibliothèque Nationale* has four boxes of letters from Clemenceau to Mme Baldensperger 1923–29, and two boxes of other correspondence and notes. The Georges Clemenceau museum in Paris has a number of letters addressed to Clemenceau. (Clemenceau himself destroyed his private papers, except for the manuscript of his memoirs, two volumes on foreign affairs and some letters.) (Source: AN, *Guide des Papiers*.)

CLEMENTEL, Etienne (1864–1936)

French politician. Colonies Minister 1905–06. Numerous ministerial offices.

Mmes Barrelet-Clémentel and Arrizoli-Clémentel deposited a collection of papers (8m) at the *Archives départementales* in Puy-de-Dôme in 1971. The material covers Clémentel's political, literary and artistic activities between 1899 and 1936, and in particular his ministerial responsibilities during the First World War. An inventory is being prepared. Access to the material is by written authorisation of either Mme Barrelet-Clémentel or Mme Arrizoli-Clémentel. In addition Mme Barrelet-Clémentel has a book of notes made by Clémentel on his tour of inspection of French arsenals and arms depots in the autumn of 1914, in his capacity as reporter on the budget for the Chamber of Deputies. (Source: AN, *Guide des Papiers*.)

CLEMM von HOHENBURG, Christian (b. 1891)

German colonel and diplomat. Military attaché at the Athens embassy 1939–41.

The German Federal Military Archive, Freiburg im Breisgau, has a collection of papers, largely consisting of files relating to his diplomatic activity and to the Greek army. There is also a manuscript on the war in Greece: *Der Krieg in Griechenland 1940–1941* (0.2m). (Source: Mommsen, *op. cit.*)

CLODIUS, Carl August (b. 1897)

German diplomat. Stationed abroad in Paris, Vienna and Sofia 1921–34; worked in Commercial Department of Foreign Office from 1934; became Deputy Director in 1938 and was Director from 1944 to 1945.

The Political Archive at the Foreign Office, Bonn, has a collection of files. (Source, Mommsen *op. cit.*)

COLD, Christian (1863–1924)

Danish naval officer and politician. Foreign Minister 1922–24.

A collection of his papers is held at the *Rigsarkiv*, Copenhagen.

COLIJN, Hendrikus (1869–1944)

Dutch statesman and politician. Chairman of the Dutch Cabinet 1925–26 and 1933–39; Minister of Defence 1911–13 and 1935–37; Minister for the Navy 1912–13; Minister for Colonies 1933–37; Foreign Minister 1937.

The *Abraham Kuyperstichting*, Free University, Amsterdam has collections of correspondence between Colijn and A.W.F. Idenburg 1908–28, and A. Kuyper 1873–1920. The *Algemeen Rijksarchief*, The Hague, has some Colijn correspondence in the archives of J.B. van Heute; correspondence 1905–08 (Inventory 2.21.08: Coll. 79): B.C. de Jonge; correspondence 1922, 1931–36 (Inventory 2.21.95: Coll. 200) and E. van Raalte; Meeting reports (Inventory 2.21.134: Coll. 285) The *Koninklijk Instituut voor Taal-, Land-, en Volkenkunde*, Leiden, has some letters written by Colijn to Th.B. Pleyte.

COLLETT, Oscar (fl. 1900s)

Swedish diplomat and legation counsellor.

The Archive of the Swedish Foreign Ministry at the *Riksarkiv*, Stockholm, has a collection of Collett's papers which cover the years 1883–1907.

COLOSIMO, Gaspare (1859–1940)

Italian Colonies Minister in the Boselli and Orlando administrations, 1916–19. Deputy Prime Minister in the last months of the Orlando administration, March–June 1919.

The provincial archive at Catanzaro has twelve files of papers covering the years 1916–19. The collection includes material related to the pacification of Cirenaica, diaries, and other documents on colonial administration. There is also material relating to the Paris Peace Conference. Other papers are reported still in private hands.

COMBES, Émile (1835–1921)

French politician. Prime Minister and Minister of the Interior 1902–05; Minister of State 1915–16.

Combes' grandsons, André and René Bron, deposited a considerable amount of material with the departmental archives in Charente-Maritime in 1972 and 1974 (twenty-two boxes, ten files, and one bound volume). The collection includes the manuscript of Combes' memoirs and original documents and notes on elections, local politics, education, the navy, political parties, religious and colonial policy, the 'fiches', the Humbert and Dreyfus affairs, and the First World War. There is also extensive correspondence. There is an inventory which may be consulted at the Archives Nationales, Paris.

COMTESSE, Robert (1847–1922)

Swiss politician. State Counsellor 1876–99; Federal Counsellor 1899–1912. Director of the International Bureau of Intellectual Property until 1921.

The State Archives of Neuchâtel Canton, Neuchâtel, has a file of notes and speeches; a file on the organisation of federal authorities; a file of correspondence; and a file of press cuttings, diplomas and certificates.

CONSTANS, Jean (1833–1913)

French diplomat. Minister to China 1886. Governor-General of French Indo-China 1887–89.

Three volumes of his papers, covering the period 1880 to 1909, are in the archives of the French Foreign Ministry, Paris.

CONTARINI, Salvatore (fl. 1914–26)

Italian public servant. During the First World War he was Head of the Department of General Affairs and later of the Department of Overseas Economic Affairs; Secretary-General of the Foreign Office 1920–26.

A small collection of his papers is held at the Historical Archive of the Italian Ministry of Foreign Affairs. It contains mainly duplicates of official documents. (Source: Cassels, op. cit.)

CONTE, Eugène (fl. 1880s)

French diplomat. Secretary of the Legation in Tokyo.

One carton of his papers, for the period 1882–83, is in the archives of the French Foreign Ministry, Paris.

COPPÉ, Albert (1911–)

High official of the EEC. Belgian Cabinet Minister.

A collection of his papers is in the General Archives of the EEC Commission, Brussels.

CORT van der LINDEN, Pieter Wilhelm Adrianus (1846–1935)

Dutch advocate, university lecturer and Minister of Justice 1897–1901. Chairman of the Dutch Cabinet and Minister for Home Affairs 1913–18.

The *Algemeen Rijksarchief*, The Hague, has a Cort van der Linden family archive (8m) which includes material on P.W.A. Cort van der Linden and his antecedents and covers the period 1634–1940 (Inventories 2.21.40 and 2.21.41: Colls 121 and 214). Reference should also be made to the Brouwer family archive (Inventory 2.21.40) and other archives of the same name in the *Rijksarchief Noord-Holland*, *Rijksarchief Drenthe*, and *Gemeentearchief Goes*. Other correspondence of P.W.A. Cort van der Linden can be found at the *Abraham Kuyperstichting*, Free University, Amsterdam, and the International Institute for Social History, Amsterdam.

COSTE, Emile (fl. 1920s)

French diplomat.

It is understood that the papers are still in family possession. See Schuker, *The End of French Supremacy*.

COT, Pierre (1895–1977)

French politician, lawyer and academic. Under-Secretary of State for Foreign Affairs 1932–33; Air Minister 1933–35 and 1936–38; Minister of Commerce 1938.

The *Service historique de l'Armée de l'Air*, Vincennes, has two 4.75m width reels, one of 15cms and one of 13cms. No copy of them exists in written form. Access to the collection is restricted.

COULONDRE, Robert (1885–1959)

French diplomat. Delegate to the Hague Conference 1929–30; London Conference 1931 and Lausanne Conference 1932. Deputy director of Political Affairs at the Quai d'Orsay, Paris 1933. Ambassador to Moscow 1936–38 and Berlin 1938–39. Director of the Minister's Cabinet 1939–40; Ambassador to Switzerland 1940.

A collection of his papers is held at the Archive of the Ministry of Foreign Affairs, Quai d'Orsay, Paris, in the Collection *Papiers d'Agents* (6) (Cote 51). (Source: Young, *op. cit.*)

CRAMM-BURGDORF, Burghard Freiherr von (1837–1913)

German diplomat. Counsellor and Ambassador of the State of Brunswick to the Prussian Court.

The *Staatsarchiv*, Wolfenbüttel, has a collection of personal papers, diaries, manuscripts, records of his candidacy for *Reichstag* elections, and correspondence (0.9m). (Source: Mommsen, *op. cit.*)

CREDARO, Luigi (1860–1939)

Italian politician. Under-Secretary of State 1906; Civilian Commissioner General of Venezia Tridentia 1919–22.

The *Archivio Centrale dello Stato*, Rome, holds forty-one files of papers covering the period 1892–1922, including material relevant to the political history of Trento, 1919–22. (Source: *Guida Generale*.)

CREMER, Jacob Theodor (1847–1923)

Dutch Minister for the Colonies 1897–1901. President of the *Nederlandsche Handels-Maatschappij* (Netherlands Trading Company) 1907–12, and later Ambassador to Washington, DC 1918–20.

The *Algemeen Rijksarchief*, The Hague, has an extensive collection (6m) of Cremer family papers (Inventory 2.21.43: Coll. 157). Some correspondence between J.T. Cremer and A.W.F. Idenburg, covering the period 1905–14 can be found in the Idenburg Collection at the *Abraham Kuyperstichting*, Free University, Amsterdam.

CREMIEUX, Benjamin (1888–1944)

French public servant. Director of the Italian information service at the Foreign Ministry.

The *Archives Départementales de l'Aude*, Carcassone, has a collection of his papers.

CRISPI, Francesco (1819–1901)

Italian politician. Prime Minister, Foreign Minister, and Interior Minister 1887–89 and 1889–91; Prime Minister and Interior Minister 1893–96.

The *Archivio Centrale dello Stato*, Rome, has a collection of Crispi's papers. The collection is divided into seven series, named after the provenance of the seven original collections. The first series, *Roma-Archivio Centrale dello Stato*, covering the period 1842–98, comprises forty-eight boxes; the second series, *Reggio-Emilia*, covering the period 1844–1901, comprises twelve boxes; the third series, *Archivio di Stato di Palermo*, covering the period 1848–95, comprises twenty-nine boxes; the fourth series, *Biblioteca nazionale di Palermo*, covering the period 1849–79, comprises two boxes; the fifth series, *Deputazione di storia patria di Palermo*, covering the period 1877–96, comprises 185 boxes; the sixth series, *Primo e secondo gabinetto*, covering the period 1887–96, comprises seventy boxes and eight registers. (The seventh series is held at the *Istituto per la storia italiana del risorgimento*, Rome.)

The first and fifth series are primarily made up of official documents relating to the activity of the government; the second and the sixth consist of personal correspondence and non-official documents concerning political events. The other two series (the third and fourth) contain letters relating to the *risorgimento*. The archive comprises 346 boxes and eight registers in total, and covers the period from 1842 to Crispi's death.

CUETKOVIĆ, Dragiša (1893–1969)

Prime Minister of Yugoslavia 1939–41.

Two boxes of papers, covering the period 1928 to 1965, are in the Hoover Institution, Stanford University, California. The collection includes correspondence and writings on Yugoslav politics and foreign affairs. Topics covered include the Regency of Prince Paul 1934–41, the Cuetković-Maček agreement, the March 1941 *coup d'état* and Yugoslavia during the Second World War. The correspondence is closed until 1992.

CUNO, Wilhelm (1876–1933)

German Chancellor.

The Hapag Archive, Hamburg, has some twenty files of material relating to reparations after the First World War, the conferences of Brussels, London, Genoa and Locarno and Hapag business. (Source: Mommsen, *op. cit.*)

CURTIUS, Julius (1877–1948)

German politician. Foreign Minister 1930–31.

Most of his papers were lost in 1945, but some copies, relating to reparations, have survived and are privately owned. The *Bundesarchiv*, Koblenz, has a further collection of papers from the years 1920–30, including material on German-Polish relations (0.25m). (Source: Mommsen, *op. cit.*)

CZAPSKI-HUTTEN, Emeryk (1897–1979)

Polish soldier, administrator and diplomat. Member of the *Sejm*. Consul-General, then Minister, in Algiers, 1943. Political Adviser, Polish Military Mission at SHAEF 1944–45. Liaison Officer, Civilian Affairs, Allied General Headquarters in Italy.

A very extensive collection of papers, covering the period 1939–44, has been deposited in the Polish Institute, London. There is material on his diplomatic and military duties in Algiers and Italy, correspondence with Cardinal Hlond, Primate of Poland and some family correspondence.

CZERNIN und zu CHUDENITZ, Ottokar Count (1872–1932)

Austro-Hungarian diplomat and politician. Ambassador to Bucharest 1913–16; recalled to Vienna following the Romanian declaration of war on the Central Powers; Minister-President and Foreign Minister of Austria-Hungary 1916–18.

Some of Czernin's papers are at the *Státni ústredni archiv*, Prague.

CZIBULINSKI, Alfred (b. 1893)

German diplomat.

The Political Archive of the West German Foreign Office, Bonn, has a very small collection of material, relating mainly to relations between Germany and Japan and Russia and Japan. (Source: Mommsen, *op. cit.*)

D

DAAE, Ludvig (1829–93)

Norwegian government minister 1884–85.

The Manuscript Collection, Oslo University Library, has a collection of manuscripts.

DALADIER, Édouard (1884–1970)

French politician. Minister of Colonies, 1924–25; War Minister, 1925, 1932–33. 1933–34; Prime Minister and War Minister, 1933; Prime Minister and Foreign Minister, 1934; Deputy Prime Minister, Minister of National Defence and War Minister, 1936–37, 1938; Minister of National Defence and War Minister, 1937–38, 1940; Prime Minister, Minister of National Defence and War Minister, 1938–40; Foreign Minister, 1938–40.

Eighty-two boxes of his papers, covering the period 1919–58, are deposited at the FNSP, Paris. The collection deals with preparations for war, the fall of France, and the Riom trials.

The collection is divided into four sections. The first section covers the inter-war years, and contains material on the Daladier and Blum administrations, and the *Front Populaire*. The second section covers the immediate pre-war period (April 1938–September 1939). The first part of this section deals with events between the invasion of Austria and the Munich crisis; the second part deals with French diplomatic relations with Poland, the Balkans, Spain, Italy, and with Anglo–French–Soviet negotiations. The third part covers August and September 1939 and includes material on the German–Soviet pact and its consequences, and general documents relating to the outbreak of war.

The third section covers the Second World War, and is sub-divided into four parts. Part 1 (September–December 1939) contains material relating to Supreme Interallied Councils, Franco-British collaboration, the invasion of Poland and Finland, and relations with the Axis powers, neutrals, the Netherlands, Belgium, and south-east Europe. Part 2 covers January to May 1940 and contains material on the international situation in January, Supreme Interallied Councils, and French foreign relations, particularly Franco-British and Franco-Italian relations. This part also contains documents relating to French domestic politics, and Scandinavia. The third and fourth parts contain material relating to the defeat of France and the French Communist Party.

The fourth section contains documents on National Defence policy and French rearmament, together with material relating to the Riom trials.

In addition to the papers in the FNSP, other papers, which concern political and military problems in relation to the origins of the Second World War (July 1936–June 1940) are available in the Ministry of Foreign Affairs Archive, Paris. These are photocopies recovered from Germany after 1945.

DAMIANI, Abele (1835–1905)

Under-Secretary of State for Foreign Affairs 1887–89 and 1889–91.

The *Archivio Centrale dello Stato*, Rome, has three boxes of miscellaneous material covering the period 1861–1904. (Source: *Guida Generale*.)

D'ANETHAN, Jules (fl. 1840s–70s)

Belgian Catholic politician. Minister of Justice 1843–47; Head of government and Minister of Foreign Affairs, 2 July 1870 to 1 December 1871.

The *Archives Générales du Royaume*, Brussels, has D'Anethan's archive on microfilm, and an inventory is due to be published shortly. A further collection is held at the *Ministère des Affaires Etrangères* (see H. Haag, *Les archives personnelles des anciens ministres belges*).

DANIELSSON, Ivan (fl. 1930s)

Swedish diplomat and envoy to Lisbon and Madrid.

The Archive of the Swedish Foreign Ministry at the *Riksarkiv*, Stockholm, has a collection of Danielsson's papers which consists of his correspondence for the years 1936 and 1937.

D'ANNUNZIO, Gabriele (1863–1938)

Italian nationalist and patriot. Led raid on Fiume, 1919.

There are three collections of his papers. The first is a large collection at the *Archivio della Fondazione del Vittoriale Gardone*. The second is a collection of three files of letters from the years 1919–37, and five volumes of photographic reproductions of the same letters. Material from both these collections has been published in De Felice and Mariano (eds) *Carteggio D'Annunzio–Mussolini* (Milan, 1971). Finally, Trinity College, Hartford, Connecticut, has nine volumes of letters, eight of which are to Mussolini. (Source: Cassels, *op. cit.*)

DÁRANYI, Kálmán (fl. 1930s)

Hungarian Prime Minister 1936–38.

The Hungarian National Archives, Budapest, have a small collection of papers (0.17m) covering the period 1930–36.

DAUTRY, Raoul (1880–1951)

French politician. Armaments Minister 1939–40; Minister for Reconstruction and Town Planning 1944–46.

The *Archives Nationales* has 260 boxes of papers deposited by Mmes Lucius, Philipott and Desbordes (*née* Dautry) between 1969 and 1976 (ref. 307 AP). The collection includes material relating to Dautry's ministerial activities, and to his personal and professional interests. Access is by written authorisation of Mmes Lucius, Philipott and Desbordes. (Source: AN, *Guide des Papiers*.)

DAVID, Eduard Heinrich (1863–1930)

German politician. President of the Weimar National Assembly and Interior Minister.

The *Bundesarchiv*, Koblenz, has his diaries from 1914 to 1919 and from 1922 (0.25m). In addition, the US National Archives, Washington, DC, have material from 1918 and 1919 on microfilm. The rest of his papers were lost during the Second World War.

DEAT, Marcel (1894–1955)

French politician. Air Minister 1936; Under-Secretary of State for Labour and Solidarity 1944.

The *Bibliothèque Nationale* has material in the manuscripts department, donated by Mme Marcel Déat in 1973. Access is by authorisation of Mme Déat. (Source: AN, *Guide des Papiers*.)

DEBICKI, Roman (1896–1980)

Polish diplomat. Served Vienna, Budapest, Belgrade and Havana.

Eleven folders of his papers have been placed on permanent deposit in the Pilsudski Institute of America, New York. The collection includes documents, diaries and correspondence (including correspondence with Jan Szembek) relating to his diplomatic postings.

DE BONO, Emilio (1866–1944)

Italian General and politician. Commandant-General of Voluntary Militia for National Security 1923–24; Governor of Tripolitania 1925–28; Under-Secretary of State 1928–29; Minister of Colonies 1929–35; High Commissioner for East African Colonies 1935.

The *Archivio Centrale dello Stato*, Rome, has two boxes of papers from the years 1915–44, including diaries for the years 1915–43.

DE BORCHGRAVE, Emile (1837–1917)

Belgian diplomat. Posted in The Hague 1863–66; Frankfurt 1866; Berne 1867; worked in the Ministry of Foreign Affairs, Brussels 1868–75; *Chef de Cabinet* to the Minister 1870–75; Consul, and then Ambassador (Minister) to Berlin 1875–79; Belgrade 1879–85; Constantinople 1885; Vienna 1892. Retired 1909.

The *Archives Générales du Royaume*, Brussels, has papers covering de Borchgrave's entire career, including correspondence, numerous notes and press articles, relating to the various posts he held and his travels. It includes correspondence with Lambermont, Banning, D'Anethan, Greindl and Charles Woeste, among others. The *Ministère des Affaires Etrangères* has his personal file, and the *Musée Royal de l'Armée* has a Famille de Borchgrave collection, although it is not known whether it contains relevant material. Finally, the *Archief en Museum voor het Vlaamse Cultuurleven*, Antwerp, has a collection containing some letters (B.74). The extent of the collection is not known. Permission is needed for consultation.

DE BORCHGRAVE, Baron Roger (b. 1871)

Belgian diplomat. The son of Emile de Borchgrave, he joined the Ministry of Foreign Affairs 1894. Held diplomatic posts in various European capitals 1895–1911, and was then appointed Belgian Minister in Tehran. Returned to Europe in 1917 and was attached to the Foreign Ministry at Sainte-Adresse. He was briefly King Albert's *Chef de Cabinet* on the latter's return to Belgium, then (December 1918 to November 1919) *Chef de Cabinet* to Foreign Minister Paul Hymans. Ambassador in Madrid 1919–32; Belgian delegate to the International Commission on the Elbe 1933; Ambassador to the Holy See 1935–38.

The *Archives Générales du Royaume*, Brussels, contains De Borchgrave's papers together with his father's, covering the period 1899–1935. They include some notes and documents concerning his diplomatic posts abroad and correspondence and notes (1918–19) concerning the post-war situation, among others. It is not known whether there is any relevant material in the Famille de Borchgrave collection at the *Musée Royal de l'Armée*.

DE BOSDARI, Alessandro (fl. 1912–26)

Italian diplomat. Minister, Athens 1912–18; Ambassador to Rio de Janeiro 1918–21; Governor of Rhodes 1921–22; Ambassador to Berlin 1922–26.

The State Archive in Bologna has his unpublished memoirs of Germany in the 1920s. (Source: Cassels, *op. cit.*)

DE BROQUEVILLE, Charles (1860–1940)

Belgian Catholic politician. In the course of his career, he was head of government from June 1911 to June 1918, during which time he took the post of Minister of Defence twice, first briefly from 23 February to 3 April 1912, and then from 11 November 1912 to 4 August 1917, when he exchanged it for the Ministry of Foreign Affairs, until 1 January 1918. After the war he was again Minister of Defence from 20 May 1926 to 21 May 1931 (two terms) and Prime Minister from 22 October 1932 to 13 November 1934.

The *Archives Générales du Royaume*, Brussels, holds De Broqueville's papers, which are available on microfilm or as photocopies, covering the period 1892–1939. The collection includes voluminous correspondence with numerous Belgian politicians, diplomats and military figures, particularly for the First World War and later, also foreign politicians and diplomats for the First World War (Briand, Millerand, Sir Francis Villiers, Brand Whitlock, Churchill); diplomatic reports on the international situation 1911–14, dossiers (including correspondence) on colonial policy, the start of the First World War, minutes of cabinet meetings of the government in Le Havre; critiques of Beyens' foreign policy; diplomatic reports 1914–17; notes and memoranda on Belgian post-war territorial demands. There are also dossiers on initiatives for a separate peace with Germany (the Coppée-von der Lancken affair); military operations 1914–18; the situation of the army; defence 1932–34; foreign policy and disarmament, and relations with Italy. Access is free, except for correspondence with the royal family.

The *Archief en Museum voor het Vlaamse Cultuurleven*, Antwerp, has a collection on de Broqueville (B.8908), apparently including letters and documents. The extent of the collection is not known. Permission is needed for consultation.

DE CARAMAN-CHIMAY, J. (fl. 1880s–90s)

Belgian politician. Minister of Foreign Affairs, October 1884 to March 1892.

J. de Caraman-Chimay's papers are held in the family's archive at the Château de Chimay. No further details available.

DE CARTIER DE MARCHIENNE, Baron Emile (1871–1946)

Belgian diplomat. Ambassador in London 1927–45. Played an important role in relations between the Belgian government and the King in 1940, and the development of the 'royal question'.

A collection of papers is held at the *Ministère des Affaires Etrangères*, Brussels.

DECAZES, Louis, duc de Glücksberg, duc (1819–86)

French diplomat and politician. Minister of Foreign Affairs 1873–77.

The *Bibliothèque Thiers* has a collection of seventy boxes of papers, purchased in 1920 (ref. Manuscrits 681 to 751). The collection includes confidential letters received from French diplomats abroad (ref. Manuscrits 687 to 720). These are from the period 1874–77, and classified chronologically. The archive of the Foreign Ministry has a collection of papers handed over to the Ministry at the personal request of Freycinet (ref. *Fonds nominatifs*, no. 54). The collection includes reports of the diplomatic agents of the French minister in Vienna above all, but also of agents in Rome, Berlin and Constantinople. There are also typed copies of letters sent to the principal diplomatic agents of the period, and a few notes. The material covers the period 1873–77. (Source: AN, *Guide des Papiers*.)

DE CEUNINCK, Baron A. (1858–1935)

Belgian officer and politician. Embarked on a military career in 1878, becoming Chief of Staff 1905–12, Major-General 1914, Lieutenant-General 1915. He was appointed joint Minister of Defence, with Emile Vandervelde, from 4 August 1917 to 21 November 1918. Retired 1923.

The *Musée Royal de l'Armée et d'Histoire Militaire*, Brussels, has some correspondence and documents of de Ceuninck's, used by M. Corvilain for his biography, *Le Général Baron de Ceuninck*, (Brussels, 1954). Details are given in R. Boijen (ed.), *Inventaris van het archieffonds 'Personalia-I'* (Brussels: MRAHM, *Inventaires/Inventarissen*, no. 15, 1981.)

DECKERS, L. (fl. 1930s)

Dutch Minister of Defence 1929–35.

The *Universiteitsbibliotheek*, Nijmegen, has a collection of Decker's correspondence. For details of other papers, contact the Central Register of Private Archives, The Hague.

DE CUVELIER, Baron Alphonse

Belgian public servant. Responsible for the foreign affairs of the Congo Free State.

A collection of his papers is at the *Musée de la Dynastie*, Rue Bréderode 21, B-1000, Brussels.

DEDEM, W.K. Baron van (1839–95)

Dutch Minister for the Colonies.

The *Algemeen Rijksarchief*, The Hague, has a collection of papers (0.1m) covering the period 1891–94 (Inventory 2.21.49: Coll. 56).
    The *Rijksarchief*, Overijssel has a collection of family papers and other correspondence can be found in a number of private archives. For further details, contact the Central Register of Private Archives, The Hague.

DE GAULLE, Charles (1890–1970)

French statesman and general. Raised and commanded Free French forces after 1940. Came to power in France 1958. Architect and first President of the Fifth Republic 1959–69. Granted independence to Algeria 1962. Advocate of closer ties with West Germany.

There are papers, which are not yet available for research, in the *Institut de Gaulle*, Paris. Other papers are in the *Archives Nationales*, Paris, whilst the *Bibliothèque Nationale* has his literary papers.

DE GEER af FINSPANG, frih. Gerard Louis (b. 1854)

Swedish Minister of State 1920–21.

A collection of De Geer's papers is held in private hands.

DE GEER af FINSPÅNG, frih. Louis Gerard (1818–96)

Swedish Minister of State 1875–76 and 1876–80.

The *Riksarkiv*, Stockholm, has a collection of De Geer's private papers.

De GERBAIX, de SONNAZ, d'HABERES, Charles-Albert, Count (1839–1920)

Italian diplomat. Legation Attaché, Foreign Ministry, Turin; First Secretary, Brussels 1869; Chargé d'Affaires, The Hague 1878–79; Legation Counsellor, The Hague 1880; Consul General, Sofia 1884; Italian delegate at the Conferences on International Law, The Hague 1891, 1894 and 1895; Plenipotentiary Minister, Lisbon 1896, charged with re-establishing diplomatic relations between Italy and Portugal; member of the Interparliamentary peace conferences of Brussels, London and Berlin.

The *Archives Départementales de la Haute-Savoie* has a collection of correspondence, press cuttings, and manuscripts.

DE GROOTE, Paul (b. 1862)

Belgian diplomat. Joined the Foreign Ministry 1884 and posted to Belgrade 1886, then Yokohama 1888–95, Constantinople, The Hague and Tehran. In 1903 he was sent to Athens, then Copenhagen. Belgian minister in Berne 1910–17, when he left office after a disagreement with foreign minister Charles de Broqueville. Member of the Ukrainian delegation to the peace conference 1919, as financial adviser. Joined the foreign ministry again 1920, posted to Lima 1921, to Stockholm 1925–28, where he was responsible for negotiating arrangements for the marriage between Leopold III and Princess Astrid of Sweden.

The *Archives Générales du Royaume*, Brussels, possesses the family archive which contains De Groote's papers 1892–1941, including considerable correspondence, among others with Baron Beyens, Emile Waxweiler, and Jules Vanden Heuvel. The archive is particularly interesting for the First World War, Latin America 1921–25 and Stockholm. Permission is required. An inventory has been published: Martina Ni Cheallaigh, *Inventaire des papiers De Groote* (Brussels: AGR, 1981).

DE GRUBEN, Baron Hervé (fl. 1920s–40s)

Belgian diplomat. Joined Ministry of Foreign Affairs 1926, posted to Berlin 1927–36; briefly *Chef de Cabinet* to Van Zeeland; then counsellor, Belgian embassy in Washington, DC, 1937–45. Assistant, then Director-General, and finally General Secretary of the political division of the Ministry of Foreign Affairs; Ambassador to Bonn 1953–56.

The *Centre de Récherches et d'Etudes Historiques de la Seconde Guerre Mondiale*, Brussels, has his archive 1926–67. It contains private papers, correspondence, documents, notes, press cuttings and articles, published and unpublished, and is particularly rich for his period in Washington. It reflects his particular interest in relations between Leopold III and the Belgian government in 1940, and the development of the 'royal question', including correspondence with Cartier de Marchienne, de Kerchove de Denterghem, de Vleeschauwer, Pierlot, Spaak, Theunis, van der Straten-Ponthoz and Van Langenhove. An inventory has been published: José Gotovitch (ed.), *Archives Baron Hervé de Gruben* (Brussels: CREHSGM, *Inventaires no. 13*, 1982).

DEJEAN, François (1871–1949)

French diplomat. Commercial Attaché, United States 1911; attached to missions in Bucharest 1914 and Washington, DC 1915; Chargé d'Affaires, Mexico 1918; Deputy Director of the American section at the Quai d'Orsay, Paris, 1920; Ambassador to Brazil 1928 and Moscow 1931–33.

A collection of his papers is held at the Archive of the Ministry of Foreign Affairs, Quai d'Orsay, Paris, in the Collection *Papiers d'Agents* (6). There are two boxes, covering the years 1916–27. (Source: Young, *op. cit.*)

DE KERCHOVE DE DENTERGHEM, Comte André (1885–1945)

Belgian diplomat. Attaché in Tokyo 1908; London 1909; then posts in Berlin 1912; Bucharest 1914; The Hague, August 1916; London 1919; Chargé d'Affaires, briefly, in Berlin 1920. He resigned to become Provincial Governor of East Flanders and became a senator in 1929. Returned to his diplomatic career as ambassador to Berlin in December 1931 and moved to Paris in 1935, and Rome in March 1938. In 1940 he left for Switzerland, before being given new duties in Portugal co-ordinating food aid for Belgium, until 1945.

The *Centre de Récherches et d'Etudes Historiques de la Seconde Guerre Mondiale*, Brussels, has a limited collection of papers relating to the period May 1940–45, consisting of correspondence with Spaak (mainly), Gutt and others, notes, speeches and reports. There is a further collection at the *Ministère des Affaires Etrangères*.

DELAVIGNETTE, Robert (fl. 1949–60)

French colonial official. Governor of Cameroun.

One box of his papers, covering the period 1949–60, has been acquired by the Hoover Institution, Stanford University, California.

DEL BO, Rinaldo (1916–)

High official of the European Community.

A collection of his papers is in the General Archives of the EEC Commission, Brussels.

DEL BONO, Alberto (1866–1944)

Italian politician. General Secretary, then Navy Minister 1916–17, 1917–19.

The *Archivio Centrale dello Stato*, Rome, has four files from 1876 and from the period 1904 to 1925. (Source: *Guida Generale*.)

DELCASSÉ, Théophile (1852–1923)

French diplomat and politician. Under-Secretary of State for Colonies 1893; Minister for Colonies 1894–95; Foreign Minister 1898–1905, 1914–15; Navy Minister 1911–13; War Minister 1914; Ambassador to St Petersburg 1913–14.

Delcassé's daughter, Mme Noguès, donated his papers to the archives of the foreign ministry in 1960 (ref. *Fonds nominatifs*). The collection consists of nine boxes and twenty-six volumes and includes dossiers on Germany, Russia, Great Britain, the United States, the Middle East and Spain, and on the Foreign Ministry, the Navy Ministry and the French embassy in St Petersburg. There are also letters from diplomats, journalists and political informers. The material covers the period 1898–1915, although there are a few documents going up to 1952. (Source: AN, *Guide des Papiers*.)

DE MARINIS, Alberto (fl. 1920s)

Italian General. Involved in foreign missions. Italian commissioner in the Government Commission and at the Plebiscite in Upper Silesia.

The *Archivio Centrale dello Stato*, Rome, has one file containing correspondence relating to the Italian delegation and the Apostolic Nunciate in Poland, from the years 1920–37.

DE PONT [junior]

Austrian. Personal service to Archduke Ferdinand Max as governor general of the Veneto-Lombard Kingdom in Miramar, 1857–64.

The *Haus-, Hof- und Staatsarchiv*, Vienna, has a collection of *Einlaufstücke* (diplomatic papers) from the Archduke's chancellery in Lombardy–Venice. There is also correspondence from the years 1849–78, and a memorandum on the internal affairs of Turkey, along with other miscellaneous items.

DEPRETIS, Agostino (1822–87)

Italian politician. Prime Minister and Finance Minister 1876–77; Prime Minister and Foreign Minister 1877–78 and 1878–79; Prime Minister and Interior Minister 1881–83, 1883–84, 1884–85 and 1885–87; Prime Minister and Foreign Minister 1887.

There is a Depretis family archive in the *Archivio Centrale dello Stato*, Rome, which is subdivided into four series. The first series covers the period 1847–87, and comprises thirty-six boxes of papers and a collection of letters relating to Depretis' public life; there are also documents on the Expedition of the Thousand, on colonial policy, and on the Battle of Lissa. The second series, comprising twenty-nine boxes, covers the period 1715 to 1922 and contains family letters and letters relating to Depretis' professional activities. The third series comprises three boxes, covering the period 1879–1918, and contains the letters of Amalia Depretis. The fourth series covers the period 1860–87 and consists of twelve boxes of letters relating predominantly to Italian domestic policy.

DERNBURG, Bernhard (1865–1937)

German politician. Director of Colonial Section of German Foreign Office 1906; State Secretary at the Reich Colonial Office 1907–10; Finance Minister 1919.

The *Bundesarchiv*, Koblenz, has a collection of papers covering the years 1900–37, including speeches, documents related to travel, in particular in the service of the Reich Colonial Office, and personal and service correspondence. (Source: Mommsen, *op. cit.*)

DESCHANEL, Paul (1856–1922)

French politician. President of the Republic, 17 February to 21 September 1920.

The *Archives Nationales* has a family archive containing the papers of Deschanel and those of his father (ref. 151 AP 35 and 36, 38 and 39, 42 to 48). The collection consists of eleven boxes of papers, including political correspondence and files on international politics. Access is by written authorisation of Mme Jacques Dupin. (Source: AN, *Guide des Papiers*.)

DESPREZ, Félix (fl. 1870s)

French diplomat. Political Director of the Foreign Office 1866–82.

A collection of papers is available in the archives of the French Foreign Ministry, Paris.

D'ESTE, Franz Ferdinand von (1863–1914)

Austrian archduke. Heir to throne of Austria–Hungary; Inspector-General of the armed forces 1913; assassinated at Sarajevo 1914.

The *Haus-, Hof- und Staatsarchiv*, Vienna, has a collection of d'Este's papers.

D'ESTOURNELLES de CONSTANT Paul H.B.B. (fl. 1900s)

French diplomat and winner of the Nobel Peace Prize 1909.

The *Archives Départementales de la Sarthe*, Le Mans, has a large collection of his papers (24.30m). A published inventory is available: Henri Boullier de Branche and Gérard Naud, *Les archives d'Estournelles de Constant (12 J), répertoire numérique détaillé*, Archives Départementales de la Sarthe, (Le Mans, 1981).

DEUNTZER, J.H. (1845–1918)

Danish politician. Prime Minister and Foreign Minister 1901–05.

A collection of his papers is held at the *Rigsarkiv*, Copenhagen (ref. RA 5333).

DEVELLE, Jules (1845–1919)

French politician. Under-Secretary of State to the Prime Minister and for the Interior 1883; Foreign Minister 1893.

The Foreign Ministry archives have one file of correspondence relating to the Franco-Russian alliance, Siam and Morocco, covering the period 14 January to 31 October 1893. The Departmental Archives, Meuse, has one file containing photocopies of letters by Develle between 1872 and 1914. (Source: AN, *Guide des Papiers.*)

DEVENTER, M.L. van (1832–95)

Counsellor to the Dutch Foreign Ministry and later Consul in Rio de Janiero.

The *Algemeen Rijksarchief*, The Hague, has a collection of papers related to van Deventer's career and other members of his family (1.8m). The archive covers the period 1854–1913 (Inventory 2.21.51: Coll. 252).

DEVÈZE, Albert (1881–1959)

Belgian liberal politician. Minister of Defence 20 November 1920 to 6 August 1923, and again 17 December 1932 to 26 May 1936.

The *Archives Générales du Royaume*, Brussels, has the family archive which contains some of Devèze's correspondence, notably with Paul Hymans, M.-L. Gérard, Adolphe Max and F. Bovesse, but apparently very little else relating to his period as Minister of Defence. An inventory has been published: R. Wellens (ed.), *Inventaire des papiers d'Albert Devèze, ministre d'Etat* (Brussels: AGR, 1978).

The *Archief en Museum voor het Vlaamse Cultuurleven*, Antwerp, has some documents and letters (D.3922). The extent of the collection is not known. Permission is needed for consultation.

DE VLEESCHAUWER, Albert (1897–1971)

Belgian Catholic politician. Minister of Colonies 15 May 1938 to 9 February 1939; 18 April 1939 to 1944.

The *Centre de Récherches et d'Etudes Historiques de la Seconde Guerre Mondiale*, Brussels, has papers largely relating to the war period. These include dossiers on subjects discussed in the cabinet, information and propaganda about Belgium and the Congo, documents relating to problems of transport to, from and via Africa in the context of the war effort. An inventory has been published: D. Martin (ed.), *Archief Albert De Vleeschauwer* (Brussels: CREHSGM, 1981), 142 pp. The *Archief en Museum voor het Vlaamse Cultuurleven*, Antwerp, also has a collection relating to De Vleeschauwer (V.7045), containing letters and documents. The extent and nature of the collection is not known. Permission is needed for consultation.

DIECKHOFF, Hans Heinrich (1884–1952)

German diplomat. Counsellor of Embassy, Washington 1922–26; London 1926–30; Director of Section III (United Kingdom and United States), Foreign Office 1930–36; acting State Secretary 1936–37; Ambassador, Washington, DC 1937–41, Madrid 1943–45.

The Political Archive of the German Foreign Office, Bonn, has a collection of papers, including diaries, manuscripts and documents and correspondence relating to Dieckhoff's diplomatic activity. Other papers have been lost. (Source: Mommsen, *op. cit.*)

DIENSTMANN, Karl (1885–1962)

German diplomat. Consul, Leningrad 1922–25; Counsellor to the Moscow embassy 1925–26; Consul, Odessa 1926–31; Consul-General, Tbilisi 1931–36; Foreign Office 1936–40; Consul-General, Leningrad 1940–41, Zürich 1943–45.

Most of his papers are privately owned, but some are held by the Political Archive of the Federal German Foreign Office in Bonn, which also has copies of some of the documents in private hands. The papers include material on German-Soviet and Polish-Soviet relations, copies of diaries, memoirs and notes (0.35m). (Source: Mommsen, *op. cit.*)

DIEPENHORST, I.N.Th. (1907–76)

State Secretary at the Dutch Foreign Ministry.

The *Algemeen Rijksarchief*, The Hague, has a collection of family papers (3m), covering the period 1904–76 (Inventory 2.21.52: Coll. 300). See also a published guide; F.J.M. van Zutphen, *Inventaris van de papieren afkomstig van P.A. Diepenhorst en I.N.Th. Diepenhorst en van enige van hun verwanten* (The Hague, 1978).

DIESEN, Unni Elisabeth (1908–)

Secretary to the Norwegian Foreign Minister 1940.

The *Riksarkiv*, Oslo, has a collection of letters and manuscripts which are kept with the papers of Henry Edward Diesen and total 0.4m (Pa. 288).

DIJK, J.J.C. van (fl. 1918–39)

Dutch Minister of Defence 1921–25 and 1937–39. Minister for the Navy 1921–22.

The *Abraham Kuyperstichting*, Free University, Amsterdam, has a small collection (one envelope) of van Dijk papers.

DIOUF, Gallandou (fl. 1930s)

French politician. Representative from Senegal 1934–39, in the Chamber of Deputies.

A collection of his papers was purchased by the *Archives Nationales*, Paris, in 1954 (ref. 110 AP 1–3). The collection includes correspondence with the Colonies Minister and the President of the Council 1934–36, material on the '*parti dioufiste*' and other parliamentary material.

DIRKSEN, Herbert von (1882–1955)

German diplomat. Chargé d'Affaires, Warsaw; subsequently Foreign Office 1921–22; Consul-General, Danzig 1923–25; Foreign Office 1925–28; Ambassador, Moscow 1928–33, Tokyo 1933–38, London 1938–39.

The *Deutsches Zentralarchiv*, Potsdam, has the larger part of his papers. The Political Archive of the Foreign Office, Bonn, has a manuscript about his ambassadorship in Moscow, and service correspondence. (Source: Mommsen, *op. cit.*)

DITTEN, Thor von (1860–1936)

Swedish Cabinet Secretary 1900–03.

The *Riksarkiv*, Stockholm, has a collection of Ditten's private papers. In addition, the Archives of the Swedish Foreign Ministry, also housed in the *Riksarkiv*, have a collection of documents related to his period in office 1900–03.

DOCKUM, C.E. von (1804–93)

Danish politician. Navy Minister 1850–52 and 1866–67.

A collection of his papers is held at the *Rigsarkiv*, Copenhagen (ref. 5340).

DOES de WILLEBOIS, P.J.A.M. van der (fl. 1870s)

Dutch Minister of Foreign Affairs 1874–77 and 1883–85.

There exists a private van der Does de Willebois archive which contains material which is largely of a genealogical nature. For further details contact the Central Register of Private Archives, The Hague.

DOMELA NIEUWENHUIS, Ferdinand Jacobus (1864–1935)

Dutch Ambassador in Pretoria 1895–1901, Bangkok 1890–94 and Sofia 1920–23.

The *Algemeen Rijksarchief*, The Hague, has an extensive collection of Domela Nieuwenhuis family papers (20m) which includes material on F.J. Domela Nieuwenhuis. The archive covers a period from the eighteenth to the twentieth century (Inventory 2.21.183: Coll. 352).

Further papers can be found at the *Rijksarchief Noord-Brabant*, 's-Hertogenbosch, and in the Ferdinand Domela Nieuwenhuis (1846–1919) archive at the International Institute for Social History, Amsterdam.

DÖNITZ, Karl (1891–1980)

German Admiral, Commander-in-Chief of the Navy. Succeeded Hitler.

The German Federal Military Archive at Freiburg im Breisgau has a collection of notes, diaries and correspondence (0.1m). (Source: Mommsen, *op. cit.*)

DONNER, Ossian (1866–1957)

Finnish ambassador and diplomat.

The *Valtionsarkisto*, Helsinki, has a collection of two boxes of letters to Donner covering the years 1919 to 1927. This collection forms part of the Donner family archive.

DOUGLAS, Ludvig Wilhelm August, Greve (1849–1916)

Swedish Foreign Minister 1895–99.

A collection of Douglas' papers is in private hands.

DOULCET, Jean (fl. 1914–18)

French diplomat. Served in Petrograd, First World War.

There are papers in the Archive of the French Foreign Ministry at the Quai d'Orsay, Paris.

DOUMERGUE, Gaston (1863–1937)

French politician. Colonies Minister 1902–05, 1914–17; Minister of Education 1908–09, and 1909–10; Prime Minister and Foreign Minister 1913–14; Foreign Minister, August 1914; Prime Minister 1934; President of the Republic 1924–31.

Doumergue's papers were left to the commune of Aigues-Vives in his will and are held at his birth-place. They include election files from the period 1893–1910 and letters received by him 1934. Access is by written authorisation of the mayor of Aigues-Vives and Doumergue's heirs.
  The Foreign Ministry archives have four volumes (ref. *Fonds nominatifs*, no. 64). These include a file on the Franco-Turkish accord of 11 September 1913; notes on Tirard's economic and financial mission to Russia in 1916; documents on the allies' conference at Petrograd in January 1917, and on Doumergue's mission to Russia; a file of information on the year 1934, and on Germany in particular; and a file on the Abyssinian affair 1935–36. (Source: AN, *Guide des Papiers*.)

DROZ, Numa (1844–99)

Swiss politician. Deputy of States Council; Federal Counsellor 1875–92. Responsible for foreign affairs from 1887. Director of the International Bureau of Railways from 1892.

The State Archive of Neuchâtel Canton has a collection of forty-nine files of his papers. The material includes published articles; documents relating to cantonal and federal affairs, railways and German socialists; and papers relating to the Wohlgemut affair. There are a further twenty-eight files containing letters received by Droz between 1869 and 1899.

DUCA, George I. (1905–   )

Romanian diplomat. Chief of Mission to Sweden 1944–47.

A large collection of sixty boxes of papers has been deposited in the Hoover Institution, Stanford University, California. The collection includes diaries, correspondence, reports and writings on Romanian politics and foreign policy. Most of the collection remains closed until twenty years after Duca's death. Some other material will be available in 1995.

DUCA, Ion George (1879–1933)

Romanian politician. Prime Minister 1933.

Three boxes of his papers covering the period 1914–26, are in the Hoover Institution, Stanford University, California.

DUCOMMUN, Elie (1833–1906)

Swiss politician. Secretary General of International Peace Bureau. Awarded Nobel Peace Prize 1902.

The Swiss National Library, Berne, has a collection of fifty-four documents from the years 1860–80. The material consists mainly of letters and notes. The United Nations Library, Geneva, also has some material in the archives of the International Peace Bureau.

DUFOUR von FERONCE, Albert (1868–1945)

German diplomat. Joined foreign service, 1919; embassy counsellor, London 1920–24; Minister, London 1924–26; Under-Secretary General, League of Nations 1926–32; Ambassador, Belgrade 1932–33.

The Political Archive of the Federal German Foreign Office, Bonn, has a very small collection of papers, including material on the domestic and foreign policies of the United Kingdom from 1925; private service correspondence with Foreign Office officials, German diplomats and other German and British politicians, businessmen and scientists, on various aspects of Anglo-German relations. (Source: Mommsen, *op. cit.*)

DUMESNIL, Jacques-Louis (1882–1956)

French politician. Under-Secretary of State for the Navy 1917; Under-Secretary of State for military and maritime aeronautics 1917–19; Navy Minister 1924–25 and 1930; Under-Secretary of State for War 1926; Air Minister 1931–32.

The Departmental Archive of Seine-et-Marne has eighty-seven boxes of Dumesnil's papers, donated by Mme Dumesnil in 1957 (ref. 769 F 1 to 87). The collection consists mainly of material relating to the *département* of Seine-et-Marne, to Fontainebleau, where Dumesnil was mayor, and to elections from municipal to senatorial level.

The *Archives Nationales* has a further thirty boxes of papers, donated by Mme Dumesnil in 1957 and 1958 (ref. 130 AP 1 to 30). These contain documents on Morocco 1908–13; aeronautics; the reorganisation of the army in 1920; the Navy and Air Force 1924–32; and the international conferences at Washington, London and Geneva between 1908 and 1923. There is also some correspondence. (Source: AN, *Guide des Papiers.*)

DUYMAER van TWIST, A.J. (1809–87)

Governor-General of the Netherlands Indies.

The *Algemeen Rijksarchief*, The Hague, has a collection of papers (0.4m) covering the period 1850–90 (Inventory 2.21.58: Coll. 101). Other correspondence with W.C. Mees can be found in the *Gemeentearchief*, Rotterdam.

E

EBERT, Friedrich (1871–1925)

President of the Weimar Republic.

No surviving papers can be located. (See Mommsen, *op. cit.*, for details of the loss of Ebert's papers.)

ECKARDSTEIN, Hermann Freiherr von (1864–1933)

German diplomat. Legation Counsellor and Chargé d'Affaires, London.

The Foreign Office Political Archive, Bonn, has a collection of papers, including the notes of Professor Rheindorf and abstracts of correspondence with Holstein from 1900 to 1901 (0.25m). These documents are also available on microfilm at the US National Archives in Washington, DC.

ECKEL, Norbert (1879–1965)

German diplomat. Consulate-General, Paris 1909–13; Vice-Consul, Consulate-General, Buenos Aires and then legation counsellor, Buenos Aires embassy 1913–20; Foreign Office, Berlin 1923; Consul, St Gallen, Switzerland 1923–26, and Lyons 1926–30; Consul, later Consul-General, Bordeaux 1932–38.

The Foreign Office Political Archive, Bonn, has a small collection of papers relating to his diplomatic career, and in particular to Paris and Buenos Aires. (Source: Mommsen, *op. cit.*)

ECKHARDT, Heinrich von (1861–1944)

German ambassador to Mexico 1914–19.

His papers are privately owned, but the Political Archive of the Federal German Foreign Office in Bonn, has a collection of copies of his memoirs (0.04m). (Source: Mommsen, *op. cit.*)

EDÉN, Nils (1871–1945)

Swedish Minister of State 1917–20.

The University Library, Uppsala, has a collection of Edén's personal papers.

EHRENSVÄRD, greve Albert Carl August Lars (1821–1901)

Swedish Foreign Minister 1885–89.

A collection of Ehrensvärd's papers can be found at the *Riksarkiv*, Stockholm.

EHRENSVÄRD, greve Johan Jakob Albert (1867–1940)

Swedish Foreign Minister 1911–14. Secretary to the Cabinet 1906–08. Later Envoy to Paris 1918–34.

The *Riksarkiv*, Stockholm, has a collection of Ehrensvärd's papers. The Archive of the Swedish Foreign Ministry, also housed at the *Riksarkiv*, has a collection of documents related to his periods of office in 1906 and 1911–14. There is also a separate holding of papers (three volumes) relating to his period as envoy to Paris. These include personal papers and other correspondence from the years 1922 to 1934.

EHRNROOTH, Johan Casimir (1833–1913)

Finnish Secretary of State and General.

The *Valtionsarkisto*, Helsinki, has one box of letters and other documents concerned primarily with his career as War Minister in Bulgaria, 1880–81.

EHRNROOTH, Leo Reinhold (1877–1951)

Finnish Senator.

The *Valtionsarkisto*, Helsinki, has a collection consisting of one box of documents relating to the negotiations between Finland and the Russian Provisional Government in St Petersburg on 29 March 1917. In addition, the Library of the Åbo Academy has a collection of Ehrnrooth's correspondence.

EINEM, *genannt* von Rothmaler, Ernst-Günther von (b. 1894)

German politician and officer. Westphalian district leader of *Freikorps Oberland* 1922–24; officer in the Second World War; German Nationalist DNVP member until 1933; Founding member of *Deutsche Partei* 1949–50; FDP member 1953.

The *Hauptstaatsarchiv*, Düsseldorf, has a collection of his papers covering the years 1949–53. The material includes correspondence with Heinrich Brüning and Hans-Christoph Seebohm about the foundation of the DP. (Source: Mommsen, *op. cit.*)

EISENDECHER, Karl von (1841–1934)

German vice-admiral and diplomat. Prussian envoy in Karlsruhe.

The Political Archive of the German Foreign Office has four packets of his papers, covering the years 1868–1925. The collection contains correspondence with, *inter alia*, Bethmann Hollweg and Wilhelm II. The material is also available on microfilm at the US National Archives, Washington, DC. (Source: Mommsen, *op. cit.*)

EISENLOHR, Ernst (b. 1882)

German diplomat. Embassy Counsellor, London 1920–22, Belgrade 1923–25; Foreign Ministry 1926–31; German Minister, Athens 1931–36, and Prague 1936–39; Chief of Extraordinary Commission on Economic Questions (*Sonderkommission für Wirtschaftsfragen*), 1939–40; Foreign Ministry 1940–43.

Eisenlohr's papers are at the Political Archive of the Federal German Foreign Office in Bonn. (Source: Kimmich, *German Foreign Policy 1918–45*.)

EISNER, Kurt (1867–1919)

German revolutionary leader. *Ministerpräsident* and Foreign Minister, independent Bavarian People's State, November 1918 to January 1919.

For details of his surviving papers, see *Sources in European Political History, Vol. I, pp. 56–7.*

EKMAN, Carl Gustaf (fl. 1920s)

Swedish Minister of State 1926–28 and 1930–32.

There is a collection of Ekman's papers in the Royal Library, Stockholm.

EMIN PASCHA* (1840–92)

German colonial administrator. Governor of Equatorial Sudan.

The *Deutsches Zentralarchiv*, Potsdam, has a file containing his diary notes, letters from Georg Schweiter and King Muanga of Uganda, and press cuttings. The material covers the period 1840–1917. The *Staatsarchiv*, Hamburg, also has a collection of his papers. The material includes diaries, notes, and correspondence in Arabic (2m). In addition the library of the *Geographisch–Karthographische Anstalt*, Gotha, has a collection of letters concerning Emin Pascha, who was also a doctor and an explorer. There are also letters in the British Library, London.

*Eduard Schnitzer.

ENCKELL, Carl Johan Alexis (1876–1959)

Finnish diplomat, ambassador and Foreign Minister 1918–20, 1924 and 1944–50.

There is a substantial collection of Enckell's papers housed at the *Valtionsarkisto*, Helsinki. The archive consists of 119 boxes and includes correspondence and other documents. Access to the collection is restricted.

ENGELHART, Thomas von Westen (1850–1905)

Norwegian member of parliament and government minister 1891–93 and 1895–98.

The *Riksarkiv*, Oslo, has a collection of documents (0.06m) consisting of diaries, correspondence and manuscripts mainly from the 1890s (Pa. 223).

EPP, Franz Xaver Ritter von (1868–1947)

German officer and politician. Colonial service in China 1901–02; military service in South-West Africa 1904–07; founder of Epp *Freikorps*, and briefly military dictator of Bavaria; his troops were used against the Left in Bavaria and the Ruhr; NSDAP member from 1928, and Nazi deputy for Upper Bavaria–Swabia; head of Colonial Policy Office of Reich Leadership from 1934; infantry general from 1935; died in a US internment camp in 1947.

According to Mommsen, there are four collections of von Epp's papers. The first was handed over to archive authorities in Bavaria in the 1960s and comprises 3.5m of documents including material relating to the Boxer Rebellion, South-West Africa and the First World War; diaries 1919–26 and 1929–31; material on the *Freikorps Epp* and the *Reichswehr*; political speeches; and material on German domestic and colonial policy and the Saar plebiscite. The second collection (0.10m) is at the German Federal Archive, Koblenz, and contains correspondence with *inter alia* Hitler, von Schleicher, and Ludendorff. The third collection was returned from the Berlin Document Centre to the Federal Archive in Koblenz, where it was combined with the first. It contains personal and historical material (0.1m) The fourth collection of papers contains his memoirs of the Nazi dictatorship and writings from the time of his imprisonment by the Americans. It is held at the *Hauptstaatsarchiv*, Munich. (Source: Mommsen, *op. cit.*)

ERDMANNSDORFF, Otto von (b. 1888)

German diplomat. Legation counsellor, Mexico 1920–23; Foreign Ministry and President's Office 1923–28; embassy counsellor, Peking 1928–33; Deputy Director *Abteilung IV*, 1934–37; Ambassador in Budapest 1937–41; Deputy Director of Political Department 1941–43.

The Political Archive of the Federal German Foreign Office in Bonn has a very small collection (0.04m) of papers, which contains a draft entitled *Die politischen Ereignisse in Ungarn, 1937–1941* and copies of reports from the Baltic 1918–19. (Source: Mommsen, *op. cit.*)

ERICH, Rafael Waldemar (1879–1946)

Finnish Professor and Ambassador. Prime Minister 1920–21.

The *Valtionsarkisto*, Helsinki, has a substantial collection of papers totalling fifty boxes. These include correspondence, political drafts and notes as well as other documents covering the years 1910 to 1945. Access to this collection is restricted. In addition, the *Valtionsarkisto* also has two boxes of correspondence between Erich and Juuso Hedberg (1851–1919), these boxes being part of the Hedberg archive.

The Library of the Åbo Academy has a collection of Erich's correspondence. Further details can be obtained from this library.

ERIKSSON, Bernhard (1878–1952)

Swedish social democratic politician. Minister for the Navy.

Four boxes of Eriksson's papers are in the ARAB, Stockholm.

ERLER, Fritz (1913–67)

German social democratic politician. Member of the Bundestag 1949. Expert on foreign and defence policy. Founder member of the German Council of the European Movement 1949. Member of the Advisory Assembly of the European Council 1950; voted on to SPD Executive 1956; Vice-Chairman of Bundestag group 1957; Vice-Chairman of SPD 1964, and as successor to Erich Ollenhauer, Chairman of the Bundestag group. Supporter of the Grand Coalition.

The AdsD at the Friedrich-Ebert-Stiftung, Bonn, has an extensive collection (including one volume from before 1945) of Erler's personal papers, correspondence and publications.

ERZBERGER, Matthias (1875–1921)

German politician. Vice-Chancellor and Finance Minister.

A collection of his papers is held at the *Bundesarchiv*, Koblenz. It contains material on many problems of the years 1914–18 (0.75m). Other papers have been lost. (Source: Mommsen, *op. cit.*)

ESSEN, Hans Henrik von (1820–94)

Secretary to the Swedish Cabinet 1870–73.

There is a collection of von Essen's papers in the Royal Library, Stockholm.

ESTRUP, J.B.S. (fl. 1865–94)

Danish politician. Interior Minister 1865–69; Navy Minister 1866; Prime Minister and Finance Minister 1875–94.

A collection of his papers is held at the *Rigsarkiv*, Copenhagen (ref. 559). Other papers are privately owned.

ETTEL, Erwin (1895–1971)

German diplomat. Ambassador in Tehran 1939–41.

The Political Archive of the German Foreign Office, Bonn, has a collection of personal papers from the years 1919–60. This material is supplemented by Ettel's own collection of material on the German radio service, and the news-sheet of the Tehran embassy. (Source: Mommsen, *op. cit.*)

ETZDORFF, Hasso von (b. 1900)

German diplomat. Representative of Foreign Ministry, Army High Command 1939–44; Consul General, Genoa 1945.

His papers are at the Political Archive of the German Foreign Office in Bonn. (Source: Kimmich, *German Foreign Policy 1918–1945*.)

EULENBERG, Friedrich Graf zu (1815–81)

German diplomat and politician. Prussian Interior Minister.

Most of his papers are at the Brandenburg provincial archive in Potsdam. The collection contains personal papers and material relating to his diplomatic activity in the Far East. (Source: Mommsen, *op. cit.*)

EULENBERG und HERTEFELD, Philipp Fürst zu (1847–1921)

German officer and diplomat. Ambassador in Vienna 1894–1902.

Many papers were destroyed when the family seat in Brandenburg was plundered in 1945. Others have been deposited at the provincial archive in Potsdam. This collection contains, *inter alia*, material on his diplomatic service in Vienna; correspondence; family papers. A further collection, now at the German Federal Archive in Koblenz, contains copies of correspondence with leading political figures of the Wilhelmine period, including the emperor himself, who was a personal friend of the prince (0.7m). A separate collection, also at Koblenz, contains literary manuscripts, material on the Eulenberg trial, and copies of further correspondence (0.3m). (Source: Mommsen, *op. cit.*)

EULER, August (1868–1957)

German politician. State Secretary and leader of the Reich Office for air and motor vehicles; founder of the first German aircraft factory.

The German Federal Archive, Koblenz, has a substantial collection of his papers, including material relating to air matters, 1910–23; the Euler aircraft factory, 1907–22; correspondence with military organisations about military aircraft, 1908–20; papers from his time as under state secretary and state secretary; and documents relating to the seizure of his factory by the French. The collection covers the period 1907–26 (3.5m). (Source: Mommsen, *op. cit.*)

EWERLÖF, Oskar Anton Herman (1876–1934)

Secretary to the Swedish Cabinet 1913–17.

The *Riksarkiv*, Stockholm, has a collection of Ewerlöf's papers. The Archives of the Swedish Foreign Ministry, also housed at the *Riksarkiv*, has a collection of documents relating to his period of service between 1907 and 1917.

EYNAC (LAURENT-EYNAC), Laurent (1886–1970)

French politician. Under-Secretary of State for aeronautics and air transport 1921–24 and 1925–26; High Commissioner for Public Works (aeronautics and air transport) 1925; Air Minister 1928–30 and 1940.

The Town Hall at Monastier (Haute-Loire) has a number of items (2.50m): the Laurent-Eynac family papers; three files of manuscript notes by Laurent-Eynac on the creation of the Air Ministry; the history of French aeronautics between 1920 and 1940; a file put together by Laurent-Eynac on his attitude in 1940 and during the occupation. Information on access may be obtained from Yves Soulingeas, Directeur des Services d'Archives de la Haute-Loire, Rue Étienne-Delcambre, B.P. 113, 43000 le Puy-en-Velay. (Source: AN, *Guide des Papiers.*)

F

FABER DU FAUR, Moritz von (1886–1971)

German lieutenant general and diplomat. Military attaché at the German embassy in Belgrade 1936–39.

The German Federal Military Archive in Freiburg im Breisgau has a small collection of papers relating to Faber du Faur's diplomatic service in Belgrade, covering the years 1935–40. (Source: Mommsen, *op. cit.*)

FABRY, Jean (1876–1968)

French politician and journalist. Lieutenant-colonel. Minister for Colonies 1924; Minister of National Defence and War 1934; Minister of War 1935–36.

The *Service historique de l'Armée de Terre*, Vincennes, has six boxes of papers donated by Jean Fabry in 1968. These contain documents on the First World War, and in particular on Joffre; material on French politics between 1920 and 1950; correspondence and notes. (Source, AN, *Guide des Papiers.*)

FAGERHOLM, Karl-August (b. 1902)

Finnish social democratic leader. Member of Parliament 1930–66; Prime Minister 1948–50, 1956–57 and 1958.

Fagerholm has deposited his papers for the years 1917–78 in the Finnish Labour Archives, Helsinki. These comprise correspondence, speeches, lectures and statements, notes from the last period of the war (autumn 1944) and, in particular, material concerning the Ministry of Social Affairs, Fagerholm's governments, and also intergovernmental agreements and cooperation between the Nordic countries. This collection is fully catalogued, but may be consulted only with Fagerholm's personal permission.

FALKENBERG, Peder Christen Jens (1892–   )

Finnish Vice-Consul and diplomat.

The *Valtionsarkisto*, Helsinki, has a small collection of documents consisting of a report on the Finnish consulate in Denmark in 1933.

FALKENHAYN, Erich von (1861–1922)

German officer. Infantry general; Prussian War Minister; Turkish marshal.

His diary and correspondence are presumed to have been destroyed. One file of other papers is at the *Deutsches Zentralarchiv*, Potsdam. (Source: Mommsen, *op. cit.*)

FANTI, Manfredo (1808–65)

Italian General. War Minister in Cavour's last administration.

The *Archivio Centrale dello Stato*, Rome, has one box of correspondence and military documents from the period 1848 to 1862. (Source: *Guida Generale*.)

FARRE, Jean (1816–87)

French General. Minister of War 1879–81.

The *Service historique de l'Armée de Terre*, Vincennes, has one file (ref. 1 K 204) containing papers relating to Farre's time as War Minister, and in particular the Tunisia expedition. The papers consist mainly of correspondence with the Foreign Minister, the Navy Minister and the Minister for Colonies, and letters from Jules Ferry. The material covers the period 1880–81. (Source: AN, *Guide des Papiers*.)

FAURE, Félix (1841–99)

French politician. Under-Secretary of State for Commerce and the Colonies 1881–82; Under-Secretary of State for the Navy and for Colonies 1883–85 and 1888; Navy Minister 1894–95. President of the Republic 1895–99.

The *Archives Nationales* (*archives privées*) has a collection of twenty-two boxes of papers deposited by Faure's grandsons, MM. François and André Berge, in 1977 (ref. Entrée 2711, provisional classification). The collection includes correspondence, material on Faure's periods in office as deputy, Secretary of State, Minister and President; notes on Indo-China; press-cuttings on the Dreyfus affair. Access is by written authorisation of the depositors. In addition the *Archives Nationales* Overseas Section has one file of official letters on Madagascar, Oceania, the Comoros and Guyana. (Source: AN, *Guide des Papiers*.)

FAURE, Paul (1878–1960)

French socialist politician. General Secretary of the SFIO until 1949. Minister of State under Blum and Chautemps June 1936 to January 1938 and March to April 1938 (responsible for liaison between the Government and the SFIO and the nationalisation of the war industries). Differed with Blum over foreign policy (recommended negotiations with Hitler and caution in relation to Franco-Russian alliance) and opposed Blum's policy of a National Government.

A part of Faure's private papers are to be found in the OURS, Paris. This comprises, in particular, his correspondence in the years 1929–35 and 1940–44.

FAVRE, Jules (1809–80)

French politician. Deputy, Senator. Minister of Foreign Affairs and Vice-President of the Government of National Defence 1870–71; Foreign Minister, February–August 1871.

The archive of the Foreign Ministry has twenty-two volumes relating to the period when Favre was Foreign Minister. The collection includes diplomatic and other correspondence; information on military operations, the condition of the army and civilian morale, and also on the siege of Paris, the armistice and the Frankfurt negotiations (ref. *Fonds nominatifs*, no. 70). Further material can be found in the manuscripts department of the *Bibliothèque Nationale*, which has nine folio volumes and a case containing eleven boxed or bound volumes (ref. *Nouvelles acquisitions françaises*, 24107–26). The collection consists of miscellaneous material including family papers; correspondence; and material on judicial reform. The first collection covers the period 1870–71, and there is a typed inventory by J. Paz. The second collection covers the period 1834–79 and there is an inventory by Jean Porcher, *Nouvelles acquisitions latines et françaises du Département des manuscrits de la Bibliothèque nationale pendant les années 1941–1945*, in the *Bibliothèque de l'École des Chartes, vol. CVI, années 1945–1946,* pp. 258–60. (Source: AN, *Guide des Papiers.*)

FEDERZONI, Luigi (fl. 1920s)

Italian politician. Colonies Minister in Mussolini's first administration, 1922–24 and during the first two years of his second administration, 1924–26.

Federzoni's papers are in the possession of his family.

FEIERABEND, Ladislaw K. (1891–1969)

Czech politician. Cabinet Minister in the Government-in-Exile 1941–45.

A large collection of papers (*c.* twenty boxes), covering the period from 1922 onwards, has been deposited in the Hoover Institution, Stanford University, California.

FELDMANS, Jules (1889–1953)

Latvian diplomat.

A collection of papers (*c.* eighteen boxes), covering the period 1919–55, is in the Hoover Institution, Stanford University, California. The collection includes material on the Russian occupation of the Baltic states in 1940 and Latvian émigré politics.

FERRY, Abel (fl. 1881–1918)

French politician. Under-Secretary of State for Foreign Affairs 1914–15.

Ferry's daughter, Mme Pisani-Ferry has a collection of his papers. The collection includes material on his time as Under-Secretary, and in particular documents relating to Africa; private and official correspondence; material on the First World War and on Ferry's mission to Italy in 1917–18; and memoirs. There is an inventory by Ferry's wife, revised by his daughter, which is available on microfilm at the *Archives Nationales* (*archives privées*, ref. 456 Mi). The archive of the Foreign Ministry has a file containing ten photocopies of documents relating to the period immediately before France's entry into the First World War (27 July to 2 August 1914). (Source: AN, *Guide des Papiers.*)

FERRY, Jules (1832–93)

French politician and diplomat. Member of Government of National Defence 1870–71; Prime Minister and Minister of Education and Arts 1880–81 and 1883; Prime Minister and Foreign Minister 1883–85.

The *Foyer des Ferry*, annexed to the municipal library in Saint-Dié has a collection made up of a bequest of Mme Jules Ferry to the Sorbonne, which was then deposited in Saint-Dié in 1955, and gifts of Mme Abel Ferry and Mme Pisani-Ferry. The collection comprises sixty-one boxes and includes a collection of files compiled by Ferry in the course of his journalistic and political career, and relating in particular to education, colonial policy and economic problems. The rest of the collection is correspondence. Mme Pisani-Ferry has a further collection of correspondence, including that of ambassadors with Ferry 1883–85, family papers, and other documents, including material on the Tonkin campaign. The Foreign Ministry archive has three volumes of papers (ref. *Fonds nominatifs*, no. 71) containing notes on Tunisia, correspondence on the Congo, and a file on Madagascar. The material covers the period 1881–85. (Source: AN, *Guide des Papiers*.)

FIEDLER-ALBERTI, Stefan (b. 1891)

Polish diplomat. Served Berlin, Belgrade, Zagreb. Consul-General in Nicosia, 1940–41. Later served in Rhodesia and South Africa.

A collection of papers, mainly relating to his diplomatic service, is in the Polish Institute, London.

FLANDIN, Pierre-Étienne (1889–1958)

French politician. Under-Secretary of State for Public Works (aeronautics and air transport) 1920–21; Prime Minister 1934–35; Foreign Minister 1936.

The Foreign Ministry archive has a file covering the period 1924–39, containing documents on Czechoslovakia and Munich, including a letter from Lord Runciman, 28 September 1938. There is further material available in the manuscripts department of the *Bibliothèque Nationale*, Paris. (Source: AN, *Guide des Papiers*.)

FLEETWOOD, Carl Reinhold Axel Georgsson (1859–92)

Head of the Political Department of the Swedish Foreign Ministry 1889–92.

The *Riksarkiv*, Stockholm, has a collection of Fleetwood's papers. Other papers and documents are still in private hands although some diaries have been published.

FLEURIAN, Aimé-Joseph de (1870–1938)

French diplomat. Minister in London 1913 and Peking 1921–24. Ambassador in London 1924–33.

A collection of his papers is held at the Archive of the Ministry of Foreign Affairs, Quai d'Orsay, Paris, in the collection *Papiers d'Agents* (6). The collection comprises three volumes covering the years 1913–33. (Source: Young, *op. cit.*)

FORRER, Ludwig (1845–1921)

Swiss politician. Federal Counsellor. President of the Confederation.

His papers are at the Central Library, Zürich. The collection comprises personal papers; letters; lecture manuscripts; and written material on juridical and political themes. The collection runs to 2.85m and covers the whole of Forrer's life.

FORSTER, Dirk (1884–1975)

German diplomat. Legation counsellor, then ambassador in Paris; deputy director of the German Office for Peace Issues (*Deutsches Büro für Friedensfragen*) 1947–49.

The Institute of Contemporary History, Munich, has a collection of his papers from the years 1947–50, relating to the structure, organisation and activity of the Peace Office (0.8m). (Source: Mommsen, *op. cit.*)

FORTHOMME, Pierre (b. 1877)

Belgian diplomat. Vice-Consul in Guatemala 1899; Consul in Natal 1903–07; Consul in Johannesburg 1907–19, where he maintained an interest in the Congo. In 1909 he accompanied Prince Albert on his visit to central and southern Africa. Took part in the campaign in favour of the colonisation of Katanga 1910–11. After the First World War briefly in Prague, then Foreign Ministry in Brussels before entering parliament in 1921 as a Liberal. Became Minister of Defence 1923–25. Out of parliament between 1925 and 1929, he was appointed Belgian High Commissioner in the Rhineland. After several different ministerial posts (1929–34), he was involved in various diplomatic negotiations – with the US, Luxembourg, at the Montreux conference. In 1936 his appointment as ambassador to Berlin was vetoed by Hitler. In 1939 he headed the Belgian mission to Latin America. Ambassador to Tokyo. Allowed to leave Japan in 1942, he stayed in Johannesburg until 1946. In 1946–47 he headed the Belgian delegation to the FAO in Washington.

The *Archives Générales du Royaume*, Brussels, has Forthomme's papers 1895–1950. These include copies of his diplomatic and political reports 1902–20 (mainly southern and central Africa); notes on the post-war situation 1921; dossiers on military questions 1922–25, including the occupation of the Rhineland, the Franco-Belgian military accord, the 'German question'; commercial agreements with the US; negotiations 1933–38; Belgian–Italian relations 1932; reports on Japan 1941–43; and the FAO. Permission is needed to use the material.

FOTITCH, Konstantin (1891–1959)

Yugoslav diplomat. Minister and Ambassador to the United States 1934–44.

An extensive collection of papers (*c.* fifty-six boxes), covering the period 1934–64, is in the Hoover Institution, Stanford University, California. The collection, closed until August 1989, includes material on political and military conditions in Yugoslavia during the Second World War, Yugoslav relations with the United States and émigré politics.

FOUCHET, Maurice (fl. 1920s)

French diplomat. Served Afghanistan, Indo-China, etc.

A collection of papers for the early 1920s is available in the archives of the French Foreign Ministry, Paris.

FRAGNITO, Giorgio (fl. 1950–70)

Italian diplomat.

The *Archivio Centrale dello Stato*, Rome, has twenty-two files covering the period 1950 to 1971. The collection comprises correspondence and documents on foreign policy, and particularly on Mauretania, Senegal, Portuguese Guinea, Egypt, Tunisia and other states. (Source: *Guida Generale.*)

FRANDIN, Hippolyte (fl. 1890s)

French diplomat. Served China, Korea, etc.

One carton of papers, covering the period 1883 to 1902, is available in the archives of the French Foreign Ministry, Paris.

FRANK, Hans (1900–46)

German politician. Frank was the leading jurist of the NSDAP, and defended Hitler in a number of actions before 1933. He became Reich Minister of Justice, and was appointed Governor General of Poland, a position which he retained even after he was stripped of all his party and legal offices in 1942. Frank was executed as a war criminal at Nuremberg in 1946.

A collection of his papers is at the German Federal Archive, Koblenz. The material includes his diaries for the years 1918–25, 1937 and 1942; personal papers; documents from the years 1927–29; and press cuttings about the Government General of Poland (0.4m). Copies of a further thirty-eight volumes of his diary are available at the Federal Archive; the originals are held by the Commission for the Investigation of Nazi crimes in Poland, and this collection is possibly identical with a collection at the Archive of New Documents, Warsaw. A further collection, consisting mainly of legal documents and correspondence relating to the Government General is at the Berlin Document Centre (1.6m). A study of Himmler and memories of Hitler, written in 1945–46 in Nuremberg are in private ownership in the United States. (Source: Mommsen, *op. cit.*)

FRANK, Karl-Hermann (1898–1946)

German politician. Sudeten *Freikorps* leader; member of Czech parliament from 1937; Chief of Police in Bohemia after Nazi occupation of Prague in 1939; Reich Protector of Bohemia and Moravia, and from 1943 Minister of State with rank of Reich Minister for Bohemia and Moravia. Executed in Prague 1946.

A collection of papers is held by the Czech Interior Ministry, Prague. (Source: Mommsen, *op. cit.*)

FRANSEN van de PUTTE, I.D. (1822–1902)

Dutch planter on Java and later Minister for the Colonies.

The *Algemeen Rijksarchief*, The Hague, has a collection of Fransen van de Putte papers (0.5m) covering the period 1838–1900 (Inventory 2.21.66: Coll. 191A). Additional correspondence with Fransen van de Putte can be found in the collections of E. van Raalte, A.J. Duymaer van Twist, jhr. J. Loudon and the Lansberge family all housed in the same archive. Other papers can be found in the L.H. Cornets de Groot collection at the *Koninklijk Bibliotheek*, The Hague, and in the H. Muller collection at the *Gemeentearchief*, Rotterdam. In addition, there is a collection of letters to N.G. Pierson at the *Universiteitsbibliotheek*, Amsterdam. There is also a Fransen van de Putte archive in private hands, consisting of personal and other correspondence. Other items can be found in the private archives of van de Maesen, Tellegen and Geertsma. Further details of these archives can be obtained from the Central Register of Private Archives, The Hague.

FRÈRE, Maurice (1890–1970)

Belgian economist and international finance specialist. Governor of the National Bank. Appointed director of the Office des Questions Commerciales in Economics Ministry 1917. Involved in reparations negotiations; appointed director of information service, Reparations Commission 1919. Committee on monetary stabilisation 1924. Involved in League of Nations' recovery plan for Austria and Hungary. Appointed financial adviser to Belgian Legation in Berlin 1930. Advised Chinese government; took part in negotiations for the end of reparations. Adviser to Austrian National Bank 1933–37; involved in international negotiations for freer trade 1937–39. Appointed president of the International Banking Commission 1938. President of the Belgian National Bank 1944; represented Belgium in the IMF and International Reconstruction and Development Bank.

The *Archives Générales du Royaume*, Brussels, has Frère's papers, covering the period 1916–56. They are particularly relevant to international finance in the inter-war period, and include correspondence; notes and reports on reparations, on the economic and financial situation of Germany from Versailles to Lausanne; notes on economic and financial questions in the League of Nations 1927–1939; on the financial situation of Austria and Hungary; on China, and on international trade. An inventory has been published: Robert Wellens (ed.), *Inventaire des Papiers de Maurice Frère, Gouverneur de la Banque Nationale de Belgique* (Brussels, 1976).

FRÈRE-ORBAN, H.J.W. (1812–96)

Belgian Liberal politician. Head of government 1857–67 and 1868–70. Head of government and Minister of Foreign Affairs 18 June 1878 to 10 June 1884.

The *Archives Générales du Royaume*, Brussels, has Frère-Orban's papers, covering the period 1840–94, including considerable correspondence with other prominent politicians, civil servants, the King, and documents relating to his political career, including defence and foreign policy. An inventory has been published: R. Boumans (ed.), *Inventaire des papiers de H.J.W. Frère-Orban* (Brussels: 1958), 88 pp.

FREY, Emil (1838–1922)

Swiss politician. Federal counsellor; President of National Council 1875–76; Head of Military Department; President of the Confederation 1894; Vice-President of the Special Conference for the International Protection of Labour, Paris 1905; major in Swiss army; commander of II division 1890.

Frey's personal papers are at the Canton State Archive of the city of Basle (*Staatsarchiv des Kantons Basel-Stadt*), in the Frey family archive (ref. *Privatarchive* 485). The papers cover private, political, academic and military subjects, and include a collection of correspondence. There is a detailed register of both personal papers and correspondence.

FREY, Remigius Emil (1803–89)

Swiss politician. President of Council of State 1855–56.

Some correspondence is to be found at Basle University Library. All the letters are dated before 1870. There are also lecture manuscripts and private papers from the period 1820–40.

FREY-HEROSÉ, Friedrich (1801–73)

Swiss officer and politician. President of the Confederation 1860.

The State Archive of the Canton Aargau, Aarau has one file of Frey-Herosé's private papers. The Aargau Canton Library has his Paris diary of 1820 and 1821 (ref. Ms BN F 91). The Swiss Federal Archives also have some of his private papers.

FREYCINET, Charles (1828–1923)

French politician. Prime Minister and Foreign Minister 1879–80, 1882 and 1886; Foreign Minister 1885; Minister of War 1888–90, 1892–93 and 1898–99; Prime Minister and Minister of War 1890–92; Minister of State 1915–16.

The *Bibliothèque de l'Ecole polytechnique*, Paris, has eighteen boxes of papers, including correspondence, reports, press cuttings and speeches. Access is possible with the written authorisation of the principal at the school. The Foreign Ministry archive has one box and sixteen volumes (ref. *Fonds nominatifs*, no. 77). The collection contains a number of documents on foreign affairs questions, above all in Africa, between 1880 and 1883; exploration in French East Africa; French penetration of the Sudan; the Balkans, the Ottoman Empire and Greece. There is also some material on legal questions. (Source: AN, *Guide des Papiers*.)

FRICK, Wilhelm (1877–1946)

German politician. Reich Minister of the Interior 1933–1943; Reich Protector of Bohemia 1943–45; executed at Nuremberg 1946.

The German Federal Archive, Koblenz, has twelve files of personal documents and private correspondence. (Source: Mommsen, *op. cit.*)

FRIETSCH, Carl Olof (Ole) (1901–74)

Finnish diplomat and legation counsellor.

The *Valtionsarkisto*, Helsinki, has a substantial collection of papers totalling forty-one boxes. Included are correspondence and other documents from the years 1912 to 1973 as well as material related to his career in the Finnish Parliament, foreign affairs and family matters from the years 1862 to 1927.

FRIIS, Michael Petersen (1857–1944)

Danish politician. Prime Minister and Defence Minister 5 April to 5 May 1940.

A collection of one packet of his papers from the years 1885–1932, including some letters, is held at the *Rigsarkiv*, Copenhagen (ref. 6624).

FRIJS, C.E. (1817–96)

Danish politician. Prime Minister and Foreign Minister 1865–70. War Minister and Navy Minister 1870.

A collection of his papers is held at the *Rigsarkiv*, Copenhagen (ref. 2541).

FROHWEIN, Hans (b. 1887)

German diplomat. Consular service in USA 1924–26; Foreign Office 1926–36; Minister in Reval, 1936–40.

A collection of documents relating to him is held at the Political Archive of the Federal German Foreign Office in Bonn.

FRYLING, Jan (fl. 1940s)

Polish diplomat, lawyer and politician. Counsellor, Polish Embassy in China.

Six boxes of his papers covering the period 1939 to 1977, have been acquired by the Hoover Institution, Stanford University, California.

FUCHS, Martin (b. 1904)

Austrian diplomat. Press attaché, Paris, before the German occupation of Austria; political émigré; Austrian consul general after the Second World War.

The DÖW, Vienna, has a collection of correspondence and drafts relating to post-war Austrian politics (three volumes).

FÜRSTENBERG, Max Egon Prince (1863–1941)

Austrian officer and politician. Member of *Herrenhaus* (Upper Chamber) in both Austria and Prussia; Royal Prussian colonel-marshal. His close personal relationships with both Wilhelm II of Germany and Archduke Franz Ferdinand made him an important figure in Austro-German relations.

His papers are at the *Fürstlich Fürstenbergisches Archiv* in Donaueschingen. Much of the material was typewritten by Fürstenberg himself. Incoming letters were usually date-stamped.

G

GAISSER, Karl (1880–1958)

German police colonel. District director in the German protectorates of Togo and Cameroon. Adviser to the Croatian police 1943–44.

The German Federal Military Archive, Freiburg im Breisgau, has a collection of papers from the years 1907–50. The material includes memoirs of his service in Togo, Cameroon, and Croatia; correspondence; and reports from Togo and Cameroon. (Source: Mommsen, *op. cit.*)

GALLENGA, Antonio Carlo Napoleone (1810–95)

Italian politician.

The Times archive in London has a collection of his papers from the years 1859–84.

GALLENGA, Romeo (fl. 1917–24)

Italian politician.

The *Archivio Centrale dello Stato*, Rome, has one box of papers referring to international questions during the First World War. The collection dates from the years 1917 to 1924. (Source: *Guida Generale*.)

GALLI, Carlo (fl. 1918–39)

Italian diplomat. Delegate to numerous conferences in the early 1920s. Minister, Tehran 1924–26; Lisbon 1926–28; Belgrade 1928–34. Ambassador, Ankara 1934–38.

His papers are at the private *Archivio dell'ambasciatore Carlo Galli*, Venice. (Source: Cassels, *op. cit.*)

GALLIÉNI, Joseph (1849–1916)

French Field-Marshal; Minister of War, October 1915 to March 1916.

The overseas section of the *Archives Nationales* has one file on Galliéni's time in the Sudan, covering the period 1887–95 (ref. APC 20). The archive also has twelve boxes of unclassified material on Gallieni's activities in Tonkin 1893–95, in Madagascar 1896–1905, and as War Minister 1915.

    The *Service historique de l'Armée de Terre*, Vincennes, has a further twelve boxes of material. The collection includes the accounts of the Governor-General of Madagascar; documents on manoeuvres between 1906 and 1912; the defence of the colonies 1910–14; projects, proposals for legislation and ministerial circulars from 1915 and 1916; material on the fortifications of Paris 1914–15 and on the re-organisation of the War Ministry 1910–16. See Devos *et al. Inventaire sommaire des archives de la Guerre* (Troyes, 1974), pp. 103–06. There are also some letters 1897–1914, in the *Bibliothèque Nationale* (ref. NAF 13295). (Source: AN, *Guide des Papiers*.)

GAMBETTA, Léon (1838–82)

French politician. Interior Minister and War Minister 1870–71; Prime Minister and Foreign Minister 1881–82.

The principal collection of Gambetta's papers relating to political matters can be found in the archives of the Foreign Ministry (ref. *Fonds nominatifs*, no. 79) and comprises sixty-one volumes of material in eighteen boxes. The collection covers the period 1870 to 1882 and contains documents relating to the Government of National Defence, military operations, the capitulation of Paris, and relations between Gambetta and the National Assembly. Further material, mainly correspondence, can be found among the papers of Joseph Reinach in the manuscript department of the *Bibliothèque Nationale*, (ref. *Nouvelles acquisitions françaises* 13527 to 13618 and 24874 to 24913). Further details are to be found in Solente, *Nouvelles acquisitions*, pp. 197–200, 251–52, 254. Copies of 496 letters to Gambetta from Léonie Léon were purchased by the library of the National Assembly in 1938, and are located under ref. U3491. (Source: AN, *Guide des Papiers*.)

GARIBALDI, Giuseppe (1807–82)

Italian general and politician.

The *Archivio Centrale dello Stato*, Rome, has one volume of Garibaldi's memoirs from the years 1871 to 1875.

GASPARINI, Jacopo (fl. 1918–29)

Italian colonial administrator. Governor of Eritrea after the First World War.

Gasparini's papers are in the care of Professor Renzo De Felice at the Institute of Historical and Political Studies in Rome. The collection includes material on Anglo-Italian relations in the Middle East. (Source: Cassels, *op. cit.*)

GAUS, Friedrich Wilhelm Otto (b. 1881)

German diplomat. Delegate at Brest-Litovsk and Versailles 1918–19, Genoa 1922, London 1924, Locarno 1925 and the League of Nations 1926 as representative of the German Foreign Office, where he was deputy director 1921–23 and then director 1923–43 of the legal department.

A collection of documents relating to him is held at the Political Archive of the Federal German Foreign Office in Bonn.

GAVRILOVIĆ, Milan (1882–1976)

Yugoslav diplomat, politician and journalist. Ambassador to the Soviet Union 1940–41.

A large collection of his papers (*c.* fifty-five boxes), covering the period 1939 to 1976, is in the Hoover Institution, Stanford University, California. There is material on Yugoslav politics and the government in exile, Draza Mihailović and the Chetnik resistance, and relations with the Soviet Union. The collection remains closed until 1995.

GAY, Francisque (1885–1963)

French politician and diplomat. Minister of State 1945–46. Deputy Prime Minister, January–June 1946. Ambassador to Canada 1948–49.

Gay's papers are in the possession of his wife. They include documents relating to his political and diplomatic careers; correspondence; miscellaneous documents on his publishing activities on the *Action française*, and the resistance (12m). (Source: AN, *Guide des Papiers*.)

GEER, Dirk Jan de (1870–1960)

Chairman of the Dutch Cabinet 1926–29 and 1939–40. During his second term of office, he took the cabinet to London but, because of his advocacy of a compromise peace with Hitler, he was persuaded to step down and later returned to the Netherlands via Lisbon. In 1947 he was dismissed as a Minister of State and given a suspended sentence for collaboration.

The *Algemeen Rijksarchief*, The Hague, has a small collection of papers (0.3m) relating to the de Geer family and covering the period 1864–1962 (Inventories 2.21.183 and 2.21.115: Coll. 286). Other papers can be found in the Mackay van Ophemert family collection.

GEERTSMA, J.H. (fl. 1870s)

Chairman of the Dutch Cabinet and Minister for Home Affairs 1872–74.

A family archive covering the period from the seventeenth to the twentieth century exists. For further details contact the Central Register of Private Archives. Other papers may be found at the *Rijksarchief*, Groningen, and in the H. Muller collection at the *Gemeentearchief*, Rotterdam.

Other letters to and from Geertsma can be found in the Fock, Lansberge and Tellegen collections at the *Algemeen Rijksarchief*, The Hague.

GEILINGER, Rudolf (1848–1911)

Swiss officer and politician. President of Grand Council 1896; National Councillor 1884; President of National Council 1896.

The Municipal Library, Winterthur, has an incomplete collection of his papers. The material includes correspondence 1898–1907; a lecture; reports concerning the Gotthard fortifications 1897–1909; and military correspondence (three pages, 1898 and 1903). The library also has a separate collection of correspondence from the years 1848–1911.

GÉRARD, Auguste (fl. 1894–1920)

French diplomat. Served China, Japan.

A collection of papers is housed in the *Archives Nationales*, Paris. A further 16 volumes of papers, covering the period 1894 to 1920, are reported in the archives of the French Foreign Ministry, Paris.

GERBRANDY, Pieter Sjoerds (1885–1961)

Chairman of the Dutch Cabinet and the government in exile in London, 1940–46. Also Minister of Justice 1939–46 and Minister of General Affairs and Colonies 1940–46.

The *Algemeen Rijksarchief*, The Hague, has a substantial collection of Gerbrandy papers (4.5m) covering the period 1904–60 (Inventory 2.21.68: Coll. 155). Most of the material comes from the post-1940 period.

GERICKE van HERWIJNEN, J.L.H.A. (fl. 1870s)

Dutch Minister of Foreign Affairs 1871–74. As a Roman Catholic he opposed the removal of diplomatic representation to the Vatican after its incorporation into Italy.

An extensive archive exists in family hands and includes correspondence with W.F. Rochussen, v.d. Bosse and Johan Rudolf Thorbecke. For further details contact the Central Register of Private Archives, The Hague.

Other papers can be found in the collections of J.W. van Lansberge and I.D. Fransen van de Putte at the *Algemeen Rijksarchief*, The Hague.

GIANNINI, Amadeo (fl. 1918–43)

Italian diplomat. Delegate to the Paris Peace Conference 1919 and Genoa Conference 1922; the Conference of Austrian Successor States, Rome 1924 and the League of Nations 1930–31. Director-General of the Foreign Office 1936–43.

A collection of sixteen boxes of his papers covering the years 1890–1960, with material relating to the period 1607 to 1828, is at the *Archivio Centrale dello Stato* in Rome. The material includes correspondence and miscellaneous administrative documents.

GIERS, Mihail Nikolaevič (1856–1925)

Russian diplomat. Member of the Russian Political Conference, Paris 1919, and chief diplomatic representative of the Vrangel government 1920.

A collection of his papers (*c.* 131 folders) is held at the Hoover Institution, Stanford University, California. Covering the years 1919–26, the material includes reports of Russian diplomatic representatives in various countries, including Britain and the United States, and telegraphic correspondence between the representatives and the Paris Conference.

GIOLITTI, Giovanni (1841–1928)

Italian politician. Prime Minister and Interior Minister 1892–93, 1903–05, 1906–09, 1911–14 and 1920–21.

The *Archivio Centrale dello Stato*, Rome, has seventeen files and fifty-five boxes of papers covering the period 1858–1928. (Source: *Guida Generale*.)

GIPPERICH, Hermann (1882–1959)

German diplomat. Consular service in China, Hong Kong and Manchuria; Consul General, Hong Kong 1936–39 and at the German embassy in China 1939–45.

A very small collection of his papers is held by the Political Archive of the German Foreign Office, Bonn (0.02m). The collection includes sketches from his time in China and Hong Kong; and memoirs, supplemented by memoirs of his wife. (Source: Mommsen, *op. cit.*)

GOBEE, E. (1881–1954)

Dutch naval officer who served in the East Indies and later as Consul at Jeddah 1917–21.

The *Koninklijk Instituut voor Taal-, Land-, en Volkenkunde*, Leiden has a collection of papers covering the period 1908–51. Copies of these on five rolls of microfilm can be found at the *Algemeen Rijksarchief*, The Hague (Inventory 2.21.193).

Other papers are known to exist in private archives. For further details contact the Central Register of Private Archives, The Hague.

GODART, Justin (1871–1956)

French politician. Under-Secretary of State for the health of the armed forces at the War Ministry 1915–20.

Godart's papers are held at the *Musée Historique*, Lyons. There are 100 boxes of material, containing a few documents on his political career but mainly material on the history of Lyons, where Godart was mayor. (Source: AN, *Guide des Papiers*.)

GOEBBELS, Joseph (1897–1945)

German politician. Member of the NSDAP from 1922; co-author of the draft programme of the Nazi 'left' submitted at the Hanover conference of 1926, he went over to Hitler's side in the same year; *Gauleiter* of Berlin-Brandenburg from 1926; member of the *Reichstag* from 1928; propaganda leader of the NSDAP from 1929; Reich Minister for Public Enlightenment and Propaganda, and President of the Reich Chamber of Culture from 1933; Plenipotentiary General for Total War from 1944.

There are several collections of Goebbels' papers. His diaries for the years 1925–26 and 1942–43 are at the Hoover Institution, Stanford University, California, along with some personal documents. His non-political papers from the years 1917–26, including his attempts at literary composition, letters, and a will from 1920 are in private ownership. Copies of parts of both these collections are at the German Federal Archive in Koblenz. A further collection of papers was found in the safe at the Propaganda Ministry. Some of these were bought by collectors and others are reported to have found their way to the Soviet Union; there are similar unconfirmed reports that other diaries are also in the Soviet Union. Microcopies of his diaries from 1924–45 were ordered to be made by Goebbels; some 20 000 plates are said to have been made, but it is not known where these now are. It is possible that a collection acquired by the Hoffmann Campe publishing house is wholly or partly a copy of this collection. The Hoffmann Campe collection consists of microfilms, microfiches, photocopies and typed copies of Goebbels' diaries for the following periods: summer 1924 to August 1931; summer 1935 to February 1938; October 1939 to summer 1941; daily dictation in typescript from summer 1941 to August 1942; January and February 1943; May and June 1943; and February to April 1945. There are 6000 pages of diaries, and 10 000 pages of daily dictation. This collection was in duplicate and was sold to the Institute of Contemporary History in Munich, and the German Federal Archive in Koblenz. Each archive should therefore have the same material. The Institute of Contemporary History also has a collection of diary fragments from 1942 and 1943, and photocopies of the diaries from the same period. The Library of Congress, Washington, DC, has records of his speeches.

GOEPPERT, Otto (1872–1943)

German diplomat and public servant. Ambassador to Finland.

A collection of his papers is held at the Political Archive of the Federal German Foreign Office in Bonn. It contains notebooks and printed material mainly from the years between 1907 and 1935, with some notebooks from 1896. (Source: Mommsen, *op. cit.*)

GÖMBÖS, Gyula (1886–1936)

Hungarian fascist and racialist politician. Captain in the General Staff during the First World War. Minister of Defence from 1929, and Prime Minister from October 1932 until October 1936.

The Hungarian National Archives, Budapest, have a collection of papers (0.14m) covering the period 1922–36.

GÖPPERT, Otto (1872–1943)

German diplomat. Ambassador to Finland 1922; Commissar in the Foreign Office 1924.

His papers are at the Political Archive of the German Foreign Office in Bonn. They include notebooks from 1896 and from the years 1914–35, and sketches and printed material concerning various special assignments (0.50m). (Source: Mommsen, *op. cit.*)

GÖRING, Hermann (1893–1946)

German politician. Member of NSDAP; elected to the *Reichstag* 1928; president of the *Reichstag* 1932–45; Prime Minister of Prussia 1933; creator of secret state police (*Gestapo*); Minister for Aviation, Commander-in-Chief of the Air Force, and plenipotentiary for the Four-Year Plan from 1936; Reich marshal from 1940; sentenced to death at Nuremberg, he committed suicide in his cell.

There are several collections of Göring's papers. The Library of Congress in Washington has a collection which includes his personal notebook and material from the office of the Four-Year Plan. A small collection, consisting mainly of three volumes of diaries, was reported to be in the hands of Sotheby's in 1977. Part of a small collection of letters to and from Karin Göring is in private ownership in the United States. Two further collections are now missing. (Source: Mommsen, *op. cit.*)

GORRINI, Giacomo (fl. 1885–1945)

Italian diplomat and publicist.

Gorrini's personal papers, which are held by the *Archivio Centrale dello Stato*, Rome, contain some documents relating to foreign policy. The collection, which comprises five boxes, covers the period 1885 to 1945. (Source: *Guida Generale.*)

GOSSLER, Alfred von (1867–1946)

German reserve major and public servant.

A collection of his papers is held at the German Federal Military Archive, Freiburg im Breisgau. The collection includes memoirs (1867–1945); documents relating to his service as an administrator in Kurland and the Baltic; and memoranda and reports on the political situation in the Baltic (0.1m). (Source: Mommsen, *op. cit.*)

GOSSLER, Heinrich von (1841–1927)

German infantry general. Prussian War Minister.

Most of his papers were destroyed, but a collection of personal papers, letters, diaries and military-historical drafts survives. This collection is privately owned, but there are copies at the German Federal Military Archive, Freiburg im Breisgau (0.1m). (Source: Mommsen, *op. cit.*)

GOUGEARD, Auguste (1827–86)

French politician, general and naval captain. Counsellor of State. Navy Minister 1881–82.

The *Service historique de la Marine*, Vincennes, has two boxes of material, including correspondence relating to Cochin-China 1863–64, and miscellaneous items relating to the prefecture of Tanan (ref. GG227 and 228). (Source: AN, *Guide des Papiers.*)

GOUT, Jean (fl. 1900–24)

French diplomat. Deputy Director, Far East Section, Foreign Office.

Ten volumes of his papers, covering the period 1900–24, are housed in the archive of the Ministry of Foreign Affairs, Quai d'Orsay, Paris.

GRAAFF, S. de (fl. 1930s)

Dutch Minister for the Colonies 1919–25 and 1929–33.

The *Gemeentearchief*, Leiden, is understood to have a de Graaff family archive.

GRAEFF, Andries Cornelis Dirk de (1872–1957)

Dutch Foreign Minister 1933–37 and formerly Ambassador to Tokyo 1919 and to Washington 1922. Governor-General of Netherlands Indies 1926–31.

The de Graeff correspondence with A.W.F. Idenburg, covering the period 1915–31, can be found at the *Abraham Kuyperstichting*, Free University, Amsterdam. Similarly, correspondence with E. van Raalte covering the period 1933–56 can be found at the *Algemeen Rijksarchief*, The Hague.

GRAFSTRÖM, Sven Hjalmarsson (1902–55)

Head of the Political Section of the Swedish Foreign Ministry 1945–48.

A collection of Grafström's papers can be found at the *Riksarkiv*, Stockholm.

GRAM, Greger Winter Wulfsberg (1846–1929)

Norwegian diplomat and government minister 1889–91 and 1893–98.

The Manuscript Collection, Oslo University Library has in its possession a collection of manuscripts. Other papers can be found at the *Riksarkiv*, Oslo.

GRAM, Victor (1910–69)

Danish politician. Defence Minister 1962–68.

A collection of twenty packets of his papers is held at the *Rigsarkiv*, Copenhagen. The material covers the years 1927–69 and includes letters, manuscripts, political works, pocket books, and papers relating to his political career (ref. 6672).

GRANDI, Dino (b. 1895)

Italian politician and diplomat. Under-Secretary of State for Foreign Affairs 1925–29; delegate to numerous conferences in the 1920s and 1930s; Foreign Minister 1929–32; Ambassador to London 1932–39; Minister of Justice 1939–43.

A collection of his papers is in the care of Professor Renzo de Felice at the Institute of Historical and Political Studies in Rome. The extensive collection includes his diary as Under-Secretary and Foreign Minister and documents from the London embassy. A small selection of material relevant to the United States is available on microfilm at Georgetown University Library, Washington, DC. The *Archivio Centrale dello Stato*, Rome, has one box of correspondence and miscellaneous documents relating to his duties as Under-Secretary of State for Foreign Affairs between 1925 and 1929, and then as Foreign Minister between 1929 and 1932 and Italian ambassador in London between 1932 and 1939. The collection contains material on the London Naval Conference of 1930 and covers the period 1925–35.

GRANDI, Domenico (fl. 1870–1935)

Italian general. War Minister in the Salandra administration 1914.

The *Archivio Centrale dello Stato*, Rome, has six boxes of correspondence and other documents on military and political matters covering the period 1870 to 1935. (Source: *Guida Generale*.)

GRAZIANI, Rodolfo (1882–1955)

Italian Field Marshal. Governor of Cirenaica 1930–34; Governor of Somalia 1935–36; Governor-General of Italian East Africa 1936–37; Chief of Army 1937–41; Governor of Libya 1940–41; Minister of National Defence in the RSI (*Repubblica Sociale Italiana*, also known as the *Repubblica di Salò*, founded by Mussolini after his escape from Gran Sasso 1943–45).

The *Archivio Centrale dello Stato*, Rome, has ninety-three files and five packets of documents of papers covering the period 1923–48. The material includes official documents on the government of Cirenaica and Tripolitania, and documents on the political situation in East Africa.

GREINDL, Baron Jules (1835–1917)

Belgian diplomat. Secretary-General of the *Association Internationale de l'Afrique* (AIA) 1876–79. Then spent eight years as Belgian Minister in Lisbon, and twenty-four years in Berlin. Retired 1912.

The *Archives Générales du Royaume*, Brussels, has Greindl's papers 1835–1917, including personal correspondence with, among others, Baron Van der Elst, Frère-Orban, Lambermont and de Mérode-Westerloo. His private office papers are disappointingly thin for his period at the AIA and in Berlin, but include interesting correspondence and notes on colonial questions, in particular the Philippines. An inventory has been published: M.-R. Thielemans (ed.), *Inventaire des papiers Greindl* (Brussels, 1976). The *Ministère des Affaires Etrangères* has a collection entitled: *Greindl (Colonisation des Philippines)* under personal papers. No further information about the collection is available.

GREVE, Wilhelm (fl. 1920s)

Director of *Norddeutscher Lloyd c*. 1925.

A collection of his papers is held at the Political Archive of the Federal German Foreign Office in Bonn. It contains mainly correspondence with the German Foreign Office relating to the Treaty of Brest Litovsk and shipping (0.6m). (Source: Mommsen, *op. cit.*)

GRÉVY, Jules (1807–91)

French politician; deputy; President 1879–87.

The Departmental Archive in Doubs has twenty bundles of correspondence and papers relating to Grévy's career covering the period 1879–87 (Série F). (Source: AN, *Guide des Papiers*.)

GRIPENBERG, Georg Achates (1890–1975)

Finnish diplomat. Ambassador in London 1933–41.

The *Valtionsarkisto*, Helsinki, has an extensive collection of Georg Gripenberg papers contained within the Gripenberg family archive which fills 300 boxes. The collection includes his correspondence and diaries for the years 1902 to 1970. There are also documents collected by his wife Marguerites (*née* Moseley-Williams). Access to this collection is restricted.

GRISEBACH, Eduard (1845–1906)

German diplomat. Consul in Bucharest, St Petersburg, Milan and Haiti.

A collection of his letters is held at the University Library, Göttingen. (Source: Mommsen, *op. cit.*)

GUARIGLIA, Raffaele (fl. 1922–43)

Italian diplomat and politician. Delegate to the Lausanne Conference 1922–23; Director-General of the Foreign Office 1926–32; Ambassador, Madrid 1932–34; coordinator of Ethiopian policy 1935–36; ambassador, Buenos Aires 1936–38, Paris 1938–40, the Vatican 1942–43 and Ankara 1943. Foreign Minister 1943.

A collection of his papers is held by the *Commissione per la Pubblicazione dei Documenti Diplomatici Italiani*, at the Italian Ministry of Foreign Affairs, Rome. (Source: Cassels, *op. cit.*)

GUMMERUS, Herman Gregorius (1877–1948)

Finnish Professor, Ambassador and diplomat.

The *Valtionsarkisto*, Helsinki, has a large collection of papers totalling 133 boxes. These include academic papers and documents on his political career as well as other family papers.

GÜNTHER, Christian Ernst (1886–1966)

Swedish Secretary to the Cabinet 1934–37, and Foreign Minister 1939–45.

There is a collection of Günther's papers in the *Riksarkiv*, Stockholm. In addition, there is a further collection in the Archives of the Swedish Foreign Ministry, also housed at the *Riksarkiv*. This second collection relates to his period of office as Foreign Minister and includes ten volumes of correspondence, *Riksdag* speeches, radio broadcasts and press conferences.

GUSTAFSON, Carl Erik (1906–)

Swedish Captain and Head of Chancellery.

The *Riksarkiv*, Stockholm, has a small collection of documents consisting of diaries for the years 1939 to 1945.

GWIAZDOWSKI, Tadeusz (1889–1950)

Polish diplomat. Minister plenipotentiary, Paris 1939–40; Chief of the Sub-Department of International Affairs at the Ministry of Foreign Affairs and Deputy Secretary General of the Ministry of Foreign Affairs in the Polish government in exile in London 1941–44; Secretary General of the Ministry of Foreign Affairs in Exile 1945–50.

The Sikorski Museum Archive at the Polish Institute, London, has a small collection (0.15m) of his papers, covering the years 1943–49. The collection includes notes and memoranda 1943–47; documents on the situation in occupied Poland 1944–45 and on the situation in Poland 1945–49; material relating to the Dumbarton Oaks Conference, the Potsdam Conference, and the Paris Conference; material relating to Soviet-Polish relations and the arrest of Polish resistance leaders in 1945; and material concerning the crisis of the Polish Government in exile 1949. (Source: Milewski *et al.* (eds) *op. cit.*)

GYLDENSTOLPE, greve August Louis Fersen (1849–1928)

Swedish Cabinet Secretary 1889–95 and Foreign Minister 1904–05.

There is a collection of Gyldenstolpe's papers in the *Riksarkiv*, Stockholm. In addition, the Archives of the Swedish Foreign Ministry, also housed at the *Riksarkiv*, have a collection of documents relating to some of his years in office, 1892–93 and 1905.

GYLLENRAM, Carle Henric René (1884–1959)

Swedish Captain and diplomat.

The Archives of the Swedish Foreign Ministry, housed at the *Riksarkiv*, Stockholm, have an extensive collection of papers covering the years 1924 to 1944. It includes material on the Greek/Turkish population commission 1924–30; the Spanish non-intervention committee 1937–39, and Gyllenram's diary for the year 1944, written in Berlin.

H

HABSBURG-LOTHRINGEN, Crown Prince Rudolf von (1858–89)

Austrian Crown Prince. Heir to Franz Josef I. Opposed to his father's domestic and foreign policies. Sympathetic to liberals; died at Mayerling.

The *Haus-, Hof- und Staatsarchiv*, Vienna, has a collection of the Crown Prince's notebooks and diaries from 1879 and 1885; notes and memoirs of his travels; correspondence; and writings and documents of a political nature. (Note that papers of most members of the royal house of Austria are to be found in the Habsburg-Lothringen Archive at the *Haus-, Hof- und Staatsarchiv*, Vienna.)

HACKZELL, Anders Verner (Antii) (1881–1946)

Finnish Foreign Minister 1932–37. Prime Minister, August to September 1944.

The *Valtionsarkisto*, Helsinki, has a collection of twenty-one boxes of correspondence, drafts and other documents from the years 1912 to 1944. In addition, there are also copies of notes and documents about Finland 1899–1916, the originals of which are in Moscow archives. There are some restrictions on access to this collection.

HAEKKERUP, Per (1915–79)

Danish social democratic politician. Foreign Minister 1962–66.

Thirty-two boxes of Haekkerup's papers for the years 1956–79 are in the ABA, Copenhagen. Together with a small collection of letters and a collection of newspaper cuttings, these contain mainly state papers and personal notes. A summary inventory is available.

HAFFNER, Wolfgang Wenzel (1806–92)

Norwegian government minister and head of the Marine Department 1861–69.

The *Riksarkiv*, Oslo, has a collection of correspondence (0.2m) relating to Haffner's career (Pa. 60).

HAFFNER, Wolfgang (1810–87)

Danish politician. Interior Minister 1867–70; War and Navy Minister 1870–72 and 1875–77.

A collection of four packets of his papers covering the years 1845–87 is held at the *Rigsarkiv*, Copenhagen. The material includes letters and memoranda (ref. 5517).

HAGERUP, Georg Francis (1853–1921)

Norwegian lawyer, diplomat and Prime Minister.

The *Riksarkiv*, Oslo, has a box containing Hagerup's diaries for the year 1905 (Pa. 84).

HALL, Carl Christian (1812–88)

Danish politician. Minister for Slesvig 1856; Prime Minister, 1857–59; Foreign Minister 1858–59; Prime Minister and Foreign Minister 1860–63; Minister for Holsten and Lauenborg 1861–63.

A collection of Hall's papers and correspondence covering the years 1838–88 is held at the *Rigsarkiv*, Copenhagen (ref. 5522, dupl. reg.).

HAMEL, J.A. van (1880–1964)

Dutch functionary at the League of Nations.

An extensive archive (6.5m) related to the van Hamel family can be found at the *Algemeen Rijksarchief*, The Hague (Inventory 2.21.81: Coll 179). In addition to the papers of J.A. van Hamel, the collection also includes material on L.A.R.J. van Hamel, a Dutch naval officer. The whole archive covers the period from the seventeenth century to 1964. Other papers can be found in the E. van Raalte collection, also at the *Algemeen Rijksarchief*, The Hague.

HAMMARSKJÖLD, Åke

Secretary-General to the Hague Tribunal.

There is a collection of Hammarskjöld's papers in the Royal Library, Stockholm.

HAMMARSKJÖLD, Dag (1905–61)

Swedish international statesman. Academic and political career in Sweden. Secretary-General of the United Nations 1953–61. Posthumously awarded Nobel Peace Prize.

The Hammarskjöld papers were deposited with the Royal Library, Stockholm, after a group of senior officials removed those needed immediately by his successor at the United Nations. The papers in the Royal Library cover the period 1953–61 and include his personal correspondence as well as some official United Nations records.

HAMMARSKJÖLD, Knut Hjalmar Leonard (fl. 1914–18)

Swedish Minister of State 1914–17.

There is a collection of Hammarskjöld's papers in the Royal Library, Stockholm.

HAMRIN, Felix Teodor (fl. 1930s)

Swedish Minister of State 1932.

There is a collection of Hamrin's papers in the Royal Library, Stockholm.

HANIEL VON HAIMMAUSEN, Edgar Karl (1870–1955)

German diplomat and public servant. Representative of German Foreign Office at the Armistice Commission 1918–19; Secretary-General of the German peace delegation 1919; Under-Secretary of State 1919–20 and State Secretary 1920–22 in the German Foreign Office.

A collection of his papers is held at the Political Archive of the Federal German Foreign Office in Bonn. It consists of one packet of documents including political correspondence and notes relating to Versailles and covers the years 1919–23. Part of the collection is on microfilm.

HANOTAUX, Gabriel (1853–1944) •

French politician and diplomat. Foreign Minister 1894–95 and 1896–98. French delegate to the League of Nations 1918, Extraordinary Ambassador to Rome 1920.

There are thirty-three volumes and ten boxes of material in the archive of the Foreign Ministry. Apart from personal and political correspondence there are a number of documents on domestic and foreign policy. The latter relate to Tunisia, Morocco, Madagascar, Franco-Italian relations, the Franco-Russian alliance, Crete, Siam and the origins of the League of Nations (ref. *Fonds nominatifs*, no. 189). There are a further eleven boxes of material at the *Service historique de l'Armée de Terre*, Vincennes (ref. 1K 100). The material was collected for the publication of a history of the First World War. In addition, the *Archives Départementales de l'Aisne*, Laon, has further papers. (Source: AN, *Guide des Papiers*.)

HANSEN, Hans Christian (1906–60)

Danish social democratic politician. Minister of Finance 1947–50; Foreign Minister 1953–55; Prime Minister 1955–60.

Some twenty-six boxes of Hansen's papers for the years 1922–60 are in the ABA, Copenhagen. These include correspondence and important papers concerning Danish foreign policy. Part of this collection is closed.

HANSEN, Hans Peter (1872–1953)

Danish politician. Defence Minister 1932–33.

A collection of Hansen's papers is held at the ABA, Copenhagen.

HANSEN, Paul (Kalundborg) (1913–66)

Danish social democratic politician. Minister of Defence 1956–62; Minister of Finance 1962–65.

One box of Paul Hansen's papers from the years 1932–33 and 1945–52 is in the ABA, Copenhagen. Apart from letters received by Hansen, this collection comprises mainly material about him, together with correspondence and material on the journal *Verdens Gang*.

HANSEN, Rasmus (1896–1971)

Danish politician. Defence Minister 1947–50 and 1953–56.

A collection of Hansen's papers is held at the ABA, Copenhagen.

HANSSON, Per Albin (1885–1946)

Swedish social democratic politician. Prime Minister 1932–36 and 1936–46.

There are collections of Hansson's papers in the *Riksarkiv*, and the *Arbetarrorelsens Arkiv*, Stockholm. In addition, the archives of the Swedish Foreign Ministry have eight volumes of correspondence related to Hansson's years in office, 1932–46. The sixty boxes of material in the *Arbetarrorelsens Arkiv* comprise diaries, correspondence, manuscripts and other material concerning his political career. With the exception of notes from the Foreign Policy Committee during the Second World War, these papers are accessible and catalogued.

HARMAND, Jules (fl. 1890s)

French diplomat. Minister in Tokyo.

One volume of papers, for 1898, is in the archives of the French Foreign Ministry, Paris.

HARTMANN, Ludo Moritz (1865–1924)

Austrian diplomat. Ambassador to Berlin 1918–20.

The *Haus-, Hof- und Staatsarchiv*, Vienna, has a collection of nine boxes of his papers, including material relating to St Germain; his ambassadorship in Berlin; and the issue of German unification with Austria. There is also a manuscript entitled *The Diplomatic Documents of the (German) Foreign Office 1871–1914*. In addition there are personal documents; manuscripts; note-books; family papers; two boxes of correspondence, mainly from Berlin; family letters; and papers relating to Theodor Mommsen.

HARTSEN, C. (fl. 1881–91)

Dutch Minister for Foreign Affairs 1881–91.

There are some papers in private archives. For further details contact the Central Register of Private Archives, The Hague.

HASSELMAN, J.J. (1815–95)

Dutch Minister for the Colonies.

The bulk of the Hasselman papers have been lost, but a small collection of material (0.1m) related to J.J. Hasselman and C.J. Hasselman can be found at the *Algemeen Rijksarchief*, The Hague (Inventory 2.21.82: Coll. 230). Some references also exist to material in the *Universiteitsbibliotheek*, Leiden.

HASSLOCHER, Eugen (d. 1895)

Diplomat. Hawaiian Consul General in Vienna and other German capitals 1866–71.

The Public Archives in Honolulu have a collection of his papers relating to his diplomatic service in Central Europe. (Source: Mommsen, *op. cit.*)

HATZFELD [-WILDENBURG], Paul Graf von (1831–1901)

German diplomat. Ambassador to Spain 1874–78; Ambassador to Constantinople 1878–81; Secretary of State in the Foreign Office 1881–85; Ambassador to London 1885–1901.

His papers are held by the *Archiv der Grafen von Hatzfeld*, Schloss Schönstein, Westerwald. There is a substantial collection (8m) including correspondence, which is supplemented by the papers of his mother, Countess Sophie von Hatzfeld. (Source: Mommsen, *op. cit.*)

HAUG, Alfred (1873–1929)

German diplomat. Consul General in Cape Town and Pretoria 1920–29.

The Political Archive of the German Foreign Office, Bonn, has a very small collection of material covering the years 1925–26, and relating to his diplomatic service in South Africa. (Source: Mommsen, *op. cit.*)

HAUSCHILD, Herbert (1880–1928)

German public servant. Legation secretary in the Foreign Office 1920–24; director of Department IVa, dealing with the Soviet Union, Poland, the Baltic and Scandinavia; Ambassador in Helsinki, 1925–28.

The Political Archive of the German Foreign Office, Bonn, has a small collection of his papers covering the years 1919–28. The material includes correspondence with members of the Foreign Office relating to Soviet-German relations and the domestic situation in the USSR. (Source: Mommsen, *op. cit.*)

HAYMERLE, Heinrich Freiherr von (fl. 1880s)

Austrian politician. Minister-President of Austria 1879–81; a plenipotentiary at the Berlin Congress 1878, along with Andrássy and Karolyi.

The *Haus-, Hof- und Staatsarchiv*, Vienna, has one box of his papers, including miscellaneous documents relating to diplomatic relations between the great powers in the mid-nineteenth century; notes; duplicates of documents and manuscripts; and official documents relating to the Berlin Congress.

HEDERSTIERNA, Carl Fredrik Wilhelm (fl. 1920s)

Swedish Foreign Minister 1923.

There is a collection of Hederstierna's papers in the *Riksarkiv*, Stockholm. A second collection can be found in the Archives of the Swedish Foreign Ministry, also housed at the *Riksarkiv*, which includes material from his year in office, 1923.

HEDTOFF-HANSEN, Hans Christian (1903–55)

Danish social democratic politician. Prime Minister 1947–50 and 1953–55.

Some sixty-four boxes of Hedtoff-Hansen's papers covering the years 1929–55 are in the ABA, Copenhagen. The part of this collection concerning the Nordic Defence Pact and Danish membership of NATO is closed.

HEEMSKERK, Azn. J. (1818–97)

Chairman of the Dutch Cabinet 1874–77 and 1883–88. Also Minister of the Interior 1866–68, 1874–77 and 1883–88.

The *Algemeen Rijksarchief*, The Hague, has a collection of Heemskerk papers (0.4m) covering the period 1850–93. (Inventory 2.21.84: Coll. 236). There is also a private Heemskerk archive. For further details, contact the Central Register of Private Archives, The Hague.

HEEMSKERK, Theodorus (1852–1932)

Chairman of the Dutch Cabinet and Minister of the Interior 1908–13.

A private Heemskerk archive exists. For further details, contact the Central Register of Private Archives, The Hague.

HEILBRON, Friedrich Gottlieb (1872–1954)

German diplomat. Consul-General, Zurich 1926–31.

His papers are in private ownership, but two films of the collection are held at the *Bundesarchiv*, Koblenz.

HEINEMANN, Gustav (1899–1976)

German politician. Minister of the Interior in the first Adenauer administration 1949–50. Resignation from government over defence and rearmament and domestic policies 1950. Founder of the *Notgemeinschaft für den Frieden Europas* (Emergency Association for European Peace). Resignation from the CDU 1951. Co-founder of the *Gesamtdeutsche Volkspartei* (for a unified and neutral Germany) 1952. SPD member of the Bundestag and executive member of the SPD from 1957. SPD Justice Minister in the Grand Coalition 1966. Federal President 1969–74.

Most of Heinemann's papers, which cover the years 1919–69, are in the AdsD, Bonn. These comprise correspondence, notes, personal papers and collections of material, especially from the period after 1945. They concern, *inter alia*, Heinemann's disagreements with Adenauer; the *Notgemeinschaft für den Frieden Europas*; his activity as a Bundestag deputy, as Federal Justice Minister, and as President; atomic weapons, the CDU and SPD; church matters, and political and journalistic activity.

HELLNER, Johannes (fl. 1920s)

Swedish Foreign Minister 1917–20.

The *Riksarkiv*, Stockholm, has a collection of papers. In addition, the Archives of the Swedish Foreign Ministry, housed in the *Riksarkiv*, has a collection of papers relating to Hellner's period in office between 1917 and 1919. His diaries have also been published.

HELLWIG, Fritz (1912–)

High official of the European Community.

A collection of his papers is in the General Archives of the EEC Commission, Brussels.

HELO, Johan (1889–1966)

Finnish Riksdag member, minister and diplomat. Cabinet Minister 1920–27. Ambassador in Paris 1954–56.

The *Valtionsarkisto*, Helsinki, has a collection of seven boxes of letters and other documents related to Helo's career.

HEMERT tot DINGSHOF, H. Baron van (1892–1972)

Commander of Dutch Legation security in Peking.

The *Algemeen Rijksarchief*, The Hague, has a collection of papers (0.5m) covering the period 1913–30 (Inventory 2.21.86: Coll. 283).

HENCKE, Andor (b. 1895)

German diplomat. Consul, Kiev 1933–35. Hencke held a large number of minor diplomatic and Foreign Office posts between joining the foreign service in 1922 and 1945. Among these were posts in Prague between 1936 and 1939; on the German-Soviet Commission, 1939, which he headed; at the Franco-German armistice negotiations, 1940–41; and in Denmark and Spain during the Second World War.

A collection of documents relating to Hencke is held at the Political Archive of the Federal German Foreign Office in Bonn.

HENTIG, Werner Otto von (b. 1886)

German diplomat. Attaché at the German embassy in Peking; Consul General in Constantinople and Tehran; ambassador in Bogota; Far East adviser in the Foreign Office 1939; ambassador to Jakarta 1951.

The Institute of Contemporary History in Munich has a very small collection of his papers covering the years 1934–68 (0.07m). The collection contains material on his youth; on the diplomatic service; and on the Foreign Office. There are also notes on German policy on the Far East 1934–41, and on the American Occupation Zone in 1945. Notes relating to an expedition to Afghanistan in 1915–16 are at the German Federal Military Archive, Freiburg im Breisgau. (Source: Mommsen, *op. cit.*)

HERRIOT, Édouard (1872–1957)

French politician. Minister of Public Works, Transport and Provisioning 1916–17; Prime Minister and Foreign Minister 1924–25, 1926 and 1932; Minister of State 1934–36.

The archives of the Foreign Ministry have forty-one volumes of Herriot's papers, including material on provisioning during the First World War; the recognition by France of the Soviet Union; Germany (Alsace–Lorraine, the Saar and reparations); the League of Nations and the London disarmament conference of 1924 and some letters from French Ambassadors in Moscow, from Léon Blum and from the French Ambassador in London. The collection covers the period 1915–61. (Source: AN, *Guide des Papiers.*)

HERTLING, Georg Graf von (1843–1919)

German Chancellor and Prussian Minister President.

A collection of his papers is held at the *Bundesarchiv*, Koblenz. It contains personal papers, publications, speeches, political material and correspondence (0.5m). A list of further relevant primary source material is contained in W. Beck, *Georg von Hertling 1843–1919 (1)* (Mainz: 1981)

HERTZBERG, Ebbe Carsten Hornemann (1847–1912)

Norwegian historian. Director of the National Archives and government Minister in 1884.

The *Riksarkiv*, Oslo, has a collection of papers (0.3m) consisting of correspondence and political documents relating to the trade and maritime commerce agreements with Switzerland and Belgium (Pa. 98).

HEUSS, Theodor (1884–1963)

German liberal politician and journalist. First president of the Federal Republic of Germany 1949–59. Editor of the *Frankfurter Zeitung*.

Heuss's papers from the years before 1933 were destroyed by Heuss himself. The main collection of his extant papers are at the Theodor Heuss Archive in Stuttgart. They form an extensive holding (34m) containing material from his entire political, parliamentary and journalistic career, but above all from the post-1945 period. In addition, a small collection of letters is in the family archive at the *Bundesarchiv*, Koblenz. (Source: Mommsen, *op. cit.*)

HEUTZ, Johannes Benedictus (1851–1924)

Dutch army officer and Governor-General of Achin 1904–09. Associated with an aggressive policy in the Dutch East Indies.

The *Algemeen Rijksarchief*, The Hague, has a collection of papers (0.1m) consisting largely of correspondence 1905–09 (Inventory 2.21.08: Coll. 79). Other correspondence with A.W.F. Idenburg, covering the period 1903–19 can be found at the *Abraham Kuyperstichting*, Free University, Amsterdam. There is also some correspondence dating from 1924–27 in the *Gemeentearchief*, Amsterdam relating to a Heutz memorial.

HEWEL, Walther (b. 1904)

German diplomat. Hewel was a Nazi who took part in Hitler's abortive putsch at Munich in 1923 and was subsequently imprisoned at Landsberg, Bavaria. He joined Ribbentrop's office, the Foreign Office and later Ribbentrop's personal staff as a specialist on England. From 1940–45 he was Ribbentrop's representative at Hitler's headquarters.

A collection of documents relating to Hewel is held at the Political Archive of the Federal German Foreign Office in Bonn.

HIITONEN (HIDÉN), Kaarlo Ensio Paulus (1900–70)

Finnish politician. Specialist in foreign affairs.

The *Valtionsarkisto*, Helsinki, has a major collection of Hiitonen's papers consisting of 215 files. This includes correspondence, speeches, notes, documents and printed works on his career in foreign affairs, party and communal politics. Other documents relate to his connection with the film industry and his period as editor of '*Vapaa Pohjola*'. There are also letters and documents of his wife. Access to this collection is restricted and part of the archive remains closed.

HINDENBURG, Paul von Beneckendorff und von (1847–1934)

German officer and politician. Service in the Austro-Prussian War 1866 and the Franco-Prussian War 1870–71; head of infantry division in the Prussian War Ministry 1889; general 1903–11; following his retirement in 1911, he was recalled as Supreme Commander of Armed Forces in East Prussia and promoted to the rank of Field Marshal 1914; Chief of General Staff and Head of Supreme Command of the Army 1916–19; President of the Reich 1925–34. Increasingly under the influence of the extreme Right he appointed chancellors Brüning, von Papen, von Schleicher, and Hitler in a space of less than three years. He died on his East Prussian estate in 1934.

The German Federal Military Archive at Freiburg im Breisgau has a collection of his papers covering the years 1847–1934. The material includes correspondence; part of a manuscript by Hermann Ritter Mertz von Quirnheim on his memoirs; and press cuttings referring to him. A further collection of his papers is in private ownership. (Source: Mommsen, *op. cit.*)

HINTZE, Paul von (1864–1941)

German officer and diplomat. Rear-admiral; military plenipotentiary in St Petersburg 1908–11; aide-de-camp to Wilhelm II 1911; Ambassador to Mexico 1911–14; Ambassador to Peking 1914–17; Ambassador to Norway 1917–18; Secretary of State in the Foreign Office 1918.

A substantial collection of his papers is held at the German Federal Military Archive, Freiburg im Breisgau. Covering the years 1882–1941, the material includes service documents relating to his entire naval and diplomatic career and his own work on naval and military history. There is also correspondence with parties and associations from the period after 1919 (3.50m). In addition the Political Archive of the Foreign Office in Bonn has a packet of papers relating to a Parliamentary Committee investigating the possibilities for peace in 1917. (Source: Mommsen, *op. cit.*)

HIRSCHFELD, Ludwig von (1842–95)

German Foreign Office official.

A collection of 136 letters from, *inter alia*, the Bismarck family, Bülow and Eulenburg is held at the Political Archive of the Federal German Foreign Office in Bonn. The letters date from the years 1874–94. (Source: Mommsen, *op. cit.*)

HITLER, Adolf (1889–1945)

German dictator. Born in Upper Austria 1889; left Austria for Munich 1913; served in the Sixteenth Bavarian Infantry Regiment during the First World War; he reached the rank of lance corporal and was awarded the Iron Cross (First Class); political informer for the *Reichswehr*, Munich 1919; leader of the NSDAP in Munich from 1920; appointed Chancellor 1933; became Supreme Commander of the Armed Forces 1938; assumed personal control of all military operations 1941.

Hitler's papers were destroyed in 1945. A few fragments remain. The US National Archives returned a collection of papers to the German Federal Archive, Koblenz, in 1962 (0.25m). This collection contains material relating to internal party matters, and the manuscript of his *Second Book*. Personal documents, including his political testament are still at the US National Archives. A further collection containing personal papers and speeches is held by the *Allgemeines Staatsarchiv* in Munich. A collection of material by Hitler, together with material about him, is in the Manuscripts Division of the Library of Congress, Washington, DC. (Source: Mommsen, *op. cit.*)

HJELT, Edvard Immanuel (1855–1921)

Finnish professor, diplomat and Secretary of State.

The *Valtionsarkisto*, Helsinki, has a substantial collection of papers totalling fifty-four boxes. This includes notes and diaries from the years 1871–1917 as well as manuscripts, notes and collected printed works covering his academic and political career. There are some restrictions on access to this collection.

HOCHSCHILD, Carl Fredrik Lotharius frih. (fl. 1880s)

Swedish Foreign Minister 1880–85.

A collection of Hochschild's papers is in private hands.

HOEGNER, Wilhelm (b. 1887)

German social democratic politician. Prime Minister of Bavaria 1945–46.

The *Institut für Zeitgeschichte*, Munich, has a very large collection of Hoegner's papers. These concern the fate of exiles; US occupation policy after the war; bi-zonal administration; political and economic reconstruction in Bavaria; the making of the Bavarian constitution; denazification; and the construction of the SPD in Bavaria 1945–71. In addition, there is correspondence from his period of exile, together with speeches and articles, political, legal and journalistic works and printed manuscripts. (Source: Mommsen, *op. cit.*)

HOHENLOHE-LANGENBURG, Ernst Fürst zu (1863–1950)

German public servant in the Ministry for Alsace–Lorraine 1894–95, and the colonial department of the Foreign Office, where he was deputy director in 1905 and 1906.

A substantial collection (18m) of his papers is held at the Hohenlohe Central Archive, Schloss Neuenstein, in the Hohenlohe district of Württemberg. The material includes diaries, documents and correspondence relating to his service in the colonial office and his regency of Saxe-Coburg-Gotha (1900–05), together with other correspondence with, among others, Hindenburg and Cosima Wagner. A further collection of papers was destroyed in a fire at Schloss Langenburg, Württemberg, in 1945. (Source: Mommsen, *op. cit.*)

HOHENLOHE-LANGENBURG, Hermann Fürst zu (1832–1913)

German cavalry general. Founder of the German Colonial Association and President of the German Colonial Society; governor of Alsace–Lorraine 1894–1907. Member of both the Württemberg Diet and the Reichstag.

A collection of his papers is at the Hohenlohe Central Archive at Schloss Langenburg. The material includes diaries, documents and correspondence from his service as governor of Alsace–Lorraine and from his career as a colonial politician (10.8m). (Source: Mommsen, *op. cit.*)

HOHENLOHE-SCHILLINGFÜRST, Chlodwig Fürst zu (1819–1901)

German politician and diplomat. Reich Chancellor and Prussian Minister President; Reich governor of Alsace–Lorraine.

A substantial collection of his papers (15m) is held at the *Bundesarchiv*, Koblenz. It contains material relating to his political and diplomatic career, and correspondence, chiefly with diplomats. (Source: Mommsen, *op. cit.*)

HOHENWART, Carl Count (1824–99)

Austrian politician. Minister-President of Austria 1871.

The *Allgemeines Verwaltungsarchiv*, Vienna, has two boxes of his papers. The collection includes diary notes; personal documents; manuscripts on legal and political themes; and correspondence.

HÖJER, Torvald Magnusson (1876–1937)

Head of the Political Section of the Swedish Foreign Ministry 1919–23. Later Legation Counsellor. An influential figure in Swedish foreign policy.

The University Library, Uppsala, has an extensive collection of Höjer's papers which includes memoranda on political and foreign policy questions, 1911–25; drafts and letters; documents on treaties; letters to Höjer (a collection of papers which includes five files of letters from King Gustaf Adolf); sundry newspapers and newspaper cuttings. The whole collection amounts to nineteen files. In addition, there are other collections at the *Riksarkiv*, and also in the Archives of the Swedish Foreign Ministry where there are documents related to the years 1910–15.

HOLMA, Harri Gustaf (1886–1954)

Finnish scholar and diplomat. Minister in Paris 1927–40.

The *Valtionsarkisto*, Helsinki, has a substantial collection of fifty-four boxes of papers which include copies and drafts of reports and documents on his diplomatic career. There are some restrictions on access to this collection. In addition, Holma's academic correspondence as an Assyrian specialist can be found in the Helsingfors University Library.

HOLST, Christian (1809–90)

Norwegian Chamberlain. Secretary to the Vice-Regent and Prime Minister.

The *Riksarkiv*, Oslo, has a collection of personal and political papers (22m) covering the period 1854 to 1890 (Pa. 40).

HOLSTEIN, Friedrich von (1837–1909)

German Foreign Office official.

There are two known collections of his extant papers. One collection is held at the Political Archive of the Federal German Foreign Office in Bonn, and contains mainly correspondence with some diary fragments. Photocopies of this collection are available both at the Public Record Office, London, and the US National Archives, Washington, DC. A further collection of personal papers is at the *Deutsches Zentralarchiv*, Potsdam. (Source: Mommsen, *op. cit.*)

HOLSTEIN VON HOLSTEINBORG, Ludvig Carl Herman (1815–92)

Danish politician. Prime Minister 1870–74.

A collection of thirty-two packets of his papers, covering the years 1831–92 is held at the *Rigsarkiv*, Copenhagen. The material includes correspondence, drafts and personal papers (ref. 5650).

HOLSTEIN-LEDREBORG, L. von (fl. 1900s)

Danish politician. Prime Minister and Defence Minister 1909.

His papers are in private hands.

HOLSTI, Eino Rudolf Woldemar (1881–1945)

Finnish statesman, diplomat and Foreign Minister 1920–22 and 1937–38.

The *Valtionsarkisto*, Helsinki, has an extensive collection of Holsti's papers, comprising a total of 119 boxes. The collection includes material on his career as a lecturer at Helsingfors University 1914–23; as Finnish representative in London 1918–19; as Finnish delegate to the Paris Peace Conference; as Foreign Minister 1920–22 and 1937–38; as Ambassador in Reval 1923–27 and as Finland's permanent representative to the League of Nations and ambassador to Switzerland 1927–40. The collection also contains some material on his stay in the United States 1940–45. Access to this archive is restricted.

HOLTFODT, Christian Theodor (1863–1930)

Norwegian Minister of Defence 1914–19.

Holtfodt's collected papers for the years 1892–1930 are held in private hands. For further details, contact the *Norsk Privatarkivinstitutt*, Oslo.

HOLZHAUSEN, Rudolf (1889–1963)

German diplomat and public servant. Served at the Foreign Office from 1919; embassy counsellor 1934; served in the Air Ministry 1940–45; Consul General 1950–52, and Ambassador 1952–54, in South Africa.

A collection of his papers is held at the Political Archive of the Federal German Foreign Office in Bonn. The collection contains material relating to the First World War; the history of National Socialism and the Nazi dictatorship; the Second World War; and German relations with South Africa and Switzerland, where he was leader of a German delegation on frontier questions (1.75m). (Source: Mommsen, *op. cit.*)

HOMAN, Johanes Linthorst (1903–)

High Official of the European Community.

A collection of his papers is in the General Archives of the EEC Commission, Brussels.

HØRRING, H.E. (1842–1909)

Danish politician. Prime Minister, Finance Minister, Justice Minister and Minister for Iceland 1897–1900.

A collection of his papers is held at the *Rigsarkiv*, Copenhagen (ref. 2404).

HORST, Julius Freiherr von (fl. 1870–80)

Austrian politician. Official adviser in the War Ministry; Defence Minister 1870–80.

The *Haus-, Hof- und Staatsarchiv*, Vienna, has six boxes of his papers. The collection includes correspondence; a *Memorandum on my Mission to Bavaria*, and material relating to his activity in the War Ministry. There is also a collection of memoirs, documents, draft laws and memoranda relating to his public activity, and his retirement.

HORTHY, Miklos (1868–1957)

Hungarian Admiral and politician. Leader of the counter-revolutionary movement in 1919 and Regent of Hungary from March 1920 until October 1944. He resigned under German pressure in favour of Ferenc Szálasi, and was exiled in Portugal after the Second World War.

The Hungarian National Archives, Budapest, have a collection of papers (1.29m) which cover the period of his regency, 1920–44.

HOSSBACH, Friedrich (1894–1980)

German infantry general. *Wehrmacht* adjutant to Hitler 1934–38; head of the Central Section of the General Staff and *Wehrmacht* 1935–38; dismissed in 1938, he was brought back to the General Staff in 1939, promoted to infantry general 1943, and served on the eastern front until January 1945. He gave his name to the 'Hossbach memorandum', a record of a conference of 5 November 1937, at which Hitler put forward a framework for continental expansion to the chiefs of the armed forces, the Foreign Minister, Baron von Neurath, and the War Minister, von Blomberg. The memorandum, which was composed from notes five days after the conference has been the subject of much controversy; it was used at Nuremberg as evidence that Germany intended to wage a war of aggression, in order to establish German war guilt.

A substantial collection of his papers is held at the German Federal Military Archive, Freiburg im Breisgau. The collection, which covers the years 1914–69, contains diary notes; memoirs; war diaries of individual units 1939–43; documents on the attempted coup of 20 July 1944, and on Fritsch and Beck; material on the Nuremberg trials; work on military history; and correspondence (4m). A further collection was destroyed in 1945. (Source: Mommsen, *op. cit.*)

HOUVEN van OORDT, J.B. van der (1867–1955)

Adviser to Governor-General J.P. graaf van Limburg Stirum.

The *Algemeen Rijksarchief*, The Hague, has a collection of archivalia (0.5m) covering the period 1888–1946. Other papers can be found in the *Gemeentearchief*, Rotterdam and the Houven van Oordt correspondence with A.W.F. Idenburg can be found at the *Abraham Kuyperstichting*, Free University, Amsterdam.

HOYNINGEN*, Oswald Baron von (1885–1963)

German diplomat. Ambassador in Lisbon 1934–44.

A collection of his papers is held at the Political Archive of the German Foreign Office in Bonn. The collection includes material relating to his service in Portugal, including files and correspondence with the German Foreign Office, with foreign diplomats, with German naval staff, and with Nazi functionaries (0.3m). (Source: Mommsen, *op. cit.*)

*Known as Heune.

HÜBBE-SCHLEIDEN, Wilhelm (1846–1916)

German lawyer and colonial politician.

A collection of his papers is held at the *Staatsarchiv*, Hamburg. The material includes papers relating to his legal career, publications, and correspondence (0.2m). (Source: Mommsen, *op. cit.*)

HUBER, Max (1874–1960)

Swiss politician. Federal councillor; Member of the International Institute of Law; President of the International Committee of the Red Cross; President of the International Court of Justice.

Zürich Central Library holds a substantial (4m) but incomplete collection of Huber's private papers. The material includes correspondence; personal papers; lectures; legal documents; and the manuscript copy of *Handbuch des Kriegsrechts*.

HUITFELDT, Arild Christopher (fl. 1880s)

Head of the Political Department of the Swedish Foreign Ministry 1884–89.

The *Riksarkiv*, Stockholm, has a collection of papers, and the Archives of the Swedish Foreign Ministry has a collection of documents related to the years 1889–90.

HUMMELAUER, Karl von (d. 1874)

Austrian diplomat. Service in Paris, London and at the Congress of Aachen.

The *Haus-, Hof- und Staatsarchiv*, Vienna, has one box of his papers.

HYMANS, Paul (1865–1941)

Belgian Liberal politician. Entered parliament 1900. Ambassador in London 1914–17. Appointed Minister without Portfolio 1916–18 (though he remained in London at first). Foreign Minister 1918–20, 1924–25, 1927–34 (through three administrations), and finally 1934–35. Minister without Portfolio 25 March 1935 to 26 May 1936.

The *Archives Générales du Royaume*, Brussels has Hymans' papers for the years 1891–1940, but these are very incomplete. They include correspondence, publications, speeches, personal dossiers on the First World War, refugees, relations with Le Havre, the peace treaties, post-war Belgian foreign policy, defence, inter-war international relations, and the Congo. Permission is needed for certain dossiers. The *Archief en Museum voor het Vlaamse Cultuurleven*, Antwerp, has a collection on Hymans (H. 987), including letters and documents. The extent and nature of the collection is not known, and permission is needed for consultation.

HYNNINEN, Paavo Juho (1883–1960)

Finnish statesman and diplomat.

The *Valtionsarkisto*, Helsinki, has a collection of correspondence and other documents from the years 1900–27. These can be found in the Armas Saastamoinen archive.

I

IDENBURG, A.W.F. (1861–1935)

Dutch Minister for the Colonies 1902–05, 1908 and 1918–19. Governor-General of East Indies 1909–16.

The *Algemeen Rijksarchief*, The Hague, has a small collection of papers (0.1m) covering the period 1915–34. It includes letters to van Heutz (1905–09) and Pleyte (1913–15) (Inventory 2.21.183: Coll. 359). Other papers can be found in the Middleburg family archive (Inventory 2.21.183: Coll. 295). The *Abraham Kuyperstichting*, Free University, Amsterdam has an extensive collection of Idenburg papers.

IDMAN, Karl Gustaf (1885–1961)

Finnish politician and diplomat.

There is a small collection of Idman's correspondence with Finnish Foreign Ministers and diplomats at the *Valtionsarkisto*, Helsinki. The archive consists of one box.

IMRÉDY, Béla (1891–1946)

Hungarian Finance Minister in the Gombos Ministry 1932–35 and later Prime Minister between May 1938 and February 1939. Also acted as Foreign Minister for a short period between November and December 1938. A supporter of German foreign policy, he was forced to resign the premiership on account of his Jewish ancestry. Later formed the Hungarian Revival Party and acted as Minister for Economic Affairs during the German occupation. After the liberation, he was sentenced to death and executed.

The Hungarian National Archives, Budapest, have a collection of papers (3.22m) which cover the period 1932–39.

INGMAN, Lauri Johannes (1868–1934)

Finnish Archbishop and Prime Minister 1918–19 and 1924–26.

The *Valtionsarkisto*, Helsinki, has an extensive collection of documents comprising seventy-seven boxes. These include correspondence from the years 1887–1934 as well as notes and drafts of parliamentary documents. There are also documents and papers on his political career as well as material on church matters and his university career. Access to the collection is restricted.

IRIMESCU, Radu (fl. 1930s)

Romanian politician and diplomat. Minister of Air and Navy 1932–38. Ambassador to the United States 1938–40.

A collection of papers, covering the period 1918–40, is in the Hoover Institution, Stanford University, California. The papers (in Romanian) include correspondence, reports, and despatches on Romanian domestic politics and foreign policy.

J

JACOBSSON, Per (1894–1963)

International economist. Chairman, International Monetary Fund.

A collection of papers has been placed in the British Library of Political and Economic Science, London.

JAENICKE, Wolfgang (1881–1968)

German politician and diplomat. Adviser to Chiang Kai-shek; Bavarian Secretary of State for Refugees. Ambassador in Pakistan and the Vatican.

A substantial collection of his papers (5.25m) is held at the *Bundesarchiv* Koblenz. The holding contains essays and articles 1904–33; and documents and correspondence from his entire life. (Source: Mommsen, *op. cit.*)

JANSEN, M.H. (1817–93)

Dutch naval officer and adviser to the Dutch Foreign Office.

The *Algemeen Rijksarchief*, The Hague, has a small collection of Jansen papers (0.3m) covering the period 1819–89. (Summary Inventory 2.21.183: Coll. 239)

JANSON, P.E. (1872–1944)

Belgian Liberal politician. Minister of Defence February to November 1920; Minister of Justice 1927–31 and 1932–34; Prime Minister November 1937 to May 1938; Foreign Minister January to February 1939; Minister of Justice April to September 1939 and January to May 1940; Minister without Portfolio in London 1940–44.

The *Archief en Museum voor het Vlaamse Cultuurleven*, Antwerp, has a collection relating to Janson (J. 247), including letters. The extent and nature of the collection is not known, and permission is needed for consultation.

JARLSBERG, Fredrik Hartvig Herman Wedel (1855–1942)

Norwegian diplomat.

Jarlsberg's private papers and a collection of manuscripts are held in private hands. For further details, contact the *Norsk Privatarkivinstitutt*, Oslo.

JASPAR, Henri (1870–1939)

Belgian Catholic politician. Among other ministerial posts, was Minister of Foreign Affairs 1920 to 1924 and again briefly in 1934. Was Prime Minister from 20 May 1926 to 21 May 1931, and Minister of Colonies 1927–29. Retired from politics 1936.

The *Archives Générales du Royaume*, Brussels has Henri Jaspar's papers 19[14]–39. These are very incomplete, but include correspondence with, among others, de Gaiffier (Belgian Ambassador in Paris), and some of his correspondence as Prime Minister. There are also personal dossiers, documents and correspondence on colonial policy, notes on foreign policy, dossiers on the peace treaties, reparations and war debts, the occupation of the Ruhr and the League of Nations. Access is restricted.

The *Archief en Museum voor het Vlaamse Cultuurleven*, Antwerp, has a collection on Jaspar (J. 276) which includes letters and documents. The extent and nature of the collection is not known, and permission is needed for consultation.

JASPAR, Marcel-Henri (1901–82)

Belgian Liberal politician and diplomat. Entered parliament 1929, and served as a Minister in the late 1930s. Appointed Chargé d'Affaires to the Czech government in exile (1942 *Ministre Plénipotentiaire*) in London, 1940; June 1945 to June 1946 was Belgian Ambassador in Prague, then Ambassador to Buenos Aires; appointed Ambassador to Brazil in 1951; Ambassador to Sweden 1954–59, and to France 1959–66.

The *Archives Générales du Royaume*, Brussels, has Jaspar's papers. See R. Wellens, *Inventaire des papiers de M.-H. Jaspar: député, ministre et ambassadeur de Belgique* (Brussels: AGR, 1982).

JAURÉGUIBERRY, Jean (1815–87)

French vice-admiral and Minister for the Navy and Colonies 1879–80 and 1882–83.

The *Service historique de la Marine*, Vincennes, has nine boxes of Jauréguiberry's papers (ref. GG2991 to 9). The collection comprises mainly correspondence, including material relating to expeditions to Saigon and China, his governorship of Senegal, and from the period when he was marine prefect of Toulon. (Source: AN *Guide des Papiers*.)

JØHNKE, Ferdinand Henrik (1837–1908)

Danish politician. Navy Minister 1901–05.

A collection of his papers is held at the *Rigsarkiv*, Copenhagen (ref. 5730).

JOMINI, Alexander Michael (1817–88)

Russian diplomat and politician.

Miscellaneous letters and papers, including diplomatic, official and personal correspondence, are in the British Library, London (ref. Egerton MSS, 3166–3243). The British Library also possesses the papers of his father.

JONGE, Bonifacius Cornelis jhr. de (1875–1958)

Dutch lawyer and head of the legal department at the War Ministry, 1910. Minister of War, 1917–18. Director of the Batavian Petroleum Company 1918–22 and Governor-General of the Netherlands Indies, 1931–36.

The *Algemeen Rijksarchief*, The Hague, has an extensive collection of de Jonge papers (4m), covering the period 1885–1958. (Inventory 2.21.95: Coll. 200). For further details see F.J.M. Otten, *Inventaris van de papieren van jhr. mr. B.C. de Jonge* and S.L. van der Wal, *Herinneringen van jhr. mr. B.C. de Jonge, met brieven uit zijn nalatenschap* (Utrecht: 1968).

JONNART, Charles (1857–1927)

French politician and diplomat. Foreign Minister 1913; Minister for the blockade and the liberated regions 1917; Governor-General of Algeria 1900–11 and 1918–19; Ambassador to the Holy See 1921–23.

Jonnart's papers are held at the departmental archives of Pas-de-Calais (ref. 26 J 1 to 24), and comprise twenty-two boxes of material including documentation on the provisioning of the civil population in the battle zone 1915–17; the Governor-Generalship of Algeria; entente diplomacy in Greece; the Ambassadorship to the Vatican. (Source: AN, *Guide des Papiers*.)

JOUVENEL DES URSINS, Henry (1876–1935)

French politician and diplomat. Minister of Education, Arts and Technical Education 1924; Minister for 'overseas France' (la France d'Outre-mer) 1934; French delegate to the League of Nations 1920 and 1924–26; French High Commissioner, Syria and Lebanon 1925–26; Ambassador to Rome 1933.

The departmental archive of Corréze, which he represented as a senator, has 125 bundles and six boxes of papers, including documents on Syrian and Lebanese matters (ref. 5 J 1 to 31). The Foreign Ministry archive has a further eight volumes in two boxes. These relate to the Geneva Conference, the League of Nations, disarmament, and Jouvenel's activities in Syria and Rome. The manuscripts department of the *Bibliothèque Nationale* has five boxes of speeches, manuscripts, notes and political papers. (Sources, AN, *Guide des Papiers*, and Young, *op. cit.*)

JUSSERAND, Jean Jules (1855–1932)

French diplomat. Ambassador to Washington after 1902.

There are papers in the Archive of the French Foreign Ministry at the Quai d'Orsay, Paris.

JUTILA, Kalle Teodor (1891–1966)

Finnish professor and politician. Ambassador to the United States, 1945–51.

The *Valtionsarkisto*, Helsinki, has a collection of fifty-six files containing documents and correspondence on Jutila's career as an agricultural expert and as a member of the Finland Bank directorate 1938–58. There is also material on his service in various governments 1927–54 and as Finnish Ambassador to the United States 1945–51.

K

KÁLLAY, Benjamin (1839–1903)

Hungarian politician. Consul-General, Belgrade 1868–75; section chief in Foreign Ministry 1879–80; Austro-Hungarian Finance Minister 1882–1903.

Kállay's papers are in the Hungarian National Archives (*Orszagos Leveltár*) in Budapest. The *Haus-, Hof- und Staatsarchiv*, Vienna, has two boxes of private and two boxes of political letters. Both collections cover the period 1879–82.

KALLAY, Miklos (1887–1967)

Hungarian politician and Minister of Agriculture in the Gombos government 1932–35. Prime Minister between March 1942 and March 1944. Attempted to loosen Hungarian ties with Germany but imprisoned in November 1944. Exiled in the United States after the Second World War.

The Hungarian National Archives, Budapest, have a collection of papers (1.96m) which cover the years of his premiership, 1942–44.

KAMPMANN, Viggo (1910–76)

Danish politician. Prime Minister 1960–62.

One packet of his papers from 1972 is held at the *Rigsarkiv*, Copenhagen (ref. 6832). The material concerns Danish entry to the European Community. A further collection is held at the State Ministry.

KAPPEYNE van de COPPELLO, Joannes (1822–95)

Chairman of the Dutch Cabinet and Minister of the Interior 1877–79.

The main archive has apparently been destroyed but the *Algemeen Rijksarchief*, The Hague, has a collection of eight letters to A. Schimmelpenninck covering the period 1874–88. In addition, the *Abraham Kuyperstichting*, Free University, Amsterdam has a collection of forty letters to A. Kuyper dated between 1874 and 1889.

KARNEBEEK, Abraham Pieter Cornelis van (1836–1925)

Dutch Minister of Foreign Affairs 1885–88.

The *Algemeen Rijksarchief*, The Hague, has a small collection of Karnebeek family papers (0.2m), covering the period 1708–1940 (Summary Inventory 2.21.183: Coll. 245). There is also some correspondence in the papers of E. van Raalte.

KARNEBEEK, Herman Adriaan van (1874–1942)

Dutch Minister for Foreign Affairs 1918–27.

The *Algemeen Rijksarchief*, The Hague, has a small collection of Karnebeek family papers (0.2m), covering the period 1708–1940 (Summary Inventory 2.21.183: Coll. 245). There is also some correspondence in the papers of E. van Raalte. In addition, there is a collection of archivalia from the Ministry of Foreign Affairs. For further details, contact the Central Register of Private Archives, The Hague.

KÁROLYI, Count Gyula (1871–1947)

Hungarian landowner and counter-revolutionary politician. Headed the National government during the Soviet Republic and became head of government again between August 1931 and October 1932.

The Hungarian National Archives, Budapest, have a collection of papers (0.1m) covering the period of his second ministry between 1931 and 1932.

KASCHE, Siegfried (1903–47)

German diplomat. Ambassador to the German puppet state of Croatia 1941–44, after a career in the Nazi paramilitary *Sturmabteilung* (SA).

A collection of twenty-one packets of his papers is held at the Political Archive of the Federal German Foreign Office in Bonn. The material includes political correspondence during his ambassadorship in Zagreb. (Source: Mommsen, *op. cit.*)

KASLAS, Boris J. (1910–   )

Lithuanian historian.

In 1976 Kaslas presented a large collection of writings and printed material relating to the Baltic countries and the Russian occupation of Lithuania to the Hoover Institution, Stanford University, California.

KAUFMANN, Henrik (1888–1963)

Danish diplomat.

A collection of his papers is held at the *Rigsarkiv*, Copenhagen. It comprises two packets of material from the years 1941–58 and includes personal papers and documents relating to his diplomatic career (ref. 5754).

KAUFMANN, Wilhelm (1821–92)

Danish politician. War Minister 1879–81.

A collection of his papers is held at the *Rigsarkiv*, Copenhagen (ref. 1039).

KAUZIK, Stanisław (fl. 1920s)

Polish financial diplomat.

A collection of papers containing material on the financial diplomacy of the Grabski government, 1923–25, is in the *Archiwum Akt Nowych*, Warsaw.

KEMPE, Richard (b. 1906)

German diplomat. Occupied various minor diplomatic posts in China to 1939; Legation Counsellor in the Foreign Office 1939–41; Embassy Counsellor, Madrid 1941–45.

A collection of his papers is at the Political Archive of the West German Foreign Office in Bonn. The material includes lectures and lecture notes and correspondence from China, Berlin and Madrid. (Source: Mommsen, *op. cit.*)

KEMPEN, C.J. van (1872–1955)

Dutch Assistant-Resident in Timor, and later Resident in S.E. Borneo.

The *Algemeen Rijksarchief*, The Hague, has a small collection of papers (0.2m), covering the period 1917–55 (Inventory 2.21.97: Coll. 134). Other papers can be found at the *Gemeentearchief*, Vlaardingen.

KERN, Johann Konrad (fl. 1850s)

Swiss diplomat. Chargé d'Affaires, Vienna 1848; Ambassador Extraordinary for Neuchâtel affair 1857; Plenipotentiary Minister, Paris, from 1857.

A large but incomplete collection of his papers is at the State Archive of Thurgau Canton, Frauenfeld. Another collection is at the Canton Library in Frauenfeld. According to the archivist at the State Archive there is also a privately owned collection to which there is no access. The papers in the State Archive include correspondence; personal papers; and diaries. They have formed the basis of a two-volume biography of Kern: *Johann Konrad Kern, Jurist, Politiker, Staatsmann* (Frauenfeld/Stuttgart; 1968); and *Johann Konrad Kern, Die Gesandschaft in Paris* (Frauenfeld/Stuttgart; 1976).

KERN, R.A. (1875–1958)

Controller and Assistant Dutch Resident on Java.

The *Koninklijk Instituut voor Taal-, Land-, en Volkenkunde*, Leiden has a collection of Kern papers. The collection includes notes, memoranda, letters and reports covering the period 1897–1955, but mainly concerned with the years 1900–37. The *Algemeen Rijksarchief*, The Hague, has copies of the above, consisting of twelve microfilm rolls (Inventory 2.21.193). For further details see: Y.S. Hidayat, *Inventaris van de papieren van R.A. Kern* (Leiden – The Hague: 1977).

KEUDELL, Robert von (1824–1903)

German Ambassador to Rome.

A collection of Keudell's papers, containing mainly private and political correspondence from the 1860s, is held at the Merseburg division of the *Deutsches Zentralarchiv*. (Source: Mommsen, *op. cit.*)

KHUEN-HÉDERVÁRY, Count Károly (fl. 1910s)

Hungarian Prime Minister, June to November 1903 and January 1910 to January 1912.

The Hungarian National Archives, Budapest, have a small collection of papers (0.01m) covering the years of his two ministries, 1903 and 1910–12.

KIDERLIN-WÄCHTER, Alfred von (1852–1912)

German Foreign Office official.

Kiderlin-Wächter's papers are at the Sterling Library, Yale University, Connecticut. The holding is substantial and includes political correspondence and memoranda. (Source: Mommsen, *op. cit.*)

KIEŁCZYNSKI, Apolinary (1904–68)

Polish diplomat and journalist. Press and Cultural Attaché, Sofia 1928–41, Vice-Consul, Istanbul 1941–43. Representative in Istanbul of Government in Exile 1945–56.

An extensive collection of papers, covering the period 1928 to 1956, has been placed on permanent deposit in the Pilsudski Institute of America, New York. The collection includes correspondence and other records of his diplomatic career.

KIEP, Otto (1886–1944)

German diplomat. Consul-General 1931–33, and Ambassador 1934–37, in New York. Head of various trade delegations to Latin American and Far Eastern countries.

A collection of his papers is at the Political Archive of the Federal German Foreign Office in Bonn. The material includes papers relating to trade relations with South Africa, India and Manchuria. (Source: Mommsen, *op. cit.*)

KIHLMAN, Mauritz Lorenzo (1861–1949)

Finnish diplomat and Government Adviser.

The *Valtionsarkisto*, Helsinki, has a small collection consisting of one box of correspondence and other documents.

KIVIMÄKI, Toivo Mikael (1886–1968)

Finnish professor and Minister of State. Ambassador to Berlin 1940–44.

The *Valtionsarkisto*, Helsinki, has a collection of four boxes containing draft notes and other documents from the years 1930–60. The collection also contains material on Kivimäki's service as Ambassador to Berlin 1940–44. Access to some of the papers is restricted.

KLEFFENS, Eelco Nicolaas van (1894–)

Major figure in Dutch foreign policy since 1940. Foreign Minister 1939–46. Dutch Representative at the United Nations 1946. Ambassador to Washington 1947 and to Lisbon 1950. Head of the Dutch Permanent Delegation to NATO and OEEC. Chairman of the United Nations Council, 1954.

There is a collection of archivalia from the Ministry of Foreign Affairs, including two volumes of memoirs. For further details, contact the Central Register of Private Archives, The Hague. Other correspondence can be found in the E. van Raalte collection at the *Algemeen Rijksarchief*, The Hague.

KLOTZ, Louis-Lucien (fl. 1920s)

French politician. Minister of Finance.

His papers are in the *Bibliothèque de Documentation Internationale*, Nanterre. These consist of thirty-eight cartons dealing with the Versailles Peace Conference. Access is open, but the collection is mainly of documents assembled by Klotz rather than his private papers.

KNUDSEN, Gunnar (1848–1928)

Norwegian Prime Minister 1908–10 and 1913–20.

Knudsen's collected papers are held in private hands. For further details, contact the *Norsk Privatarkivinstitutt*, Oslo.

KOCH, Walter (1870–1942)

German politician and diplomat. Reich Minister in Prague.

The provincial archive in Dresden has a collection of his memoirs for the years 1870–1937. (Koch was mainly active in Saxony.)

KOHT, Halvdan (1873–1965)

Norwegian historian and Minister of Foreign Affairs 1935–40.

The *Riksarkiv*, Oslo, has a collection of documents (seventeen parcels) consisting of correspondence, manuscripts and notes for the years 1933 to 1964 (Pa. 258).

KOL, Henri Hubert van (1852–1925)

Dutch SDAP member who became the party's spokesman for colonial affairs. Also visited Japan between 1909 and 1914 to report on their industrialisation.

The *Abraham Kuyperstichting*, Free University, Amsterdam has a collection of letters covering the period 1907 to 1914 in the A.W.F. Idenburg archive. Other papers relating to van Kol's political career can be found in the van Kol collection at the International Institute for Social History. The collection, which covers the period 1875–1924, contains a substantial number of dossiers (2.2m) related to the Dutch Social Democratic Party (SDAP) and international socialist matters. For further details of the collection, see M. Campfens, *De Nederlandse Archieven van het Internationaal Instituut voor Sociale Geschiedenis te Amsterdam*.

KOLEMIN, Iurii Aleksandrovič (fl. 1920s)

Russian diplomat in Paris and Madrid.

His papers are at the Bakhmeteff Archive, Columbia University, New York, and contain those of his stepfather, V.P. Bakhrat, last tsarist ambassador to Switzerland. Both sets of papers deal with Russo-German and Russo-Swiss relations before 1917. The collection covers the period from 1892 to the 1950s.

KOLMODIN, Johannes Axel (1884–1933)

Swedish diplomat.

The University Library, Uppsala, has a collection of Kolmodin's papers which includes twenty-seven files containing extensive correspondence with Swedes and foreigners as well as biographical material, diplomatic reports and historical/topographical material from a number of European countries.

KOMARNICKI, Tytus (1896–1967)

Polish diplomat. Secretary-General and Deputy Head of the Polish delegation to the Geneva disarmament conference 1932–34; Minister and Permanent Delegate at the League of Nations 1934–37; Minister, Berne 1938–40; Minister to the Dutch government in London 1942–43.

The Sikorski Museum Archive at the Polish Institute, London, has a small collection (0.15m) of his papers, covering the years 1928–66. The collection contains correspondence; his report from the disarmament conference 1934; documents relating to his service at the League of Nations 1934–36; press cuttings; and material relating to his academic career after the Second World War. (Source: Milewski *et al.* (eds) *op. cit.*)

KÖNIG, Bernhard von (1858–1915)

German Foreign Office, colonial policy division.

His diaries from the First World War, which contain material on colonial policy, are at the *Deutsches Zentralarchiv* in Potsdam. (Source: Mommsen, *op. cit.*)

KONON, Henri (1862–1939)

Danish politician. Foreign and Defence Minister 1920.

A collection of his papers is held at the *Rigsarkiv*, Copenhagen (ref. 5795).

KONOW, Wollert (1845–1924)

Norwegian Prime Minister 1910–12.

The University Library, Bergen has Konow's collected papers.

KÓNYI, Manó (1842–1917)

Hungarian politician.

A collection of his papers concerning Hungarian politics and the *Ausgleich* of 1867 is in the Library of the School of Slavonic and East European Studies, University of London. The papers of Count Menyhért Lónyay are also housed in the same library.

KÖPKE, Gerhard von (b. 1873)

German Foreign Office official.

A collection of documents relating to Köpke is held at the Political Archive of the Federal German Foreign Office in Bonn. His papers are in the possession of Frau Gerda Klei.

KORDT, Erich (1903–70)

German diplomat, lawyer and academic. Diplomatic service, 1928–45; German Foreign Office 1938–40; Ambassador in Tokyo 1941; Chargé d'Affaires, Nanking 1943–45; after the Second World War with the German Peace Bureau.

There are three collections of his papers. The Political Archive of the Federal German Foreign Office has a collection containing material on alliances in the Far East, covering the years 1925–35, and some official documents. The *Haupstaatsarchiv*, Düsseldorf, has a small collection (0.1m) of papers relating to the post-war period, including documents on Germany's participation in international organisations, and the St Petersburg Agreement of 1949. A further collection is held at the Institute of Contemporary History, Munich, and contains material on the Foreign Office, National Socialism, resistance, Nuremberg (the Weizsäcker trial) and post-war reconstruction (1.8m). (Source: Mommsen, *op. cit.*)

KORDT, Theo (1893–1962)

German diplomat. Embassy counsellor in London 1938–39; Berne 1939–45. Head of Foreign Department of the Chancellor's Office and later assistant secretary 1950–53. Ambassador to Greece 1953–58.

A collection of his papers is held at the Political Archive of the Federal German Foreign Office, Bonn. The material includes documents, private and service correspondence 1946–53, and material on post-war reconstruction (1.2m). (Source: Mommsen, *op. cit.*)

KÖRNER, Theodor (1873–1957)

Austrian socialist and Federal President. Officer, First World War; Director of Army Office during the First Republic; joined SDAP 1924; arrested and imprisoned without trial for eleven months 1934; Mayor of Vienna 1949–51; Federal President 1951–57.

There are several separate extant collections of Körner's papers. The first is in the War Archive, Vienna. The Vienna City and Province Archive has three boxes of papers, including biographical notes; personal documents; correspondence 1911–32; an envelope containing a collection of material towards a history of the year 1848; and a collection of material relating to Vienna during his period of office as mayor (hospitals 1946–51; schools 1946–49; sport, youth activities and leisure 1947–51; regional planning and construction 1949–51). The VGA, Vienna, has three files. The first contains miscellaneous notes on military matters, personal documents, speeches, and articles, along with material relating to his visit to London in May 1948. The second contains essays on military subjects, and the third contains material relating to the *Republikanischer Schutzbund*, the socialist paramilitary force of the First Republic, with which he was connected for a number of years. Other papers and books were sold because none of the president's family wanted to take them. There is a collection of correspondence from the years 1943–56 in the Vienna City Library (WSLB). A collection of about 150 books and pamphlets, which were presented to the archive of the *Arbeiterzeitung* in 1957 by Senator Dr Antosch have been integrated into the library of the Association for the History of the Labour Movement in Vienna.

KÖSTER, Adolf (1883–1930)

German social democratic politician and diplomat. Appointed Prussian State Commissar for the province Schleswig–Holstein 1919. Later Reich Minister of the Interior 1921–22. Member of the Reichstag 1921–23. Appointed Ambassador to Latvia in 1923 and to Yugoslavia in 1928.

Although part of Köster's papers appear to have been lost, a small collection of his papers covering 1903–30 is in the AdsD at the Friedrich-Ebert-Stiftung, Bonn. These comprise personal papers, manuscripts, correspondence and newspaper cuttings to do with the First World War, material concerning the Schleswig–Holstein question 1919; manuscripts on the Yugoslavian labour movement and correspondence arising from his capacity as Minister and Ambassador. (Source: Mommsen, *op. cit.*)

KÖSTER, R.W.H.D. (1883–1940)

Ambassador for the Grand-Duchy of Baden in Berlin.

The *Algemeen Rijksarchief*, The Hague, has a collection of papers (0.2m) related to Köster. The archive also includes material on the town of Mühleim and covers the period from the seventeenth century to 1936 (Inventory 2.21.101: Coll. 173).

KOT, Stanisław (1888–1975)

Polish diplomat, academic and politician. Ambassador to the USSR 1940–42; Ambassador to Italy 1945–47, when he defected to the West.

The Sikorski Museum Archive at the Polish Institute, London, has a collection of his papers covering the years 1939–60 (3.75m). The collection includes official and private correspondence relating to his diplomatic and political career; material and correspondence concerning Poland's relations with the Soviet Union; material relating to broadcasting to Poland from the West; and published material from occupied Poland, along with correspondence with resistance leaders. (Source: Milewski *et al.* (eds) *op. cit.*)

KOTZE, Hans Ulrich von (1891–1941)

German diplomat and delegate to the League of Nations. Ambassador to Riga.

A collection of his papers is held at the Political Archive of the Federal German Foreign Office in Bonn. It contains notes 1927–52 and a collection of documents 1898–1914. (Source: Mommsen, *op. cit.*)

KRABBE, Christopher (1833–1913)

Danish Defence Minister 1909–10.

A collection of eleven packets of his papers is held at the *Rigsarkiv*, Copenhagen. The material covers the period 1821–1913 and includes letters, drafts, personal papers and his diary (ref. 5798).

KRACKER VON SCHWARZENFELDT, Dorotheus (1869–1935)

German diplomat. Resident Minister in Bogota, Colombia 1910–21.

A collection of his papers is held at the Political Archive of the West German Foreign Office, Bonn. The material consists of personal memoirs, and covers the period 1911–19 (0.25m). (Source: Mommsen, *op. cit.*)

KRAG, Jens Otto (1914–78)

Danish politician. Foreign Minister 1958–62 and 1966–67; Prime Minister 1962–68 and 1971–72.

A collection of his papers is held at the ABA, Copenhagen.

KRIEGE, Johannes (1857–1937)

German civil servant. Director of the legal department of the German Foreign Office.

A collection of his papers is held at the Political Archive of the Federal German Foreign Office in Bonn. The collection includes material relating to the Hague Peace conference, 1907; the parliamentary committee investigating war debts; the charges against Wilhelm II and others; and notes and letters of Wilhelm II (0.25m). (Source: Mommsen, *op. cit.*)

KRISTENSEN, Knud (1880–1962)

Danish Prime Minister 1945–47.

A collection of his papers is held at the State Ministry, Copenhagen.

KRÜMMER, Ewald (1896–1968)

German diplomat. Diplomatic service in Athens, Sweden, Turkey and Warsaw and at the Foreign Office 1922–43. FDP defence expert and member of the Bundestag.

A small collection of his papers (0.1m), covering the years 1947–68, is at the *Hauptstaatsar- chiv*, Düsseldorf. The material relates to European foreign policy after the Second World War 1947–63, and Germany's relations with the Eastern Bloc 1964–68. (Source: Mommsen, *op. cit.*)

KRUPENSKIĬ, Aleksandr Nikolaevič (fl. 1920s–30s)

Bessarabian politician. President, Bessarabian Provincial Zemstvo. Delegate to the Paris Peace Conference 1919–20.

Nine boxes of his papers, covering the period 1918–35, were given by him in 1936 to the Hoover Institution, Stanford University, California. The papers (in Russian, French and Romanian) include correspondence and a variety of other papers relating to Bessarabian relations with Russia, the annexation by Romania and the Paris Peace Conference.

KÜHLBORN, Georg (1888–1969)

German diplomat. Consul in Mukden, Manchuria 1936–39. Embassy Counsellor in Hsinking, China 1939–40; Consul-General, Vladivostok 1940–41, Consul-General, Hsinking 1941–45.

A typescript of his memoirs copied from a privately owned collection of his papers is held at the Political Archive of the West German Foreign Office in Bonn. The manuscript concerns his service in China and the Soviet Union; his imprisonment in the Soviet Union, and his return to Germany. (Source: Mommsen, *op. cit.*)

KUUSAMO, (FAGERHOLM), Kaarlo Edvin (1893–1956)

Finnish diplomat and Vice-Consul in New York and Consul-General in Montreal 1929–46.

The *Valtionsarkisto*, Helsinki, has a collection of four files of newspaper cuttings entitled *Polulta poimittua I–IV* which cover the years 1931–46.

KUUSKOSKI, Reino Iisakki (1907–65)

Finnish President and Statesman.

The *Valtionsarkisto*, Helsinki, has an extensive collection of fifty-one boxes of documents. These include manuscripts and documents from the 1920s to the 1960s related to his various cabinet functions. There are some restrictions on access to this collection.

KUYPER, Abraham (1837–1920)

Leader of the Dutch Anti-Revolutionary Party. Chairman of the Cabinet and Minister of the Interior 1901–05.

The *Abraham Kuyperstichting*, Free University, Amsterdam has a collection of Kuyper's papers. This includes his letters to A.W.F. Idenburg 1909–19, and from Idenburg 1893–1912. Some further correspondence can be found in the Groen van Prinsterer and Geisweit van der Netten collections at the *Algemeen Rijksarchief*, The Hague; the van Lynden van Sandenburg collection at the *Rijksarchief*, Utrecht; and the Aalberse collection at the Catholic Documentation Centre, Nijmegen University. The *Rijksarchief*, Gelderland also has some papers, and the Hogerzeil private collection has correspondence covering the period 1880–1910. For further details, contact the Central Register of Private Archives. Letters from Kuyper exist in the G.J. Vos collection at the *Gemeente-archief*, Amsterdam, the N. Beets collection at the *Universiteits-bibliotheek*, Leiden, and the Jan Vett private archive. The bulk of the Kuyper papers remain in the hands of his family.

L

LA CHAMBRE, Guy (1898–1965)

French politician. Under-Secretary of State for War 1932–33 and 1933–34; Minister for the Merchant Navy 1934; Air Minister 1938–40; Minister with responsibility for relations with Associated States 1954; Minister of State with responsibility for relations with Associated States 1954–55.

The *Service historique de l'Armée de l'Air*, Vincennes, has one reel of 15cm, lasting about four hours, containing an interview with La Chambre about his career. (Source: AN, *Guide des Papiers*.)

LAGERBERG, Sven (fl. 1928–46)

Swedish diplomat and vice-consul.

The Archives of the Swedish Foreign Ministry at the *Riksarkiv*, Stockholm, have a collection of documents related to Lagerberg's career in the years 1928–46. The collection comprises fifteen volumes.

LAGERHEIM, Carl Herman Theodor Alfred (1843–1929)

Swedish Foreign Minister 1899–1904. Previously Head of the Political Department of the Foreign Ministry 1871–76, and Secretary to the Cabinet 1876–86.

A collection of Lagerheim's papers can be found at the *Riksarkiv*, Stockholm.

LAMBERMONT, Baron AUGUSTE (1819–1905)

Belgian public servant. Secretary-General of the Belgian Foreign Office and adviser to Leopold II; represented Belgium at the Berlin African conference 1884–85 which recognised the Congo as a sovereign state.

A collection of his papers is held at the *Ministère des Affaires Etrangères*, Brussels.

LAMOUREUX, Lucien (fl. 1919–40)

French diplomat.

A microfilm of his memoirs is held at the *Bibliothèque de Documentation Internationale Contemporaine* at Nanterre. The memoirs are entitled *Souvenirs politiques, 1919–40*.

LANDEGREN, Carl Henrik Victor (1870–1940)

Swedish colonel and diplomat.

The *Krigsarkiv*, Stockholm, has a collection of papers totalling eighteen bundles and split into three sections. The first comprises a family archive of two bundles with documents on a visit to Russia, 1917–18 and photographs. The second section is a personal archive and includes drafts, documents and notes on Russia and the Balkan States, the Vilna affair, letters and newspaper cuttings. The third section consists of eleven bundles and deals with his period of service as a legation counsellor in Russia 1917–18; his command of the Swedish Vilna detachment 1920–21; letters; photographs and newspaper cuttings.

LANGWERTH von SIMMERN, Ernst (1865–1942)

German Foreign Office official and diplomat. Ambassador to Madrid 1920–25.

A collection of his papers is at the Political Archive of the Federal German Foreign Office. It comprises one packet of documents relating to his activity as Reich commissar for the occupied Rhineland territories. (Source: Mommsen, *op. cit.*)

LANSBERGE, Johan Wilhelm van (1830–1905)

Dutch diplomat in St Petersburg and Brussels 1857–74, and Governor-General of the Netherlands Indies 1874–81.

The *Algemeen Rijksarchief*, The Hague, has a collection of van Lansberge family papers (2.0m), which covers the period 1507–1967 (Inventory 2.21.103: Coll. 116).

LAPIE, Pierre-Olivier (b. 1901)

French politician and public servant. Under-Secretary of State for Foreign Affairs 1946–47. Governor of Chad 1940–42. Member of the High Authority of the European Steel and Coal Community 1959–67.

The *Archives Nationales* Paris had three boxes of papers, including a diary covering the years 1946–58 and notes taken at the Council of Ministers from July 1950 to July 1951 (ref. 331 AP 1 to 3). (Source: AN, *Guide des Papiers.*) In addition, papers relating to his service with the European Commission can be found in the General Archives of the EEC Commission, Brussels.

LAURENT, Charles (b. 1856)

French diplomat. Financial counsellor to the Turkish government 1908 and Ambassador to Berlin 1920–22.

The Foreign Ministry Archive at the Quai d'Orsay, Paris, has one box of his papers from 1920–22 (Cote 102) (Source: Young, *op. cit.*)

LEBRUN, Albert (1871–1950)

French politician. Minister for Colonies 1911–13 and 1913–14; Minister of War, January 1913; Minister for the Blockade and the Liberated Regions 1917–19; President of the Republic 1932–40.

The archive of the Ministry of Foreign Affairs has seven boxes of papers, including the cabinet papers of the Minister for the Blockade and the Liberated Regions; on negotiations with neutral countries; on Russia; and on the League of Nations. The collection covers the period 1917–24 (ref. *Fonds nominatifs*, no. 104). The *Service historique de l'Armée de Terre*, Vincennes, has a further five boxes, containing parliamentary documents on the First World War 1915–18, and other material on the length of French military service, the Rhine frontier, war credits, and the budget of the German army. In addition to these collections the overseas section of the *Archives Nationales* has a file of documents relating to Lebrun's activities as Colonies Minister, and in particular to the Niger, the Congo and the Franco-German treaty. Lebrun's son has a collection of documents relating to his private and public life. (Source: AN, *Guide des Papiers.*)

LECOMTE, Jean (fl. 1921–49)

Swiss militia officer. Official of the Saar, 1934–35, and Alexandrette, 1937–39, Plebiscite Commissions.

The Archive of the League of Nations, Geneva, has seven boxes of his papers, covering the period from 1921 to 1949.

LEERS, Johannes (1902–65)

German diplomat and viciously anti-semitic Nazi journalist. Employed by Nasser's foreign propaganda service after post-war exile in Argentina and conversion to Islam.

The Political Archive of the West German Foreign Office in Bonn has a collection of his papers, consisting mainly of correspondence with publishers, lectures and notes. A further collection, covering the years 1929–43, is at the *Deutsches Zentralarchiv*, Potsdam. (Source: Mommsen, *op. cit.*)

LELY, C. (1854–1929)

Dutch Governor of Surinam.

The *Algemeen Rijksarchief*, The Hague, has a collection of papers (0.4m) covering the period 1881–1968 which includes archives from 1881–1954 and archivalia, 1900–29 (Summary Inventory 2.21.183: Coll. 381).

LERCHENFELD AUF KÖFERING, Hugo Graf von (1871–1944)

German politician and diplomat. Minister President of Bavaria, 1924–26; Minister in Vienna 1926–31; Minister in Brussels 1931–33.

A collection of his papers is at the Political Archive of the Federal German Foreign Office. It includes notes on Russian matters and translations from Polish and Russian newspapers from 1915 when he was a member of the German civil administration in Warsaw. (Source: Mommsen, *op. cit.*)

LERSNER, Kurt Freiherr von (1883–1954)

German diplomat and politician. Served in Paris, Brussels and Washington before the First World War. Member, and later President, of the German Peace Delegation to Versailles.

Those of his papers not destroyed during the Second World War are at the German Federal Military Archives at Freiburg im Breisgau. They include diary notes, memoirs and documents relating both to military history and to the peace negotiations at Versailles (0.3m). (Source: Mommsen, *op. cit.*)

LE SUIRE, Günther von (1880–1950)

German diplomat. President of the civil administration of the province of Hennegau in Mons, Belgium; member of German peace delegation in Versailles and subsequent conferences.

The German Federal Archive, Koblenz, has a collection of Le Suire's papers. The material includes documents on his activity in Belgium and the peace delegation (1.8m). (Source: Mommsen, *op. cit.*)

LEUTWEIN, Paul (1882–1956)

German officer and writer on Africa.

The German Federal Archive, Koblenz, has a collection of his papers, including material on colonial questions. (Source: Mommsen, *op. cit.*)

LEUTWEIN, Theodor (1849–1921)

German officer and governor of South West Africa.

The German Federal Archive, Koblenz, has a small collection (0.3m) of his papers, including material on South West Africa. Most of his papers were lost in Silesia during the Second World War. (Source: Mommsen, *op. cit.*)

LEVENSKIOLD, Carl O. (1839–1916)

Norwegian Member of Parliament and Minister in Stockholm 1884.

The Manuscript Collection, Oslo University Library, has a collection of diaries for the years 1884–91 and memoirs of the *Storting* 1883–84.

LEWENHAUPT, greve Carl (fl. 1873–95)

Swedish Foreign Minister 1889–95. Previously Secretary to the Cabinet 1873–76.

The Archives of the Swedish Foreign Ministry at the *Riksarkiv* have a collection of his papers covering the years 1885–1905. Another collection is in private hands.

LEYDS, W.J. (1859–1940)

Confidant and adviser to Paul Kruger from 1889 until the 1930s. Accepted as a diplomatic representative in the Netherlands, France and Germany as well as in Russia, Belgium and Portugal.

The *Algemeen Rijksarchief*, The Hague has a substantial collection of Leyds papers (6m) covering the period 1884 to 1940 (Inventory 2.21.105: Coll. 97). There is also a Leyds Archive in the Transvaal Archives Depot, Pretoria, South Africa.

LEYGUES, Georges (1857–1933)

French politician. Minister for Colonies 1906; Navy Minister 1917–20, 1925–26, 1926–30 and 1932–33; Prime Minister and Foreign Minister 1920–21.

The *Service historique de la Marine* has fourteen boxes of papers. The collection largely comprises material dealing with education, but there are also documents relating to Leygues' ministries. In addition the Foreign Ministry archive has three volumes of papers. However, few of these relate to his ministerial activities. (Source: AN, *Guide des Papiers.*)

LIBRACH, Jan (1904–73)

Polish diplomat and writer.

Five folders of his papers covering the period 1939–73, have been placed on permanent deposit in the Pilsudski Institute of America, New York. The collection, which includes reports, memoranda and correspondence, relates to the Polish Embassy in Paris 1939, the Bureau of Continental Action in London 1940–44 and the Polish Ministry of Foreign Affairs in London 1944–54.

LICHNOWSKY, Karl Max, Prince (1860–1928)

German diplomat. Following minor diplomatic posts in London, Stockholm, Constantinople, Dresden and Bucharest he was Ambassador in Vienna, London, St Petersburg and Rome. Following his retirement he was recalled by Emperor Wilhelm II and sent back to London, where he tried to promote Anglo-German understanding on the eve of the First World War.

There is no collection of his papers, but papers relating to his career are to be found at the Political Archive of the Federal German Foreign Office in Bonn. Lichnowsky also published a great deal of material. See H.F. Young, *Prince Lichnowsky and the Great War* (University of Georgia, Athens, Georgia, 1977).

LIE, Trygve (1896–1968)

Norwegian Minister of Foreign Affairs in the Government in Exile 1940–45. Secretary-General of the United Nations 1946–52.

The Manuscript Collection, Oslo University Library, has a collection of Lie's personal papers. Most of his papers relating to the United Nations were destroyed after he completed his memoirs, *In the Cause of Peace*. A few were placed in the Norwegian Ministry of Foreign Affairs, Oslo.

LIEBE, Otto (1860–1920)

Danish politician. Prime Minister and Justice Minister, March–April 1920.

One packet of his papers is held at the *Rigsarkiv*, Copenhagen. It contains material from 1920 relating to the Easter Crisis (ref. 5882).

LIERES UND WILKAU, Joachim von (b. 1886)

Civil servant in the German Foreign Office 1934–38.

A substantial collection (5m) of his papers is held at the Political Archive of the Federal German Foreign Office in Bonn. It contains material on relations between Germany and Poland, and on Upper Silesia and Danzig. (Source: Mommsen, *op. cit.*)

LIMBURG STIRUM, Johan Paul, Graaf van (1873–1948)

Dutch diplomat and Ambassador to Cairo, Berlin, London and Stockholm in the period 1922–39. Governor-General of the Netherlands Indies 1916–21.

The *Algemeen Rijksarchief*, The Hague, has an extensive collection of van Limburg Stirum family papers (11m) covering the period 1266–1934 (Inventories 2.21.106–8: Colls. 93, 114 and 162). The collection includes his letters to Th.B. Pleyte 1916–18 and to A.C.D. de Graeff 1910–37 which are contained in eleven files. There is also some correspondence relating to his career as Governor-General of the Netherlands Indies. His correspondence with A.W.F. Idenburg for the period 1916–21 can be found in the Idenburg collection at the *Abraham Kuyperstichting*, Free University, Amsterdam. A further collection of family papers exists in the *Rijksarchief*, Zuid-Holland, which has papers up to the year 1937.

LIMBURG STIRUM, Menno David, Graaf van (1807–91)

Dutch Minister of War.

The *Algemeen Rijksarchief* has an extensive collection of van Limburg Stirum family papers (11m), covering the period 1266–1934 (Inventories 2.21.106–8: Colls. 93, 114 and 162). A further collection of family papers can be found in the *Rijksarchief*, Zuid-Holland, which contains material up to the year 1937.

LINDMAN, Salomon Arvid Achates (fl. 1906–30)

Swedish Minister of State 1906–11 and 1928–30. Foreign Minister 1917.

There is a collection of Lindman's papers at the *Riksarkiv*, Stockholm, and the Archives of the Swedish Foreign Ministry, also housed at the *Riksarkiv*, have a collection of documents relating to his year as Foreign Minister. His diaries have been published.

LIPSKI, Józef (1894–1958)

Polish diplomat. Ambassador to Berlin 1933–39.

A collection of his papers covering the period 1933–58 was given to the Pilsudski Institute Library, New York, by his widow, Mrs Anna Lipski. The collection, in part transcripts, contains material relating to his diplomatic service in Germany, his subsequent military service in the Polish Army during the Second World War, and his time in Washington after the war. These papers were in part published in Wacław Jedrzejewicz (ed.), *Diplomat in Berlin 1933–1939: Papers and Memoirs of Józef Lipski, Ambassador of Poland* (1968). Reference should also be made to the extensive Lipski papers in the Polish Institute, London.

LOCKROY, Édouard (1840–1913)

French politician. Navy Minister 1895–96, 1898 and 1899; Provisional War Minister 1898.

The manuscripts department of the *Bibliothèque Nationale* has five boxes of material. (Source: AN, *Guide des Papiers*.)

LÖFGREN, Jonas Eliel (fl. 1920s)

Swedish Foreign Minister 1926–28.

A collection of Löfgren's papers can be found in the Royal Library, Stockholm, and the Archives of the Swedish Foreign Ministry, housed at the *Riksarkiv*, Stockholm, have a collection of correspondence related to his period in office, 1926–28.

LOGEMANN, J.H.A. (1892–1969)

Dutch administrator in the Netherlands Indies and Minister for the Colonies.

The *Algemeen Rijksarchief*, The Hague, has a collection of papers (2m) covering the period 1925 to 1969 (Inventory 2.21.111: Coll. 220). For further details see: C.M. Lont (ed.), *Inventaris van de papieren van prof. dr. J.H.A. Logemann* (The Hague: 1975).

LONG, Maurice (1866–1923)

French politician and public servant. Minister for General Provisioning 1917; Governor-General of Indo-China 1919–23.

The departmental archive of Drôme, which Long represented as a deputy 1910–23, has one box of his papers, including some documents on Indo-China (ref. J488). (Source: AN, *Guide des Papiers*.)

LOUBET, Emile (1838–1929)

French politician. Prime Minister and Interior Minister 1892. President of the Republic 1899–1906.

The departmental archive of Drôme, which Loubet represented as deputy and senator, has five reels of microfilm containing the presidential papers, including official exchanges with foreign heads of state, and material on colonial policy, especially the Chinese expedition (ref. 1 Mi 11, 408, 451). Access is by written authorisation of the documents' owner. (Source: AN, *Guide des Papiers*.)

LOUCHEUR, Louis (1872–1931)

French politician. Under-Secretary of State for War Manufactures 1916–17; Minister for Armaments and War Manufactures 1917–20; Minister for the Liberated Areas 1921–22.

The IHRIC at the University of Paris has seven reels of microfilm copies of original documents held at the Hoover Institution, Stanford University, (ref. MF 1 RI 1458–64). The collection, covering the period 1916–31, consists of correspondence, speeches, notes and assorted other papers. The papers include reports from Loucheur as industrial adviser to Russia 1916; papers on the reparations negotiations 1921–24; the Loucheur–Coudenhove–Kalergi correspondence 1927–31; an interview in 1924 with Konrad Adenauer; and notes taken by Paul Mantoux on the 1918 conversations of the allied foreign ministers in Paris prior to the armistice negotiations. An index to the collection is available.

LOUDON, jhr. dr. John (1866–1955)

Dutch diplomat. Ambassador to Tokyo 1906–08; to Washington 1908–13; to Paris 1919–40. The first Dutch delegate to the League of Nations.

The *Ministerie van Buitenlandse Zaken* has a collection of three boxes of archivalia relating to John Loudon and covering the period 1887 to 1940.

LOUIS, Georges

French diplomat.

A collection of papers is in the Archive of the French Ministry of Foreign Affairs at the Quai d'Orsay, Paris.

LØVLAND, Jørgen Gunnarsson (1848–1922)

Norwegian Foreign Minister 1905–08. Prime Minister from October 1907 until 1908.

The *Riksarkiv*, Oslo, has a collection of documents (0.01m) consisting of Løvland's political papers for the year 1905 (Pa. 162). There are other collections of Løvland's papers in Oslo University Library and in the *Aust-Agder Arkiv*, Arendal.

LÖWEN, Gerhard (fl. 1916–32)

Swedish diplomat and envoy to Argentina.

The Archives of the Swedish Foreign Ministry, housed at the *Riksarkiv*, Stockholm, have a collection of letters and press cuttings covering the years 1916–32.

LUCIUS, FREIHERR VON STOEDTEN, Hellmuth (1869–1934)

German diplomat. Ambassador to Stockholm and The Hague.

A collection of his papers is at the Political Archive of the Federal German Foreign Office. It comprises five packets of correspondence and memoranda from the years 1901–27.

LUCKWALD, Erich von (b. 1884)

German diplomat. Ambassador to Albania 1934–36. Consul-General in Danzig 1936–37. Foreign Office representative to the Reich Protector of Bohemia and Moravia.

A collection of copies of his papers, which are privately owned, is held at the Political Archive of the Federal German Foreign Office in Bonn. The material covers his diplomatic career up to 1938 (0.02m). (Source: Mommsen, *op. cit.*)

LUKASIEWICZ, Juliusz (1892–1951)

Polish diplomat. Ambassador to France 1936–39.

The papers, in part transcripts, were presented to the Pilsudski Institute of America Library, New York City, by the ambassador and his son. These papers consist of copies of correspondence, memoirs, and documents, concerning Lukasiewicz's career as Ambassador in Paris 1936–39, and his activities in London and Washington 1939–51. In part, they have been published in Waclaw Jedrzejewicz (ed.), *Diplomat in Paris, 1936–1939: Papers and Memoirs of Juliusz Lukasiewicz, Ambassador of Poland* (1970).

LUNDBERG, Knut Emil Johan (1891–1963)

Swedish Consul-General.

The *Krigsarkiv*, Stockholm, has a small collection of papers consisting primarily of notes on Soviet newspapers of the 1920s.

LUNDEBERG, Christian (fl. 1900s)

Swedish Minister of State 1905.

There is a collection of Lundeberg's papers in the University Library, Uppsala. A further collection is in private hands.

LUTHER, Hans (1879–1962)

German politician and diplomat. As Reich Finance Minister 1923–25, he led the German delegation to Locarno; Chancellor 1925–26; President of the *Reichsbank* 1930–33; and Ambassador to Washington 1933–37.

The German Federal Archive, Koblenz, has a substantial collection (7.5m) of his papers. It includes political material from the Weimar period; documents and correspondence from the post-war period; lectures and speeches; and material relating to his travel abroad, academic institutions and associations. (Source: Mommsen, *op. cit.*)

LUTHER, Martin Franz Julius (b. 1895)

German diplomat, who joined the diplomatic service in 1938 after two years in Ribbentrop's office. Participated in the Wannsee Conference on the 'final solution' to the Jewish question.

A collection of papers relating to his career is at the Political Archive of the Federal German Foreign Office.

LÜTZOW, Heinrich Count (fl. 1852–97)

Austrian diplomat. Section chief in the Foreign Ministry and Ambassador to Italy.

The *Haus-, Hof- und Staatsarchiv*, Vienna, has one bundle of memoirs for the years 1852–97.

LUZATTI, Luigi (1841–1927)

Italian politician. Prime Minister and Interior Minister 1910–11.

The *Archivio Centrale dello Stato*, Rome, has two boxes of documents on Italian domestic, foreign and colonial policy between 1885 and 1920. (Source: *Guida Generale.*)

LYAUTEY, Louis Hubert Gonzalve (1854–1934)

French Field-Marshal. Minister of War 1916–17. Resident Commissioner-General in Morocco.

The *Archives Nationales* has a substantial holding (62.5m). The collection includes material on Tonkin and Madagascar; the XIV Hussars at Alençon; Algeria and Morocco; the War Ministry and Lorraine. Access is by written authorisation of M. Le Révérend, and subject to the agreement of the *Archives Nationales*. In addition the *Service historique de l'Armée de la Terre*, Vincennes, has 107 letters addressed to Lyautey between August 1914 and January 1915 (ref. 1K 195). In addition, two boxes of material, mainly printed but with some original material 1891–1924 are in the archives of the League of Nations at Geneva. Lyautey's correspondence with Auguste Terrier is in the *Bibliothèque de L-Institut* (ref. MS 5903). (Source: AN, *Guide des Papiers.*) There is also some correspondence concerning Siam in the British Library, London.

LYKKE, Ivar (1872–1949)

Norwegian Prime Minister and Foreign Minister 1926–29.

Trondheim University Library has a collection of documents (2.4m) including private and political papers, correspondence, manuscripts and printed matter. These papers cover the years 1878–1964.

LYNDEN van SANDENBURG, C. Th. van (1826–85)

Chairman of the Dutch Cabinet 1879–83 and Minister for Foreign Affairs 1879–81.

The *Algemeen Rijksarchief*, The Hague, has a collection of thirty-four letters from van Lynden van Sandenburg to A. Schimmelpenninck from the period 1866 to 1885. These can be found in the Schimmelpenninck collection (Inventory 2.21.07: Coll. 61).

M

MACCHIO, Karl Freiherr von (fl. 1899–1915)

Austrian diplomat. Ambassador, Cetinje 1899–1903; Ambassador to Rome 1914–15.

The *Haus-, Hof- und Staatsarchiv*, Vienna, has two boxes of his papers, the first of these contains mainly correspondence from his diplomatic service in Cetinje and Rome and with Aehrenthal and others. The second box contains manuscripts and miscellaneous items.

MACKAY van OPHEMERT, Baron Aeneas (1838–1909)

Chairman of the Dutch Cabinet 1888–91. Minister of the Interior 1888–90; and Minister for the Colonies 1890–91.

The *Abraham Kuyperstichting*, Free University, Amsterdam has a collection of eighty-five letters from Mackay van Ophemert to Abraham Kuyper. The *Algemeen Rijksarchief*, The Hague, has an extensive collection of Mackay van Ophemert family papers (33m) covering the period from 1370 to 1930 (Inventories 2.21.115–6 and 2.21.183: Colls. 243 and 330). For further details see; G.J.W. de Jonghe, *Beschrijving van een verzameling stukken afkomstig van het geslacht Mackay van Ophemert en van leden van aanverwante geslachten* (The Hague; 1967) and J.A.A. Bervoets, *Supplement II* (The Hague; 1977).

MACKAY van OPHEMERT, Baron Donald Jacob (1839–1921)

Attaché at the Dutch Embassy in London. Member of the British House of Lords and later Governor of Bombay and Under-Secretary of State for India.

The *Algemeen Rijksarchief*, The Hague, has an extensive collection of Mackay van Ophemert family papers (33m) covering the period from 1370 to 1930 (Inventories 2.21.115–6 and 2.21.183: Colls. 243 and 330). For further details see; G.J.W. de Jonghe, *Beschrijving van een verzameling stukken afkomstig van het geslacht Mackay van Ophemert en van leden van aanverwante geslachten* (The Hague: 1967) and J.A.A. Bervoets, *Supplement II* (The Hague: 1977).

MACKENSEN, Hans Georg von (1883–1947)

German diplomat. Minor diplomatic posts in Copenhagen, Rome, Brussels and Tirana 1919–29; Minister in Budapest 1933–37; Ambassador in Rome 1938–43.

A collection of his papers covering the years 1938–43 is held at the Political Archive of the Federal German Foreign Office in Bonn (0.2m).

MADARIAGA Y ROJO, Salvador de (b. 1886)

Spanish diplomat, politician and writer.

The surviving papers have been deposited in the *Instituto Cornide*, La Corunna, Spain. No further details were available.

MADSEN, Wilhelm Herman Oluf (1844–1917)

Danish War Minister 1901–05.

A collection of five packets of his papers is held at the *Rigsarkiv*, Copenhagen. The material covers the years 1872–1916 and includes letters, personal papers, memoranda and material concerning defence matters (ref. 5940 dupl. reg.).

MAGNUS, Anton Freiherr von (1821–82)

Prussian ambassador in Mexico and various North German cities.

A collection of his papers is at the Political Archive of the Federal German Foreign Office. The material dates from 1866–67 and relates to Mexico. (Source: Mommsen *op. cit.*)

MAKLAKOV, Vassillii Alekseivič (1870–1957)

Russian lawyer and diplomat. Ambassador to France, appointed by the Provisional Government 1917; member of the Russian Political Conference, Paris 1919; President of the Central Office for Russian Refugees in France.

An extensive collection of papers was given by Maklakov to the Hoover Institution, Stanford University, California. One part consists of records from the Russian embassy archives in Paris. This collection, which covers the period 1917–23, comprises diplomatic correspondence, reports, memoranda and notes. The material relates chiefly to the activities of the anti-Bolshevik groups, to questions of interest to White Russian groups before the Paris Peace Conference, and to events and conditions during the civil war in Russia. The second part of the collection consists of his personal papers, and covers the period 1927–57. In addition, four volumes of his letters to Boris Elkin, 1939–57, are in the Elkin papers deposited in the Bodleian Library, Oxford.

MALTZAN, Adolf Georg Otto (b. 1877)

German public servant and diplomat. State Secretary in the Foreign Office, 1922–24; Ambassador to Washington 1925–27.

A collection of five packets of his papers is at the Political Archive of the Federal German Foreign Office.

MANNERHEIM, Friherr Carl Gustaf Emil (1867–1951)

Marshal of Finland. President of the Finnish Republic, 1944–45.

The *Valtionsarkisto*, Helsinki, has a substantial collection of 197 files which includes correspondence, writings and other material for memoirs as well as documents from the years 1867–1951 related to Mannerheim's public and private life. There is also a collection of Mannerheim's correspondence with Sven Anders Hedin in the Hedin archive at the *Valtionsarkisto*. The originals are housed at the *Riksarkiv*, Stockholm. The *Valtionsarkisto* has a further collection of 831 files which includes Mannerheim's war archive for the years 1940–59 and diaries. Further papers and documents can be found in the University Library, Helsingfors.

MANTOUX, Paul (fl. 1918)

Interpreter, Paris Peace Conference.

His papers are at the *Bibliothèque Internationale de Documentation Contemporaine*, Nantes. There are six cartons, including two on the inter-allied conferences, 1915–18, one on the Peace Conference, February-June 1919 and three dossiers on Albert Thomas, 1915–19.

MARCHET, Gustav (fl. 1900s)

Austrian politician. Minister 1906.

The *Haus-, Hof- und Staatsarchiv*, Vienna, has thirty-three boxes of his papers. The collection includes material on the Tyrolean-Italian question; on the military administration in Russian Poland, 1915; on the German civil administration in Belgium, and on relations between Austria and Hungary, 1903, 1910 and 1913.

MAREES van SWINDEREN, R. de (fl. 1908–13)

Dutch Minister for Foreign Affairs 1908–13.

The *Ministerie van Buitenlandse Zaken* has a file of correspondence between de Marees van Swinderen and J. Loudon covering the period from 1909 to 1923 in the Loudon collection. Some correspondence between de Marees van Swinderen and J.P. van Limburg Stirum for the years 1914–15 is also known to exist. For further details, contact the Central Register of Private Archives, The Hague.

MARGERIS, Pierre Jacquin de (b. 1861)

French diplomat. Secretary in Copenhagen, Constantinople, Washington and Madrid 1883–87; minister in Siam and China 1887–89; director-general of political and commercial affairs at the Quai d'Orsay 1912–19; Ambassador, Belgium 1919–22 and Germany 1922–31.

The Foreign Ministry Archive at the Quai d'Orsay, Paris, has five cartons of his papers covering the years 1902 to 1924 (Cote 113).

MARIN, Louis (1871–1960)

French politician. Minister for the Liberated Areas 1924; Minister of State 1934–36, 1940.

The *Archives Nationales* has a substantial holding (283 boxes, ref. 317 AP 1 to 283). The collection includes material on the First World War; the Treaty of Versailles; Marin's foreign missions; war damage and reconstruction after the First and Second World Wars. Boxes 1 to 103 are closed. Access to the rest of the collection is by written authorisation of Mme Marin. The Foreign Ministry archive has twenty-two boxes of printed material relating to foreign policy between 1915 and 1959. (Source: AN, *Guide des Papiers*.)

MARSCHALL VON BIEBERSTEIN, Adolf Freiherr von (1842–1912)

German politician and diplomat. State Secretary in the Foreign Office. Ambassador to Constantinople and London.

His papers were destroyed during the war, but the US National Archives, Washington, DC, has copies of his parliamentary speeches from 1892–99.

MARTINI, Ferdinando (1841–1928)

Italian left liberal politician. Minister of Education 1892–93; Colonies Minister 1914–16; Civil commissioner, Eritrea 1897–1907.

The *Archivio Centrale dello Stato*, Rome, has twenty-one boxes and one volume of documentary material from the period 1874–1925. The collection includes material on education questions and documents relating to Eritrea. (Source: *Guida Generale*.)

MARX, Wilhelm (1863–1946)

German Chancellor. Leading politician of the Roman Catholic Centre Party.

The City Archive, Cologne, has a substantial collection of his papers (57m). The material includes documents on foreign policy and National Socialism. (Source: Mommsen, *op. cit.*)

MASLOVSKII, Eugenii Vasil'evič (fl. 1900–18)

Russian general and diplomat.

The Bakhmeteff Archive has six boxes of his papers. There are around 2065 items, including his typed memoirs, covering diplomatic and military activity in northern Persia 1909–14; service on the staff on the Caucasus front in the First World War; and the Civil War in the South. There are also copies of articles, and correspondence relating to General Iudenič; drafts of reviews; and a typed diary.

MASSIGLI, René (b. 1888)

French diplomat. Delegate to the ambassadors conference 1920 and the Lausanne Conference 1922–23; Head of League Service, Quai d'Orsay, Paris 1928; Deputy Director 1933–37 and Director 1937–38 of Political Affairs in the Foreign Office; Ambassador to Turkey 1938–40; CFLN commissioner for foreign affairs 1943–44; Ambassador to London 1944–45; Secretary-General at the Quai d'Orsay, Paris 1955–56.

A collection of five volumes of his papers from the year 1919 is held at the Archive of the Ministry of Foreign Affairs, Quai d'Orsay, Paris, in the collection *Papiers d'Agents* (6). (Source: Young, *op. cit.*)

MASSON, Fulgence (1854–1942)

Belgian Liberal politician. Minister of Defence 1918–20.

A collection of his papers is held at the *Archives de l'Etat à Mons*, Mons.

MAURA, D. Antonio (fl. 1920s)

Spanish statesman. Prime Minister 1919 and 1921.

The papers are in the Antonio Maura Foundation in Madrid.

MAYER, René (1895–1972)

French politician. Commissar for Communications and the Merchant Navy on the French Committee for National Liberation, Algiers 1944; Minister of National Defence 1948; Deputy Prime Minister and Minister of Finance and Economic Affairs 1951–52; Prime Minister 1953; Commissar General for German and Austrian Affairs 1945–46; President of the High Commission of the European Coal and Steel Community 1953–57.

The *Archives Nationales* has forty-two boxes of Mayer's papers (ref. 363 AP 1 to 42). The material includes documents from the Commissariat for Communications and the Merchant Navy in Algiers 1943–44; the Commissariat General for German and Austrian affairs 1946; on national defence 1948; on the Prime Ministership 1953; on NATO 1951–52; on the OECD 1951–54; on Indo-China and Algeria 1946–58; on the Coal and Steel Community 1955–57; correspondence and diaries. Access is closed until 2022. (Source: AN, *Guide des Papiers.*)

MECHLER, Emil (1845–1923)

German privy counsellor. Director of the Central Bureau of the Foreign Office.

A collection of his papers is at the Political Archive of the Federal German Foreign Office. It comprises one packet of notes, documents and correspondence, including material on the Berlin Congress.

MEESTER, Theodoor Herman de (1851–1919)

Chairman of the Dutch Cabinet and Minister of Finance 1905–08.

The *Algemeen Rijksarchief*, The Hague, has a small collection of de Meester papers (0.1m) covering the period from 1873 to 1920 (Summary Inventory 2.21.183: Coll. 132).

MELCHERS, Wilhelm (1900–71)

German public servant and diplomat. Far East specialist in the German Foreign Office until 1945; participated in the post-war reconstruction of the German Foreign Office and foreign service before serving as Ambassador in Baghdad 1953–57, New Delhi 1957–61 and Athens 1962–65.

A collection of his papers is held at the Political Archive of the Federal German Foreign Office in Bonn. It comprises 3m of material relating to the Middle East, India, the reconstruction of the foreign service, and his post-war diplomatic postings. (Source: Mommsen, *op. cit.*)

MELLVILL van CARNBEE, P.R.A. (fl. 1910s)

Dutch Legation Counsellor in Paris and Sofia 1915–17.

The *Ministerie van Buitenlandse Zaken* has a small collection of papers related to Mellvill van Carnbee in the J. Loudon collection. For further details contact the Central Register of Private Archives, The Hague.

MELVIL van LYNDEN, Baron R. (1843–1910)

Dutch Minister for Foreign Affairs 1901–05.

The *Algemeen Rijksarchief*, The Hague, has a collection of Melvil van Lynden papers covering his period in office from 1900 to 1905 (Summary Inventory 2.21.118: Coll. 132).

A collection of forty letters to Abraham Kuyper, covering the period 1873 to 1905 can be found at the *Abraham Kuyperstichting*, Free University, Amsterdam. Other papers are known to exist in the van Notten collection at the *Rijksarchief*, Utrecht.

MENDE, Erich (b. 1916)

German officer and politician. Served as a major and regimental commander in the Second World War. One of the founders of the FDP, of which he was federal president from 1960 to 1968. Federal Vice-Chancellor and Minister for Inner German Relations, 1963. Left FDP for CDU in 1970.

A large collection of his papers (20m) is held at the Political Archive of the Federal German Foreign Office in Bonn. The material comprises documents relating to his service as a member of the West German parliament and president of the FDP, and political correspondence. (Source: Mommsen, *op. cit.*)

MENDÈS-FRANCE, Pierre (1907–82)

French politician. Member of the Provisional Government in Algiers 1943–44; Prime Minister 1954–55; Foreign Minister 1954–55; Joint Governor of the International Bank of Reconstruction, Washington 1946–58; Governor of the International Monetary Fund 1947–58.

Mendès-France's papers are still in his widow's possession, except for a collection relating to the departmental politics of the Eure, which are in the departmental archive. (Source: AN, *Guide des papiers.*)

MENNSDORF-POUILLY-DIETRICHSTEIN, Albert Graf (fl. 1900–20)

Austrian diplomat.

The *Haus-, Hof- und Staatsarchiv*, Vienna, has a collection of private papers and correspondence. The holding includes material on the action of the great powers in Macedonia 1907; the Bosnian crisis 1908–09; the ambassadors' conference of 1912–13; missions to Sweden, Norway and Denmark in 1917; a mission to Berne in 1917; a meeting with General Smuts in Geneva the same year; peace talks 1918; Brest-Litovsk; the Reparations Commission; the League of Nations 1920–35. His correspondents included Aehrental, Albert Count Apponyi, Arthur Balfour, Max Beck and Berchtold.

MERCIER, Ernest (fl. 1920s)

French diplomat.

A collection of papers is reported in the Hoover Institution, Stanford University, California.

MERENS, Allard (1899–1977)

Dutch consul and diplomat.

The *Algemeen Rijksarchief*, The Hague, has a small collection of memoirs (0.1m) covering the years 1899 to 1975 (Summary Inventory 2.21.183: Coll. 367). Other papers are known to exist at the *Stichting Centraal Bureau voor Genealogie*, The Hague.

MESSIMY, Adolphe (1869–1935)

French politician. Colonies Minister 1911. War Minister 1911–12; 1914.

The *Archives Nationales* has nine boxes of Messimy's papers (ref. Entrées 2575 and 2722). The collection includes material on the First World War, and particularly on the battle of the Somme; documents of the Senate Commission on Colonies; and memoirs. (Source: AN, *Guide des Papiers*.)

METAXAS, Ioannis (1871–1941)

Greek dictator. Prime Minister 1936–41.

An extensive but as yet uncatalogued collection of papers is in the General State Archives, Athens. The collection, arranged chronologically, contains memoranda, reports, etc. (For further details see D.H. Thomas and L. Case, *The New Guide to the Diplomatic Archives of Western Europe*.)

MEYENDORFF, Alexander (1869–1964)

Russian and Baltic statesman. Represented Baltic States at Paris Peace Conference, 1919.

The *Valtionsarkisto*, Helsinki, has a collection of thirty-five files which includes letters to Meyendorff from the years 1919–39, lecture notes and notes on his career as a lecturer in Britain 1919–34, and writings about Russia. There are also documents related to Meyendorff's work as representative for the Baltic states at the Paris Peace Conference in 1919. Other documents exist in libraries and archives in the Soviet Union, Germany and Britain.

MEYER, Ernst Wilhelm (1892–1969)

German diplomat. Embassy counsellor in Washington, DC 1931–37; exile in USA 1940–47; Ambassador to India 1952–57; SPD member of Bundestag.

A small collection of his papers (0.3m) is held at the Political Archive of the Federal German Foreign Office in Bonn. The material comprises mainly unpublished manuscripts on Nazism, Germany and Europe, and foreign policy. (Source: Mommsen, *op. cit.*)

MEYER, Richard (b. 1883)

German diplomat and public servant.

A collection of papers relating to his career is at the Political Archive of the Federal German Foreign Office.

MEYER, S. (1912–67)

Dutch administrator in Batavia, Riouw and Pontianak.

The *Algemeen Rijksarchief*, The Hague, has a collection of papers and other material (0.2m) covering the years 1936 to 1955 (Inventory 2.21.120: Coll. 187).

MEYER, Theodore (fl. 1870–1900)

French diplomat, Consul in China and Singapore 1880s.

One carton of papers, covering the period 1870 to 1900 is in the archives of the French Foreign Ministry, Paris.

MICHAELIS, Georg (1857–1936)

German Chancellor.

A collection of copies from his papers, which are now missing, is at the *Deutsches Zentralarchiv* in Potsdam (seven volumes). Copies of these are available at the German Federal Archive in Koblenz. (Source: Mommsen *op. cit.*)

MICHAELLES, Gustav (1855–1932)

German Ambassador to Peru and Brazil.

A photocopy of an unpublished manuscript and some private correspondence are at the Political Archive of the Federal German Foreign Office. The manuscript, entitled *Im kaiserlichen Dienst: Erlebnis*, is also available on microfilm from the US National Archives, Washington, DC (T-291, roll 4).

MICHAŁOWSKI, Roman (1895–1974)

Polish diplomat and army officer.

Nine folders of his papers, covering the period 1926–53, have been placed on permanent loan in the Pilsudski Institute of America, New York. The collection includes diaries, correspondence, reports and memoranda on Polish foreign policy, 1918–39.

MICHELSEN, Peter Christian Kersleb Kjerschow (1857–1925)

Norwegian Prime Minister 1905–07.

The Christian Michelsen Institute, Bergen has Michelsen's collected political papers.

MICHIELS van VERDUYNEN, jhr. E.F.M.J. (fl. 1939–45)

Dutch Ambassador to London and Minister without Portfolio in the Government in Exile 1940–45.

The *Ministerie van Buitenlandse Zaken* has a collection of Michiels van Verduynen papers.

MIKLAS, Wilhelm (1872–1956)

Austrian politician. President 1928–38.

His papers are available on microfilm at the US National Archives, Washington. A copy is held by the John Rylands University Library, Manchester. The Institute of Contemporary History, Vienna, has a further collection, consisting mainly of notes.

MIKOŁAJCZYK, Stanisław (1901–66)

Polish politician. Prime Minister, Government in Exile 1943–44; Second Vice-Premier and Minister of Agriculture 1945–47; President, International Peasant Union.

A very large collection of papers, in Polish and English covering the years 1938–66, was purchased from Marian Mikołajczyk in 1978 by the Hoover Institution, Stanford University. The collection of correspondence and other papers concerns wartime Polish politics, communism in Poland and Eastern Europe, relations with Russia and his work for the International Peasant Union.

MILLER, Karl Karlovič (fl. 1910s)

Russian diplomat. Commercial attaché in the Imperial Russian embassy in Japan.

His papers are at the Bakhmeteff Archive, Columbia University. There are about 200 items, including reports about the liquidation of the embassy and consulates in China, and financial transactions between Russia and Japan during and after the First World War.

MILLERAND, Alexandre (1859–1943)

French politician. War Minister 1912–13 and 1914–15; Commissar General at Strasbourg 1919; Prime Minister and Foreign Minister 1920; President of the Republic 1920–24.

There are two major collections of papers. The *Bibliothèque Nationale* has 102 boxes of Millerand's papers in the manuscripts department. This collection includes material relating to Millerand's various ministerial offices and the Prime Ministership and presidency. In addition, the Foreign Ministry archive has ninety-five volumes of documents seen by the President between 1920 and 1924 relating to German reparations; disarmament; interallied war debts; the Balkans; the Far East; Russia and the Geneva Conference, and Switzerland. The collection covers the period 1894–1925. An inventory has been prepared. (Source: AN, *Guide des Papiers.*)

MIQUEL, Hans von (1872–1917)

German Consul-General and Ambassador in Cairo.

A collection of his papers is at the Political Archive of the Federal German Foreign Office. It comprises one packet of essays, notes and correspondence.

MITKIEWICZ, Leon (1896–1972)

Polish military leader. Colonel and Chief of Intelligence, Polish Army. Military Attaché to Lithuania. Polish representative, Allied Combined Chiefs of Staff 1943–45.

In 1965 Mitkiewicz gave an important collection of material (in Polish, covering the period 1918–69) to the Hoover Institution, Stanford University, California. The collection includes a diary, correspondence and other papers. There is material on Poland's foreign relations, allied diplomacy in the Second World War and the 1944 Warsaw uprising.

MŁYNARSKI, Feliks (fl. 1920s)

Polish banker. Vice-President, Bank of Poland.

His manuscript recollections are in the *Biblioteka Ossolineum*, Wrocław.

MODEROW, Wlodzimierz (fl. 1940s)

International public servant. First Director of the European Office, United Nations, Geneva.

Two boxes of his papers, covering the period 1945–52, are with the League of Nations Archive at the United Nations in Geneva. Among these papers are documents concerning the United Nations Negotiating Committee on League of Nations Assets, of which Moderow was chairman, and the typescript of an unpublished book *Die Freie Stadt Danzig: Ein völkerrechtliches Experiment*. All the papers are now available for research.

MOHN, Paul Erik Alfred (1898–1957)

Swedish diplomat with extensive European experience including the non-intervention committee in Spain 1936–37; Paris and Vichy 1939–40; Rome 1942–43 and Washington 1943. His career continued after the Second World War.

The University Library, Uppsala, has a collection of Mohn's papers including notes, letters, manuscripts and documents related to his career, mainly in the post-war period.

MOHR, Otto Carl (1883–1970)

Danish diplomat.

The *Rigsarkiv*, Copenhagen, has three packets of his papers covering the years 1940–67. The collection includes material on the occupation and interned Danish citizens (ref. 5972).

MOLTKE, Carl Paul Oscar (1869–1935)

Danish diplomat and politician. Foreign Minister 1924–26.

A collection of four packets of his papers is held at the *Rigsarkiv*, Copenhagen. It covers the years 1894–1935 and includes letters, material concerning expeditions to Greenland, defence, Danish-American matters and documents relating to military history (ref. 5977). A further collection is held at the ABA, Copenhagen.

MOLTKE, Hans Adolf von (b. 1884)

German public servant and diplomat. Foreign ministry representative at the plebiscite commission in Upper Silesia 1920, and member of the mixed commission in Upper Silesia 1922; embassy counsellor, Constantinople 1924–28; Deputy Director of Department IV 1928–31; Minister in Poland 1931–39; Ambassador in Madrid 1943.

A collection of his papers is at the Political Archive of the Federal German Foreign Office in Bonn. It includes documents relating to Poland and the Baltic.

MOMMER, Karl (b. 1910)

German socialist politician. Member of the Bundestag from 1949 (on the SPD Group Executive). Expert on the Saar. Member of the Advisory Assembly of the Council of Europe 1950–58.

Mommer's papers covering the years 1945–56 are in the AdsD at the Friedrich-Ebert-Stiftung, Bonn. These comprise documents concerning the Saar, foreign policy, the Council of Europe, all-German questions, draft laws in the Bundestag (tax, finance and family law) and Bundestag elections. (Source: Mommsen, *op. cit.*)

MONNET, Jean (1888–1979)

French economist. Architect of European Unity.

Reference should be made to the Jean Monnet Foundation for Europe, University of Lausanne. Monnet donated his very extensive papers there in 1978.

MONRAD, Ditler Gothard (1811–87)

Danish bishop and politician. Prime Minister, Foreign Minister and Finance Minister 1863–64.

A collection of six packets of his papers is held at the *Rigsarkiv*, Copenhagen. It covers the years 1799–1916 and includes the papers of his first wife, Nathalie, and his second wife, Emmy. The collection contains letters, drafts, memoranda, personal papers and family documents (ref. 5982, dupl. reg.).

MOOK, H.J. van (1894–1965)

Dutch Minister for the Colonies and Lieutenant-Governor-General of the Netherlands Indies.

The *Algemeen Rijksarchief*, The Hague, has a collection of papers (2.5m) relating mainly to the years between 1942 and 1950 (Inventory 2.21.123: Coll. 176). For further details see; M. Dutilh, *Inventaris van de papieren van dr. H.J. van Mook* (The Hague: 1975).

MORGEN, Kurt von (1858–1928)

Prussian general and explorer in Africa.

The German Federal Military Archive, Freiburg im Breisgau, has a collection of memoirs, lectures, and speeches, including some material on the colonial service. There is also correspondence from 1893 to 1904 (0.35m). (Source: Mommsen *op. cit.*)

MOSCICKI, Michał (1894–1961)

Polish diplomat. Secretary, Polish delegation, Paris Peace Conference 1919.

A collection of papers, in part transcripts, has been placed on permanent deposit in the Pilsudski Institute of America, New York. The collection, covering the period 1918 to 1957, includes correspondence and documents mainly relating to the Paris Peace Conference and also Polish emigration after 1945.

MOWINCKEL, Johan Ludvig (1870–1943)

Norwegian Prime Minister 1924–26, 1928–31 and 1933–35.

The Manuscript Collection, Oslo University Library, has a collection of Mowinckel's private papers.

MÜLLER, Adolf (b. 1865)

German Minister in Berne 1919–33.

A collection of his papers is at the Political Archive of the Federal German Foreign Office in Bonn. It contains documents and political correspondence from the years 1919–31.

MÜLLER, Felix von (1857–1918)

German diplomat. Ambassador to The Hague and secretary to Chancellor von Bülow.

The *Hauptstaatsarchiv*, Stuttgart, has a collection of his papers. (Source: Mommsen, *op. cit.*)

MÜLLER, Hermann (1876–1931)

German politician. Reich Foreign Minister 1919. Chancellor, March to June 1920 and June 1928 to March 1930.

The *Deutsches Zentralarchiv*, Potsdam has four boxes of his papers from the years 1910–31. In addition, there is a second collection in the AdsD at the Friedrich-Ebert-Stiftung, Bonn. This comprises mainly files from his time as Reich Chancellor (including the process of forming governments) together with correspondence concerning his book on the November Revolution. (Source: Mommsen, *op. cit.*)

MUNCH, Peter (1870–1948)

Danish politician. Defence Minister 1913–20; Foreign Minister 1929.

A collection of about 100 packets of his papers is held at the *Rigsarkiv*, Copenhagen. It covers the years 1880–1947 and includes correspondence, diaries, material concerning his political career, the Radical Left (*radikale Venstre*) party, and documents relating to various international organisations (ref. 6663).

MUSSOLINI, Benito (1883–1945)

Italian fascist dictator 1922–43.

The *Archivio Centrale dello Stato*, Rome, has a collection of forty-eight containers of his papers covering the years 1922–45. Trinity College, Hartford, Connecticut, has two exchanges between Mussolini and Hitler from 1931 and 1944. (Source: Cassels, *op. cit.*)

MUSURUS, Stephanos (1842–1907)

Greek diplomat. Son of Konstantinos Musurus.

The Gennadeion Library, Athens, has the papers of both Stephanos Musurus and his father. Together, they constitute a rich source for Greek diplomatic history, with particular material on Konstantinos Musurus's period as Ambassador in London 1851–85.

MYCIELSKI, Kazimierz (b. 1904)

Polish diplomat in France during the Second World War.

The Sikorski Museum Archive at the Polish Institute, London, has a small collection (0.1m) of his papers covering the years 1940–44. The material includes documents concerning organisations with which he was involved: the Polish Mission of the Red Cross in Paris 1940–42 and the Association of Welfare for the Poles in France 1941–44. There is also material of the representative of the Polish government for France, Belgium and Holland 1943–44 and material relating to his arrest by the Gestapo in 1944. (Source: Milewski *et al.* (eds) *op. cit.*)

MYRDAL, Alva (b. 1902)

Swedish social scientist, social democratic politician and diplomat. Director of the Institute for Social Policy 1936–48; Head of the UNO Department for Social Questions 1949–50, and of the Social Science Department of UNESCO 1951–55; Swedish Ambassador to several countries (including India 1955–59); Member of Parliament 1962–70; Minister for Disarmament 1967–73; Head of the Swedish disarmament delegation in Geneva 1962–73. Prolific author. Wife of Gunnar Myrdal.

An enormous and continuously supplemented collection of both Alva and Gunnar Myrdal's papers from 1919 onwards is in the ARAB, Stockholm. This comprises correspondence, manuscripts, notes, drafts, transcripts and photographs, as well as other material arising out of their political and scientific activity such as pamphlets, newspaper cuttings and other printed material, and tape recordings. A two-volume inventory is available, but access to the collection is restricted.

N

NADOLNY, Rudolf (1873–1953)

German diplomat. Minister in Sweden 1921–25; Ambassador to Turkey 1924–32; head of the German delegation to the Geneva disarmament conference 1932; Ambassador to Moscow 1933–34.

A collection of his papers is held at the Political Archive of the Federal German Foreign Office in Bonn. The collection includes speeches from the 1920s, material relating to the Geneva conference, essays, manuscripts and personal and political correspondence (1.6m). The original manuscript of his memoirs is reported to be in the possession of Frau Änny Nadolny. (Source: Mommsen, *op. cit.*)

NANSEN, Fritjof (1861–1930)

Norwegian scientist, explorer and diplomat. Later head of the Nansen Office for refugees after the First World War.

The Manuscript Collection, Oslo University Library, has his collected papers.

NEBENDAHL, Peter Georg Gustav (1847–1914)

German diplomat and Vice-Consul in Bristol.

A small collection of papers, mainly of an official nature, can be found at Bristol Record Office, Bristol (ref: 21132/1–35). The collection consists of about eighty documents and includes material on his diplomatic activities as Vice-Consul for Sweden, Norway and Russia, and in Bristol.

NEERGARD, Niels Thomasius (1854–1936)

Danish politician. Prime Minister 1908–09 and 1920–24.

A collection of 124 packets of his papers is held at the *Rigsarkiv*, Copenhagen. It covers the years 1866–1935 and contains personal papers, memoranda, memoirs, correspondence, political documents and material relating to his terms of office as Prime Minister and Finance Minister (ref. 6026 *trykt reg.*)

NEUMAN, Władysław (1893–1945)

Polish diplomat and writer. Served in Paris and Mexico City.

Six folders of his papers have been placed on permanent deposit in the Pilsudski Institute of America, New York. There are correspondence, reports and memoranda on his diplomatic career.

NEURATH, Constantin Freiherr von (1873–1956)

German diplomat and politician. Minister in Copenhagen 1919–21; Ambassador in Rome 1921–30, and London 1930–32; foreign minister from 1932 until the purge of conservatives from the cabinet by Hitler in 1938; Reich protector of Bohemia and Moravia 1939–43 (on leave after 1941).

His papers are privately owned by Frau Winifred von Mackensen, (*née* von Neurath). Documents from Neurath's ministerial office are at the *Deutsches Zentralarchiv* in Potsdam. Other papers relating to Neurath's career are available at the Political Archive of the Federal German Foreign Office in Bonn. The Berlin Document Center, Berlin, has Neurath's SS personnel file.

NIKITIN, Vasilii Petrovič (1885–1960)

Russian diplomat, economist and scholar. Diplomatic service in Persia 1911–19.

The Bakhmeteff Archive, Columbia University, New York, has nineteen boxes of his papers. The collection includes diaries and memoirs relating to his diplomatic service in Persia; reminiscences and autobiographical writings; correspondence; drafts of historical works; and family papers.

NIKOLAEV, A.M. (fl. 1910s)

Russian military agent at the Tsarist embassy in the United States.

The Bakhmeteff Archive, Columbia University, New York has about fifteen boxes of his papers. The collection includes telegrams; army supply data; reports; correspondence of Tsarist agents in the United States 1917–20; petitions of US citizens to join the United States army from the First World War; a diary from 1915, when he was attached to the London embassy; memoirs; and correspondence.

NIKOL'SKII, Boris Aleksandrovič (fl. 1910s)

Russian diplomat. Commercial counsellor at the Russian embassy in Stockholm before 1914. Right-wing émigré activist.

The Bakhmeteff Archive, Columbia University, New York, has about twelve boxes of his papers.

NITTI, Francesco Saverio (1868–1953)

Italian politician. Prime Minister and Interior Minister 1919–20.

The *Archivio Centrale dello Stato*, Rome, has fifty boxes of papers covering the period 1894–1926. The collection contains documents relating to the Italian delegation at the Paris Peace Conference. Other papers of Nitti are held at the *Fondazione L. Einaudi* in Turin. See *L'Archivio di Francesco Saverio Nitti. Inventario*, in *Annali della Fondazione L. Einaudi, VIII* (1974), pp. 375–437. (Source: *Guida Generale*.)

NIUKKANEN, Juho (1888–1954)

Finnish Minister and *Riksdag* member.

The *Valtionsarkisto*, Helsinki, has a collection which includes correspondence, notes and other documents related to Niukkanen's career 1909–53.

NOEBEL, Willy (1887–1965)

German public servant and diplomat. Polish expert in German Foreign Office 1927–33. Ambassador to Tokyo 1933–38, and Lima 1938–42.

A collection of his papers is held at the Political Archive of the Federal German Foreign Office in Bonn. The collection contains material relating to relations with Poland, Japan, Peru and other countries in Latin America. (Source: Mommsen, *op. cit.*)

NOIROT, Ernest (1851–1913)

French colonial administrator. Served Senegal, Guinea.

A collection of his papers was purchased by the *Archives Nationales*, Paris, in 1957 (ref. 148 AP1–5). The collection, covering the period 1869 to 1912, includes correspondence, diaries, and minutes of reports. A fuller description is available in the article by G. Debien, 'Papiers, Ernest Noirot', *Bulletin de l'Institut français d'Afrique noire* (1964), pp. 676–93. A microfilm of these papers is in the Hoover Institution, Stanford University, California.

NOSTITZ-DRZEWIECKY, Gottfried von (1902–76)

German diplomat. Legation secretary in Vienna 1934–38; Consul in Geneva 1940–45; legation counsellor, The Hague 1953–57; Consul General, São Paolo 1957–64; Ambassador to Chile 1964–67.

A collection of his papers is held at the Political Archive of the Federal German Foreign Office in Bonn. The collection covers his diplomatic career, and contains material on, *inter alia*, the internment and deportation of Germans in Switzerland in 1945; events in Germany in the immediate post-war years; and diplomatic visits to the Netherlands, São Paolo and Santiago. (Source: Mommsen, *op. cit.*)

NOTHOMB, Jean-Baptiste (1805–81)

Belgian Liberal politician. Member of the National Congress; Secretary-General of the Ministry of Foreign Affairs until 1836, then minister of public works until 1840 when he went to Frankfurt as *envoyé extraordinaire*. Was head of Government and Minister of the Interior 1841–45. From 1845–81, *envoyé extraordinaire et ministre plenipotentiaire* (ambassador) in Berlin, and travelled extensively.

The *Archives Générales du Royaume*, Brussels has papers from the period 1830–81, including dossiers and private office papers relating to his posts as Secretary-General and as a Minister, and correspondence with, among others, Leopold I 1834–65, Leopold II 1866–80, on colonial questions mainly, and Lambermont 1860–79. An inventory has been published: M.-R. Thielemans and A.M. Pagnoul (eds), *Inventaire des papiers de J.-B. Nothomb, 1805–81* (Brussels: AGR, 1970), 71 pp.

NOUHUYS, J.W. van (1869–1963)

Dutch explorer and diplomat.

The *Algemeen Rijksarchief*, The Hague, has a small Nouhuys collection (0.1m) covering the period 1907 to 1945 but consisting primarily of an account of the Lorentz expedition to New Guinea in 1909, and of personal diaries kept during the Second World War 1939–45 (Inventory 2.21.125: Coll. 125).

NYGAARDSVOLD, Johan (1879-1952)

Norwegian Prime Minister 1935-45.

The *Riksarkiv*, Oslo, has a collection of correspondence, reports and notes from the 'London' period of the Government in Exile 1940-45. Other papers can be found in Oslo University Library, and the *Arbeiderbevegelsens Arkiv*, Oslo.

NYGREN, Oscar Eugène (1872-1960)

Swedish General. Present at Geneva Disarmament Conference.

The *Krigsarkiv*, Stockholm, has a small collection of papers which includes Nygren's diary from the Geneva disarmament conference of 1929 and notes on his visits to the Eastern Front in 1918.

O

OLLIVIER, Emile (1825–1913)

French politician. Prime Minister 1870.

An extensive collection of papers has survived in family hands. It includes extensive correspondence, seven bound volumes of diaries (1846–48, 1851–53, 1853–57, 1857–63, 1863–65, 1866–69 and 1870), pocket note-books, and other documentation such as bound collections of speeches, and newspaper cuttings.

OLSHAUSEN, Franz (b. 1872)

German diplomat. Chargé d'Affaires, Buenos Aires 1920–22; representative and then Ambassador to Lithuania 1922–24; Ambassador to Belgrade 1924–28; Ambassador to Chile 1928–32.

A copy of the manuscript of his memoirs (0.06m) is held at the Political Archive of the Federal German Foreign Office in Bonn. (Source: Mommsen, *op. cit.*)

OLSSØN, Christian Wilhelm Bredal (1844–1915)

Norwegian General and Minister of Defence 1893–98 and 1905–07.

The *Riksarkiv*, Oslo, has a collection of documents (2.6m) consisting of political correspondence and reports for the years 1867 to 1917 (Pa. 226).

ORDING, Arne (1898–1967)

Norwegian historian and government adviser.

The Manuscript Collection, Oslo University Library, has a collection of diaries, covering the years 1942–45.

ORLANDO, Vittorio Emanuele (1860–1952)

Italian politician. Prime Minister and Interior Minister 1917–19.

The *Archivio Centrale dello Stato*, Rome, has 111 files of Orlando's papers covering the period 1901–50. The collection contains material relevant to the Paris Peace Conference, and correspondence with a number of prominent Italian politicians of the first half of the twentieth century. (Source: *Guida Generale.*)

ORŁOWSKI, Leon (1891–1975)

Polish diplomat. Served Budapest 1933–41.

A collection of papers has been placed on permanent deposit in the Pilsudski Institute of America, New York. There is correspondence and other material relating to the Polish legation in Budapest 1933–41.

ORTS, Pierre (1872–1958)

Belgian diplomat. Adviser to the King of Siam in the 1890s; Cabinent Secretary, Department of the Interior, *Etat Indépendent du Congo* from 1905. Secretary-General of the Ministry of Foreign Affairs 1917 to 1920; represented Belgium at the peace conferences and was responsible for negotiating the treaty for the mandate over Rwanda-Urundi. Subsequently president of the Permanent Commission on the Mandates 1920–40 in the League of Nations, and a member of the Belgian delegation to the first meeting of the United Nations after the Second World War.

The *Archives Générales du Royaume*, Brussels has the Orts family archive, including Pierre Orts' papers 1876–1958. These include correspondence with numerous Belgian diplomats and politicians, with Leopold II and Albert I, also dossiers on French-Siamese relations, on the von der Lancken affair, territorial questions, the mandate over Rwanda-Urundi, and a collection of documents on the Second World War and the occupation of Belgium. Access is free, except for dossiers concerning the 'royal question'. An inventory has been published: M.-R. Thielemans, *Inventaire des papiers Orts* (Brussels: AGR, 1973).

OSTHEIM, Gräfin (Countess) (1886–1931)

German diplomat.

A collection of her papers is at the Political Archive of the Federal German Foreign Office in Bonn. It comprises one packet of letters from King Constantine of Greece.

OSUSKY, Stefan (fl. 1918–40)

Czech diplomat. Ambassador to Great Britain 1918–20; Ambassador to France 1920–40.

A collection of forty-two boxes of his papers is held at the Hoover Institution, Stanford University, California.

OTTER, frih. Fredrik Wilhelm von (fl. 1900s)

Swedish Minister of State 1900–02.

A collection of Otter's papers can be found at the *Riksarkiv*, Stockholm.

OUTREY, Maxime (fl. 1850–80s)

French diplomat. Minister in Tokyo, 1868–73.

Seven cartons of his papers, covering the period 1854 to 1882, are in the archives of the French Foreign Ministry, Quai d' Orsay, Paris.

OW-WACHENDORF, Wernher Melchior Freiherr von (1886–1939)

German diplomat. Embassy Counsellor in Belgrade, Brussels and London. Ambassador in Luxembourg and Egypt.

A collection of letters (one packet), from the years 1916 and 1917, is at the Political Archive of the Federal German Foreign Office in Bonn.

P

PAASIKIVI (HELLSTÉN), Juho Kusti (1870–1956)

President of the Finnish Republic 1945–56. Campaigned for Finnish Independence. Ambassador to Stockholm and to the League of Nations. Prime Minister after 1944.

The *Valtionsarkisto*, Helsinki, has an extensive collection of his private papers and other documents totalling approximately 50m. The papers were received between 1959 and 1979 and were closed until May 1984.

PABST, General van (fl. 1940s)

General of the Dutch Army and Minister in Tokyo in 1940.

A van Pabst family archive exists in the *Rijksarchief*, Gelderland.

PADEREWSKI, Ignacy Jan (1860–1941)

Polish statesman. Prime Minister 1919.

The Hoover Institution, Stanford University, California, has a collection of papers covering the period 1894–1941 (in Polish, English and French). There is material on the establishment of an independent Poland, the Paris Peace Conference and inter-war Polish politics.

PAINLEVÉ, Paul (1863–1933)

French politician. War Minister 1917; Prime Minister and War Minister 1917 and 1925; Prime Minister and Finance Minister 1925; War Minister 1925–26 and 1926–29; Air Minister 1930–31, 1932–33.

The *Archives Nationales* has 242 boxes and two linear metres of Painlevé's papers (ref. 313 AP). The collection includes files of the Prime Minister and correspondence. (Source: AN, *Guide des Papiers*.)

PALÉOLOGUE, Maurice (1859–1944)

French diplomat and public servant. Director of political and commercial affairs, Foreign Office 1912–14. Ambassador, Petrograd 1914–17. Secretary-General at the Foreign Office 1920.

A collection of his papers is held at the Archive of the Ministry of Foreign Affairs, Quai d'Orsay, Paris, in the Collection *Papiers d'Agents* (6). The material is contained in five volumes, covering the years 1914–37 (Cote 133). (Source: Young, *op. cit.*)

PALMSTIERNA, frih. Erik Kule (fl. 1920s)

Swedish diplomat. Envoy to London and Foreign Minister 1920.

The bulk of Palmstierna's papers are in private hands although his diaries have been published. Other papers can be found in the Archives of the Swedish Foreign Ministry at the *Riksarkiv* where there is a collection of documents for the years 1931 and 1935.

PANTALEONI, Maffeo (fl. 1920s)

Italian diplomat. President of the League of Nations Committee for Austrian Reconstruction 1922–23.

A collection of his papers is at the *Archivio Centrale dello Stato*, Rome. (Source: Cassels, *op. cit.*)

PAPEN, Franz von (1879–1969)

German politician and diplomat. Chancellor 1930–32; Hitler's Vice-Chancellor 1933–34; plenipotentiary for the Saar 1933–34; Minister, and then Ambassador in Vienna 1934–38; Ambassador to Turkey 1938–44.

The whereabouts of his papers is unknown. His memoirs were published in English in New York in 1953 Franz von Papen, B. Connel (trans.). *Memoirs* (New York: 1953).

PASTUHOV, Vladimir D. (1898–1967)

Secretary, League of Nations Commission of Enquiry in Manchuria 1931–34.

An extensive collection of papers concerning the investigation into the 1931 Manchuria incident has been given by the Pastuhov family to the Hoover Institution, Stanford University, California. There are fifty-eight boxes of papers and other material, in English, French, Russian and Chinese, covering the period 1927–38.

PAUL-BONCOUR, Joseph (1873–1972)

French politician. War Minister 1932; Prime Minister and Foreign Minister 1932–33; Foreign Minister 1933–34 and 1938; Minister of National Defence and War 1934; Minister of State, Permanent Delegate to the League of Nations, Geneva 1936.

The greater part of Paul-Boncour's papers (fifty-nine boxes; 11m) is in the *Archives Nationales*, and includes political files, correspondence and speeches (ref. Entrée 2699, temporary reference). Access is by written authorisation of M. François Paul-Boncour. A further five boxes of papers are held by the Foreign Ministry archive. The material includes files on the Dumbarton Oaks Conference 1944; and on the San Francisco Conference and the birth of the United Nations 1945. The collection covers the period 1924–51. (Source: AN, *Guide des Papiers*.)

PAVIE, Auguste (fl. 1880s–90s)

French diplomat. Minister in Bangkok. Headed various diplomatic missions in Indo-China.

A collection of papers (13 cartons, covering the period 1887 to 1895) is available in the archive of the French Foreign Ministry, Paris. A detailed list has been prepared.

PAYE, Lucien (1907–72)

French politician and diplomat. High representative of France in Senegal 1962; French Ambassador in Peking 1964.

The *Archives Nationales*, Paris, has ten boxes of material on the Commission for the reform of the statute of the ORTF, of which Paye was president in 1969 and 1970 (ref. 364 AP). (Source: AN, *Guide des Papiers.*)

PELLEGRINI, Antoine (fl. 1900s)

French diplomat. Served in Bangkok, 1901–04.

One dossier of his papers, covering the period 1902–03, is in the archives of the French Foreign Ministry, Quai d'Orsay, Paris.

PELLOUX, Luigi Gerolamo (1839–1924)

Italian politician. Under Secretary of State for War 1880 and 1884; Minister of War 1891–92, 1892–93 and 1896–97; Prime Minister and Interior Minister 1898–99 and 1899–1900.

The *Archivio Centrale dello Stato*, Rome has fifty-seven boxes of papers from the years 1841–1924. The collection comprises miscellaneous documentary material on Italian domestic and foreign policy, and on the assassination of Umberto I. (Source: *Guida Generale.*)

PELT, Adrien (fl. 1920–70)

International public servant. Member, later (1934–40) Director of Information Section, League of Nations.

The Archives of the League of Nations, Geneva, has twenty-three boxes of papers covering the period 1920–70, which have been classified and listed in their entirety. There is material on Libya, where Pelt was UN Commissioner from 1952–57.

PERRIER, Léon (1873–1948)

French politician. Colonies minister 1925–26 and 1926–28.

The departmental archives of Isère have thirteen boxes of material including lecture notes, political notes, and personal documents. The collection is of particular relevance to the history of the Radical Socialist Party. (Source: AN, *Guide des Papiers.*)

PETACCI, Clara (fl. 1930s)

Italian politician.

The *Archivio Centrale dello Stato* has a holding of eighteen boxes of papers dating from the period 1932–45. The collection comprises diaries, correspondence with Mussolini and other personal papers. (Source: *Guida Generale.*)

PETERS, Karl (1856–1918)

German colonial politician. Founder of the Society for German Colonisation, later the German East Africa Company. Reich commissar in the German protectorate of East Africa.

The *Deutsches Zentralarchiv*, Potsdam, has an extensive collection of personal and official correspondence. (Source: Mommsen, *op. cit.*)

PHILIPPIN, Jules (1818–82)

Swiss politician and officer. States Counsellor 1856–60; National Counsellor 1860–82; twice President of the National Council; adjutant general 1870–71; army division commander.

The State Archives of Neuchâtel canton, Neuchâtel, has four files of Philippin's papers. The material scarcely covers a fraction of his career, and relates mainly to the railways; relations between Geneva and Switzerland; and commercial treaties.

PICHON, Stéphen (1857–1933)

French politician and diplomat. Foreign Minister 1906–11, 1913 and 1917–20.

The French Foreign Ministry archive has eight volumes of files and notes on Morocco, the Belgian Congo, the Balkans, Russia, Austria–Hungary; war aims, peace conditions and armistice negotiations; the Peace Conference (including material on Alsace–Lorraine, the Saar and Fiume); and the League of Nations (ref. *Fonds Nominatifs*, no. 141). The *Bibliothèque de L'Institut*, Paris has a further four volumes of correspondence from Pichon's period as Foreign Minister and notes taken at sessions of the Senate Foreign Affairs Commission (ref. Mss 4395–98). (Source: AN, *Guide des Papiers*.)

PIERSON, Nicolaas Gerard (1839–1909)

Chairman of the Dutch Cabinet 1897–1901 and Minister of Finance 1891–94 and 1897–1901.

There is no record of Pierson's personal papers, but the *Algemeen Rijksarchief*, The Hague, has a collection of forty-six letters to Balthasar Heldring covering the years 1866 to 1904 (Inventory 2.21.85: Coll. 148). The *Abraham Kuyperstichting*, Free University, Amsterdam has ten letters written to Abraham Kuyper, and the *Gemeentearchief*, Rotterdam has letters from the years 1859 to 1895 written to H. Muller in the Muller Collection. The private archives of I.D. Fransen van de Putte and W.L.A. Roessingh also have some Pierson material. For further details, contact the Central Register of Private Archives, The Hague. The *Algemeen Rijksarchief* also has some letters sent to S. van Houten in the van Houten collection (Inventory 2.21.26: Coll. 138) and there is a collection of Pierson archivalia, including letters written to him, at the *Universiteitsbibliotheek*, Amsterdam.

PIÉTRI, François (1878–1966)

French politician and diplomat. Minister for the Navy 1934–36; Minister for Posts 1940; Vichy Ambassador to Spain 1940–44.

His papers, in private possession, were used by Anthony Adamthwaite in his book, *France and the Coming of the Second World War* (London: 1977).

PIIP, Antonius (fl. 1920s)

Estonian politician. Prime Minister 1920–21.

A small amount of material relating to such issues as Latvian independence and the diplomatic recognition of Estonia is in the Hoover Institution, Stanford University, California.

PILSUDSKI, Józef (1867–1935)

Polish statesman and soldier. Chief of State and Commander-in-Chief of the Army.

One collection of papers is available in the Pilsudski Institute of America, New York. This collection includes correspondence, manuscripts of writings and speeches, and press cuttings. The Institute also has the records of the Chief Inspectorate of Armed Forces and the Minister's Office of the Ministry of Military Affairs.

PINELLI, Giuseppe (fl. 1890s)

Italian politician. Chief of Crispi cabinet.

The *Archivio Centrale dello Stato*, Rome, has thirty files and one volume of correspondence relating to domestic and foreign policy, and documents relating to the Foreign Ministry.

PINOT, Robert

French diplomat.

His private papers are still in the possession of the family. They were used in Schuker, *The End of French Supremacy*.

PISANI DOSSI, Alberto Carlo (fl. 1860–1910)

Italian writer and diplomat.

The *Archivio Centrale dello Stato* has thirty files and one volume of papers from the years 1866–1907. The collection comprises correspondence on Italian domestic and foreign policy and documents relating to the Italian Foreign Office. (Source: *Guida Generale*.)

PLATEN, greve Baltzar Julius Ernst von (fl. 1870s)

Swedish Foreign Minister 1871–72.

A collection of Platen's papers is in private hands.

PLENNER, Ernst Freiherr von (1841–1923)

Austrian diplomat and politician. Legation secretary, Paris 1865. Legation counsellor, London 1867. *Reichstag* deputy and Bohemian *Landtag* deputy. Finance Minister. President of the Austrian group of the Parliamentary Union.

The *Haus-, Hof- und Staatsarchiv*, Vienna, has a family archive which contains Plenner's papers. Of the thirteen boxes which make up the collection, eight contain personal documents; speeches; notes; essays; material relating to the Inter-Parliamentary Union; and miscellaneous other items. The rest contain correspondence: two of them letters to his father, and three of them letters to him from prominent figures of the time. His correspondents included Aerenthal, Foreign Minister; Albert Count Apponyi, Ambassador in London; Franz Ferdinand and Carl Auersperg; Albert Count Mennsdorf, Ambassador in London; Count Welserheimb, Defence Minister; Ottakar Czernin, Foreign Minister; Karl Count Stürgkh, Prime Minister; Count Taafe, Prime Minister; and Anton Count Wolkenstein, Ambassador in Paris and St Petersburg (ref. XIX/11; boxes 8–20).

PLEYTE, Th. B. (1846–1926)

Dutch Minister for the Colonies 1913–18, and Ambassador to Brazil.

The *Algemeen Rijksarchief*, The Hague, has a small collection of papers (0.2m) from the years 1913 to 1925 (Inventory 2.21.08: Coll. 80). In addition, the *Koninklijk Instituut voor Taal-, Land-, en Volkenkunde*, Leiden has two letters and there is also some correspondence in the A.W.F. Idenburg collection at the *Abraham Kuyperstichting*, Free University, Amsterdam.

POINCARÉ, Raymond (1860–1934)

French politician. Prime Minister and Foreign Minister 1912–13 and 1922–24; Prime Minister 1926–28 and 1928–29; President of the Republic 1913–20.

There are three collections of Poincaré's papers. The manuscripts department of the *Bibliothèque Nationale* has seventy-two volumes of letters received by Poincaré, diary notes 1912–19, speeches 1894–1930, and miscellaneous other items. The *Service historique de l'Armée de Terre*, Vincennes has six boxes of material relating to the First World War; the French military mission in Poland in 1919; the situation in Germany in 1928; arms limitation 1929. (See also Devos *et al., op. cit.*) The Foreign Ministry archive has two volumes containing manuscripts of Poincaré's memoirs. (Source: AN, *Guide des Papiers*.)

PONINSKI, Alfred (1896–1968)

Polish diplomat. Director of Consulate, Istanbul 1941–42. Ambassador to China 1942–45.

The Sikorski Museum Archive at the Polish Institute, London, has a small collection (0.22m) of his papers covering the years 1918–45. The collection includes personal papers, documents and articles by Poninski from the years 1918–39, and a typescript copy of his memoirs. (Source: Milewski *et al.* (eds) *op. cit.*)

POPESCU, Dimitri G. (1908–   )

Romanian diplomat. Private Secretary to the Foreign Secretary, G. Gafencu.

Six boxes of papers, in Romanian and French, covering the period 1940–46 were given by Popescu to the Hoover Institution, Stanford University, California, in 1976. The material concerns Romanian foreign relations (especially with the Allies) during the Second World War.

PORRO, Carlo (1854–1939)

Italian general. Under-Secretary of State for War 1905–06, in the Fortis administration.

The *Archivio Centrale dello Stato*, Rome, has one box of papers from the years 1896–1926, dealing with military matters, and in particular with aviation. (Source: *Guida Generale*.)

POSSE, greve Arvid Rutger Fredriksson (fl. 1880s)

Swedish Minister of State 1880–83.

A collection of Posse's papers can be found at the University Library, Lund.

POTULICKI, Michał (b. 1897)

Polish lawyer. Principal Legal Adviser, Foreign Ministry, Polish Government in Exile, London 1941–45. Secretary-General, Inter-Allied Research Committee, London.

A collection of papers (two and a half boxes, in Polish), covering the period 1933 to 1945, was given by him to the Hoover Institution, Stanford University, California, in 1946. Numerous topics covered include Polish politics and government; the German invasion of Poland; and Polish relations with the Allies.

POULLET, Prosper (1868–1937)

Belgian Christian-Democratic politician. Led a Christian-Democratic-Socialist coalition June 1925 to May 1926; Minister of Defence, January to May 1926.

The *Archives Générales du Royaume*, Brussels, has Poullet's archive 1874–1937, including correspondence with numerous prominent Belgian politicians of the period, and (limited) dossiers on military questions 1919–34. The *Archief en Museum voor het Vlaamse Cultuur-leven*, Antwerp, has a collection relating to Poullet (P. 7954), containing letters, documents and manuscripts. The extent and nature of the collection is not known. Permission is needed for consultation.

POURTALÈS, Herr von (1853–1928)

German Ambassador to St Petersburg.

A collection of his papers is at the Political Archive of the Federal German Foreign Office in Bonn. It comprises one packet of correspondence from the years 1908–20. His correspondents included von Bülow, Bethmann-Hollweg and Jagow.

PRITTWITZ UND GAFFRON, Friedrich Wilhelm von (1884–1955)

German diplomat. Embassy counsellor, Rome 1921–27; Ambassador, Washington 1927–33.

Most of his papers are privately owned. There is a collection of correspondence 1917–33, notes 1917 and speeches (USA, 1928–33) at the Political Archive of the Federal German Foreign Office in Bonn. (Source: Mommsen, *op. cit.*)

PRÜFER, Kurt (1881–1959)

German public servant and diplomat. Foreign Office 1936–38. Ambassador in Rio de Janeiro 1938–41.

A small collection of his papers (0.2m) is held at the Political Archive of the Federal German Foreign Office in Bonn. It contains personal and official papers, including material on the history of the German Foreign Office. (Source: Mommsen, *op. cit.*)

PUSTA, Kaarel Robert (1883–1964)

Estonian diplomat. Ambassador to Spain. Foreign Minister.

Twenty boxes of his papers, covering the period 1918–64, were given by his widow in 1964 to the Hoover Institution, Stanford University, California. An unpublished list has been prepared. The collection comprises personal reminiscences, essays and printed material, relating to the diplomatic activities of Estonia and other Baltic States.

PUTTKAMMER, Jesco von (1855–1917)

German colonial administrator. Commissioner for Togo; governor of Cameroon.

The *Deutsches Zentralarchiv*, Potsdam, has one box of documents relating to his colonial activity. (Source: Mommsen, *op. cit.*)

Q

QUAADE, George Joachim (1813–89)

Danish diplomat and politician. Foreign Minister 1864.

A collection of eight packets of his papers is held at the *Rigsarkiv*, Copenhagen. It covers the years 1849–97 and includes letters, personal papers and drafts relating to foreign policy and his diplomatic career (ref. 6171, dupl. reg.).

QUISLING, Vidkun (1887–1945)

Head of the Nazi sponsored government of Norway during the German occupation 1940–45.

The *Riksarkiv*, Oslo, has two collections of Quisling papers. The first contains correspondence, manuscripts and notes from the period 1932–42 (1.4m). The second collection consists of family and private papers together with other correspondence covering the years 1843–1945 (1m).

R

RABEN-LEVETZAU, Frederik (1850–1933)

Danish politician. Foreign Minister 1905–08.

A collection of his papers is held at the *Rigsarkiv*, Copenhagen (ref. 1564).

RACZKIEWICZ, Wladyslaw (b. 1885)

Polish statesman. President of the Polish Republic 1939–47.

Some three folders of papers (in part transcripts) for the period 1939–47 are in the Pilsudski Institute of America, New York. The collection includes correspondence, diaries, memoranda, and notes.

RACZYNSKI, Edward (b. 1891)

Polish diplomat. Polish Minister to the League of Nations, 1932–34; ambassador in London 1934–45; politically active in exile since 1945; President of the Polish Republic in Exile after 1979.

The Sikorski Museum Archive at the Polish Institute, London, has a collection of his papers covering the years 1945–62 (1.5m). The collection consists largely of material relating to his post-war political activity in exile, including the documentation of war crimes, material concerning the welfare of Polish refugees and resettlement. (Source: Milewski *et al.* (eds) *op. cit.*)

RADISICS, Elmer (b. 1884)

Hungarian journalist, diplomat and statesman. Chief, Historical Department, Ministry of Foreign Affairs. Member, Secretariat, League of Nations 1931–40.

A collection of papers (six boxes, 1920–64) was deposited by him in the Hoover Institution, Stanford University, California in 1960. The material relates not only to Hungarian politics and Danube Valley questions, but also to military campaigns in the Second World War, Palestinian history and Jewish–Arab relations. Some material is closed.

RADOLIN, Hugo Fürst von (1841–1917)

German diplomat and member of Prussian royal family. Ambassador in Constantinople 1892; St Petersburg 1895; and Paris 1900–10.

His papers are at the archive of the Quai d'Orsay, Paris. (Source: Mommsen, *op. cit.*)

RADOWITZ, Josef Maria von (1839–1912)

German diplomat. Ambassador to Athens, 1874–82; Constantinople 1882–92; and Madrid 1892–1908.

A collection of Radowitz's papers is held at the Political Archive of the Federal German Foreign Office in Bonn. It contains material relating to Turkey and the Berlin Congress of 1878. A further collection is held by the Merseberg division of the *Deutsches Zentralarchiv*. (Source: Mommsen, *op. cit.*)

RAESTAD, Arnold Christian (1878–1945)

Norwegian Foreign Minister 1921–22 and director of the Bank of Norway.

The Manuscript Collection, Oslo University Library, has Raestad's collected papers, manuscripts and correspondence. Other papers can be found at the *Riksarkiv*, Oslo (ref. Pa. 277).

RAHN, Rudolf (1900–74)

German diplomat. Minor diplomatic posts in Ankara, Lisbon and Paris 1930–44, during which time he was also employed at the Foreign Ministry. Ambassador to Italy 1943–45.

A collection of his papers is at the Political Archive of the Federal German Foreign Office in Bonn. (Source: Kimmich, *op. cit.*)

RAIBERTI, Flaminius, Baron (1862–1929)

French politician. War Minister 1920–21; Navy Minister 1922–24.

Raiberti's daughter, Mme René Fatou has some correspondence and miscellaneous papers (c. 2m). (Source: AN, *Guide des Papiers.*)

RAMBONNET, J.J. (fl. 1914–18)

Dutch Minister of Defence, 1917 and Minister for the Navy 1913–18.

The *Algemeen Rijksarchief*, The Hague, has a collection of Rambonnet family papers (0.2m) which covers the period 1776 to 1932. This forms a part of the van Dam van Isselt and Marchant family archives (Inventories 2.21.47 and 2.21.117).

RAMEL, frih. Sten Gustaf Fredrik Troil (fl. 1900–40s)

Swedish Foreign Minister 1930–32. Formerly Secretary to the Cabinet 1908–13.

The Archives of the Swedish Foreign Ministry at the *Riksarkiv*, Stockholm, have a collection of papers related to Ramel's periods in office 1909–12, and three volumes of correspondence from the years 1917 and 1930–32.

RAMSAY, Carl Henrik Wolter (1886–1951)

Finnish statesman and Foreign Minister 1943–44.

The *Valtionsarkisto*, Helsinki, has an extensive collection of papers consisting of fifty-three boxes. These contain correspondence for the years 1936–50 together with documentation on war-crimes trials and his work in commerce and industry.

RAMSTEDT, Gustaf John (1873–1950)

Finnish professor and diplomat.

The *Valtionsarkisto*, Helsinki, has a collection of sixteen boxes of papers which include correspondence and other documents concerning Ramstedt's career as Finnish Chargé d'Affaires in Japan and China, 1919–29. Other literary and philological material can be found at the University of Helsinki Library.

RAMSTEDT, Johan Olof (fl. 1900s)

Swedish Minister of State 1905.

There is a collection of Ramstedt's papers at the *Riksarkiv*, Stockholm. A further collection is in private hands.

RASMUSSEN, Gustav (d. 1955)

Danish politician. Foreign Minister 1945–50.

A collection of his papers is held at the ABA, Copenhagen.

RATAJ, Maciej (fl. 1920s)

Polish politician. Marshal of the *Sejm*.

His diary is in the *Biblioteka Narodawa*, Warsaw. A published version is also available.

RATARD, Jules (fl. 1890–1910)

French diplomat. Consul in Yokohama, 1897–1901, and Shanghai, 1901–08.

Two cartons of his papers are in the archives of the French Foreign Ministry, Quai d'Orsay, Paris.

RATH, Hermann von (b. 1856)

German civil servant. Private secretary to Herbert von Bismarck and Legation Counsellor in the German Foreign Office.

The *Deutsches Zentralarchiv*, Potsdam has a collection of his papers. A further collection is also available from the US National Archives, Washington, DC.

RATHENAU, Walther (1867–1922)

German Foreign Minister, 1922. Leading industrialist. Economic director of German war economy, 1914–18. Founder of Democratic Party. Signed Rapallo Treaty, 1922. Murdered by right-wing extremists.

The German Federal Archive in Koblenz has a collection of his papers. However, most of Rathenau's papers were lost and the Koblenz collection is small (0.1m), consisting of fragments of the original collection. Other relevant papers are, of course, available in the Federal Archives and the *Deutsches Zentralarchiv*, Potsdam, in the appropriate ministerial collections. There are also papers relating to his career in the Political Archive of the Federal German Foreign Office in Bonn.

RAYBAUDI, Massiglia Annibale (fl. 1875–1915)

Italian diplomat.

The *Archivio Centrale dello Stato*, Rome, has two files of documents. The collection dates from the period 1875–1915, and comprises correspondence and speeches on foreign policy. (Source: *Guida Generale*.)

REEDTZ, Holger (1800–57)

Danish diplomat and politician. Foreign Minister 1850–51.

A collection of seven packets of his papers is held at the *Rigsarkiv*, Copenhagen. It covers the years 1800–55 and includes letters, drafts, personal papers, historical collections, manuscripts and material relating to his term as Foreign Minister and his diplomatic service (ref. 6190).

REEDTZ-THOTT, K. T. T. O. de (1839–1923)

Danish politician. Prime Minister 1894–97. Foreign Minister 1892–97.

A collection of his papers is held at the LAK.

REGULSKI, Bronisław (1886–1961)

Polish general. Deputy First Vice-Minister of War 1934–39. Military Attaché, London 1940–45.

The Sikorski Museum Archive at the Polish Institute, London, has a small collection of his papers covering the years 1934–53. It includes a report covering his service as Deputy First Vice-Minister of War 1934–39, and situation reports of the military attaché in London 1944–45. (Source: Milewski *et al.* (eds) *op. cit.*)

REICH, Christian (1822–65)

Danish War Minister 1864.

A collection of his papers is held at the *Rigsarkiv*, Copenhagen (ref. 6196).

REIJONEN, Emil Erkki (1869–1940)

Finnish politician and diplomat.

The *Valtionsarkisto*, Helsinki has a collection of thirty-one boxes which contain Reijonen's correspondence for the years 1883 to 1940 together with documents concerning his career as Ambassador in Estonia and Latvia.

RELANDER, Lauri Kristian (d. 1942)

President of the Finnish Republic 1925–31.

The *Valtionsarkisto*, Helsinki, has a collection of papers which comprises four boxes and includes diaries from Relander's period as President together with some manuscript memoirs. Access to this collection is restricted. See also E. Jutikkala, *Presidentin päiväkirja. Lauri Kristian Relanderin muistiinpanot 1925–1931* (2 vols.) (Helsinki: 1967–68).

RENKIN, Jules (1862–1934)

Belgian Christian–Democratic politician. First Minister of Colonies 1908–18.

The *Archives Générales du Royaume*, Brussels, has Renkin's papers, but these are very incomplete. Covering 1914–18, they mostly relate to the war and to internal politics in occupied Belgium, with almost nothing concerning the Congo. Authorisation is needed. The *Archief en Museum voor het Vlaamse Cultuurleven*, Antwerp, has a collection on Renkin (R.3743) which includes letters. The extent and nature of the collection is not known. Permission is needed for consultation.

RENNER, Karl (1870–1950)

Austrian Social Democrat. Marxist theorist and leader of the right wing of the SDAP. Chancellor and Foreign Minister 1918; President 1945–50.

The AVA, Vienna, has thirty-four boxes containing Renner's papers. The collection includes six boxes of correspondence; material on foreign policy, including St Germain, western Hungary, Germany and the United States; material on the labour movement, including the Prague labour party; material relating to the International Labour Organisation, Geneva and the International Association for Social Progress; and material on the constitution (ref. 27/ 31). The *Haus-, Hof- und Staatsarchiv*, Vienna, has four boxes of papers. The first contains various manuscripts. The second contains pamphlets; fly-sheets; lectures; a two part manuscript entitled '*Gesetz und Recht*'; and material on the world economy and on the '*Anschluss*'. The third box contains the manuscripts *Die Nation – Mythos und Wirklichkeit*, *Arbeit und Lohn*, *Politische Leitsätze*, *Bauers Plan für die Koalition*, *St Germain, 1919*, and *Die deutsche Revolution*. The fourth box contains various articles and correspondence. The VGA, Vienna, has a collection of correspondence 1908–50, including letters from his imprisonment in the *Landesgericht*. The Vienna City Library (WSLB) has a collection of correspondence from 1919–50; and a collection of manuscripts and draft speeches.

RENTHE-FINK, Cecil von (b. 1864)

German diplomat. Secretary-General of the Elbe Commission, 1923. Member of the political section of the League of Nations secretariat 1926–33. Minister in Copenhagen 1936–40, and then plenipotentiary in Denmark 1940–42. Plenipotentiary in Vichy France 1943.

A collection of his papers is at the Political Archive of the Federal German Foreign Office in Bonn. It contains material on Denmark and Pétain, notes and memoirs, and copies of official documents from Department II of the German Foreign Office, where he served from 1933–36. (Sources: Mommsen, *op. cit.*, Kimmich, *op. cit.*)

RETINGER, Józef (1888–1960)

Polish political *eminence grise*. Adviser to Sikorski. Advocate of European unity, and one of the pioneers of the Council of Europe.

The Sikorski Museum Archive at the Polish Institute, London, has a small collection (0.9m) of his papers covering the years 1918–47. The collection includes documents relating to Sikorski and his letters to Retinger; material relating to Retinger's political career 1918–39, and to the political situation in Poland in the 1930s; material on Jewish matters, 1937–42; material concerning British supplies to Poland, 1945–46; personal documents; and personal and official correspondence. (Source: Milewski *et al.* (eds) *op. cit.*)

REUSS, Heinrich VII, Prince of (1825–1906)

German ambassador in St Petersburg, Constantinople and Vienna. Adjutant General of Wilhelm I.

Reuss's family papers, including material on relations between Prussia and Russia, are at the State Archives in Warsaw. (Source: Mommsen, *op. cit.*)

REYNAUD, Paul (1878–1966)

French politician. Colonies Minister 1931–32; Prime Minister and Foreign Minister, March to May 1940; Prime Minister, Minister of War and National Defence, 18 May to 5 June 1940; Prime Minister, Minister of War and National Defence and Foreign Minister, 5 to 16 June 1940.

There are two collections of Reynaud's papers. By far the larger is in the *Archives Nationales*, which has 103 boxes of material relating to his professional and political career (ref. 74 AP 1 to 106). The Foreign Ministry archive has a further two boxes containing a file on the Norwegian affair; notes and telegrams on the Balkans, Finland and the Far East; files on Italy, the blockade, armaments and the armistice (ref. *Papiers* 40). (Source: AN, *Guide des Papiers*.)

REYNAUD, Roger

High official of the European Community.

A collection of his papers is in the General Archives of the EEC Commission, Brussels.

RIBOT, Alexandre (1842–1923)

French politician. Foreign Minister 1890–92 and 1917; Prime Minister and Foreign Minister 1892–93 and 1917; Prime Minister and Interior Minister 1893; Prime Minister and Finance Minister 1895; Prime Minister and Justice Minister 1914.

The Foreign Ministry archive has five volumes of material on foreign relations with Turkey, Germany, Italy, Great Britain, Portugal, and the United States, covering the period 1890–93; and material on colonial expansion in Africa. (Source: AN, *Guide des Papiers*.)

RICASOLI, Bettino (1809–80)

Italian politician. Prime Minister, Foreign Minister, Interior Minister and War Minister 1861–62; Prime Minister and Interior Minister 1866–67.

The *Archivio Centrale dello Stato*, Rome, has six files of correspondence and cabinet papers from the years 1849 to 1872. (Source: *Guida Generale*.)

RICHARD, Baron Raoul (fl. 1939–45)

Belgian politician.

The *Centre de Récherches et d'Etudes Historiques de la Seconde Guerre Mondiale*, Brussels, has Richard's papers for the period of the Second World War, largely 1940–42, including correspondence with Pierlot, Camille Gutt, Hugh Dalton, Spaak, Cartier de Marchiennes and Sir F. Leith-Ross; also notes, documents and correspondence relating to the Belgian government in London 1940–42. An inventory has been published: Alain Dantoing (ed.), *Archives Baron Raoul Richard*, CREHSGM, Inventaires, No. 12 (Brussels: 1982).

RICHTHOFEN, Baron Oswald von (1847–1946)

German diplomat, public servant and politician. Director, Colonial Department, Foreign Office 1896–97; Foreign Secretary 1900–06.

Richthofen's papers are in two parts. One collection is at the Political Archive of the Federal German Foreign Office in Bonn, and contains correspondence with other diplomats along with political material relating to the years 1879–81, originally from the papers of Frederick III. The German Federal Archive in Koblenz has another collection, containing diplomatic papers from the turn of the century. Other material, including parliámentary speeches, is on microfilm at the US National Archives, Washington, DC.

RICHTHOFEN, Hartmann Freiherr von (1878–1953)

German diplomat in Copenhagen, Tehran and Mexico. Department head in War Ministry.

The German Federal Archive in Koblenz has a small collection (0.5m) of his papers from 1890–1924. It includes speeches, essays and political documents on his activity for the (Liberal) German Democratic Party (DDP). Some material is available on microfilm at the US National Archives, Washington, DC. (Source: Mommsen, *op. cit.*)

RIEDL, Richard (fl. 1930s)

German diplomat. Ambassador in Vienna.

A collection of papers, covering the years 1939–43, is available in the Imperial War Museum, London (ref. AL2554/1–2).

RITTER, Karl (b. 1883)

German Foreign Office official and Ambassador to Rio de Janeiro 1937–38.

A collection of his papers is at the Political Archive of the Federal German Foreign Office in Bonn.

ROCHUSSEN, W.F. (fl. 1880s)

Dutch diplomat 1854–81. Minister for Foreign Affairs 1881–83.

The *Algemeen Rijksarchief*, The Hague, has a collection of Rochussen family papers (0.3m) which covers the period 1845–1918. While most of W.F. Rochussen's papers appear to have been destroyed, there is some material in the family archive (Inventory 2.21.141: Coll. 284).

RÖELL, jhr. Joan (1844–1914)

Chairman of the Dutch Cabinet and Minister for Foreign Affairs 1894–97.

The *Abraham Kuyperstichting*, Free University, Amsterdam has thirty letters from Röell to Kuyper. The *Algemeen Rijksarchief*, The Hague has a substantial collection of Röell papers (7.1m) which covers the period 1868–1914 (Inventory 2.21.183: Coll. 54a).

ROLLIN COUQUERQUE, Louis Marie (1869–1960)

Administrator at the Dutch Colonial Ministry.

The *Algemeen Rijksarchief*, The Hague, has a collection of Rollin Couquerque family papers (0.2m), covering the period 1830–1953 (Inventory 2.21.142: Coll. 90). Other family papers can be found at the *Stichting Centraal Bureau voor Genealogie*, The Hague, and at the *Gemeentearchief*, The Hague. For further information, see J.A.A. Bervoets, *Inventaris van een verzameling papieren afkomstig van het geslacht Rollin Couquerque* (The Hague: 1973).

ROMER, Tadeusz (b. 1894)

Polish diplomat and statesman. Ambassador to Moscow 1942–43; Minister of Foreign Affairs, Polish Government in Exile, London 1943–44.

The extensive papers, covering the period 1913–75, have been placed in the Public Archives of Canada. The collection includes correspondence, memoranda, reports and telegrams, minutes of meetings on Polish politics and Polish foreign relations. There are restrictions on access. A microfilm of these papers is in the Hoover Institution, Stanford University, California.

ROSEN, Friedrich (1856–1935)

German diplomat and politician. Ambassador to Bucharest, Lisbon and The Hague; Foreign Minister.

A manuscript relating to his diplomatic activity is at the Political Archive of the Federal German Foreign Office in Bonn. (Source: Mommsen, *op. cit.*)

ROSENBERG, Frederic Hans von (1874–1937)

German diplomat. Ambassador in Vienna 1920–22; Copenhagen 1922; Stockholm 1924–33; and Ankara 1933–35. Chief of German delegation to the League Assembly 1932; Foreign Minister 1922–23.

A collection of his papers is at the Political Archive of the Federal German Foreign Office in Bonn. It comprises one envelope containing political correspondence from 1918. The *Deutsches Zentralarchiv*, Potsdam also has a collection of his papers.

ROSENØRN-LEHN, Otto (1821–92)

Danish Foreign Minister 1870–75 and 1875–92.

A collection of his papers is held at the *Rigsarkiv*, Copenhagen (ref. 1717).

ROSSMANN, Erich (1884–1953)

German social democratic politician. Advocate of European unity and cooperation. General Secretary of the European Union, 1948.

The first part of Rossmann's papers for the period before 1943 was destroyed by bomb damage. The second part, covering the years 1946–53, is in the *Bundesarchiv*, Koblenz. This comprises personal papers and memoirs (1884–1945) relating to the reforming of the SPD in Thuringia after 1945, as well as his activity in the *Land* Council, and as General Secretary of the European Union and on behalf of war casualties, refugees and pensioners. (Source: Mommsen, *op. cit.*)

RUYS de BEERENBROUCK, jhr. Charles Joseph Marie (1873–1936)

Chairman of the Dutch Cabinet 1918–25 and 1929–33. Minister of the Interior 1918–25; Minister of Defence 1920; and Minister for Foreign Affairs 1933.

The *Algemeen Rijksarchief*, The Hague, has a substantial collection of Ruys de Beerenbrouck papers (5m), covering the years 1896 to 1936 (Summary Inventory 2.21.183: Coll. 372). There are also papers in the collections of J.H. Geertsma and A. Schimmelpenninck, the latter comprising eighteen letters from the years 1888–1905. There is also a family archive in the *Rijksarchief*, Limburg and correspondence in the Aalberse collection at the *Katholiek Documentatie Centrum*, Nijmegen. Some papers are still in the hands of his family.

RYDBERG, O.S. (fl. 1872–1914)

Swedish diplomat and Legation Counsellor.

The Archives of the Swedish Foreign Ministry at the *Riksarkiv*, Stockholm, have a collection of papers related to Rydberg's service with the ministry for the years 1872–1914.

RYGH, Evald (1842–1913)

Norwegian government minister 1889–91.

The *Riksarkiv*, Oslo, has a collection of papers (1m) consisting of letter-books from the years 1889–91 (Pa. 298).

RYTI, Risto Heikki (1889–1956)

President of the Finnish Republic 1940–44.

The *Valtionsarkisto*, Helsinki, has an extensive collection of papers consisting of eighty-one boxes. These include documents on his career as Director-General of the Finlands Bank, as Minister of State and as President. Also included are documents concerning the war-crimes trials 1945–46.

S

SAASTAMOINEN, Armas Herman (1886–1932)

Finnish diplomat and ambassador.

The *Valtionsarkisto*, Helsinki has a collection of fifty-one boxes which includes correspondence and other papers related to Saastamoinen's work and career as Ambassador in Copenhagen, Washington, London and The Hague. In addition, there are some family papers and one microfilm reel of a diary for the years 1926 to 1932 as well as general correspondence and documents for the years 1900 to 1927 and correspondence with P.J. Hynninen.

SABLIN, Eugenii Vasil'evič (fl. 1890–1918)

Russian diplomat. Sablin was the last Imperial Russian representative in the United Kingdom before the Bolshevik Revolution.

The Bakhmeteff Archive in Columbia University, New York has about forty-nine boxes of his papers. The collection includes some of the archive of the Imperial Embassy in London from the years 1886–90 and 1919–30.

SAGER, Robert (fl. 1890–1935)

Swedish diplomat and envoy.

The Archives of the Swedish Foreign Ministry at the *Riksarkiv*, Stockholm have a collection of papers related to Sager's diplomatic service in the years 1890–1935.

SALANDRA, Antonio (1853–1931)

Italian politician. Prime Minister and Interior Minister 1914–16.

The *Archivio Centrale dello Stato*, Rome, has a collection of correspondence relating to domestic and foreign policy during the First World War. The collection covers the period 1905–17 and comprises nine files. (Source: *Guida Generale*.)

SALNAIS, Voldemars (1886–1948)

Latvian diplomat. Delegate to the League of Nations 1921–34. Minister to Sweden, Norway and Denmark 1937–40.

A collection of his papers was given by Lilija Salnais in 1975 to the Hoover Institution, Stanford University, California. The papers, covering the period 1918–45, relate to such topics as Latvian independence movements and foreign relations.

SANDLER, Richard Johannes (1884–1964)

Swedish Minister of State 1925–26 and Foreign Minister 1932–36 and 1936–39.

There is a collection of Sandler's papers at the *Riksarkiv*, Stockholm. The Archives of the Swedish Foreign Ministry, housed at the *Riksarkiv*, have a collection of correspondence (eleven volumes) related to the years 1926 and 1932–39. Further papers can be found at the *Arbetarrörelsens Arkiv* (ARAB) Stockholm.

SARRAUT, Albert (1872–1962)

French politician and public servant. Under-Secretary of State for War 1909–10; Colonies Minister 1920–24 and 1932–33; Navy Minister 1930 and 1933–34; Prime Minister 1933 and 1936; Minister of State 1937–38; Governor General of Indo-China 1916–19; Ambassador to Turkey 1925–26.

The Departmental Archives of Aude have seventy-two bundles (84m) of material on French foreign and domestic policy between the wars. There is also material on Indo-China and on the Aude. The overseas section of the *Archives Nationales* has seventeen boxes of official papers from Sarraut's Governor-Generalship of Indo-China (ref. PA. 9). (Source: AN, *Guide des Papiers.*)

SAVORNIN LOHMAN, jhr. Alexander Frederick de (1837–1924)

Dutch politician and founder of the CHU (Christian Historical Union).

The *Algemeen Rijksarchief*, The Hague, has an extensive collection of de Savornin Lohman papers (6m) which covers the years 1867 to 1923 (Inventory 2.21.148: Coll. 87). Other papers can be found in the van Houten, van Heutz and Groen van Prinsterer papers. The *Abraham Kuyperstichting*, Free University, Amsterdam has a large amount of material related to Savornin Lohman. This includes 630 letters from de Savornin Lohman to Kuyper (1870–1920) and fifteen letters from Kuyper (1880–1903). There is also a collection of letters to A.W.F. Idenburg (1904–22). A family archive (1m) exists at the *Gemeentearchief*, Groningen, and there are some letters in the Hogerzeil private archive. For further details, contact the Central Register of Private Archives, The Hague. The *Algemeen Rijksarchief* also has the papers of the A.F. de Savornin Lohman Stichting (1955–79) which comprises 10m of archive. Access to this collection is restricted.

SAVORNIN LOHMAN, jhr. Maurits Adriaan de (1832–99)

Dutch Governor of Surinam.

The *Algemeen Rijksarchief*, The Hague, has a few items of interest in the B.C. de Savornin Lohman collection which covers the years 1832 to 1946 (Inventory 2.21.149: Coll. 272). In addition, there are fifteen letters written to Abraham Kuyper in the years 1880 to 1891 at the *Abraham Kuyperstichting*, Free University, Amsterdam.

SAZONOV, Sergei Dmietrievič (1861–1927)

Russian diplomat. Minister of Foreign Affairs 1910–16.

Four boxes of papers covering the period 1915 to 1927, including memoirs and cuttings, are in the Hoover Institution, Stanford University, California.

SCAPINI, Georges (b. 1891)

French diplomat and politician. Deputy, National Assembly 1928–40. Ambassador to Germany and Chief of the Diplomatic Service for Prisoners of War 1940–44.

A large collection of papers, covering the period 1928–63, was presented to the Hoover Institution, Stanford University, California, in 1978 by Lucie Marie Scapini. Among the correspondence, papers and other documentation is material relating to French politics, French prisoners of war and Scapini's trial in 1952 as a Nazi collaborator. Until 1998, written permission of the family is needed to use this collection.

SCAVENIUS, Erik (1877–1962)

Danish politician. Foreign Minister 1909–10, 1913–20, 1920–22 and after 1935; Prime Minister under the German occupation 1942–45.

A collection of his papers is held at the *Rigsarkiv*, Copenhagen (ref. 2467).

SCHACK, Eckhard von (1879–1961)

German public servant and diplomat. Legation counsellor in the Foreign Office and Ambassador to Lithuania.

A collection of his papers is held at the Political Archive of the Federal German Foreign Office, Bonn. It covers the years 1927–31 and contains material on Lithuania. (Source: Mommsen, *op. cit.*)

SCHANZER, Carlo (1865–1953)

Italian politician and diplomat. Minister of Foreign Affairs 1922; Italian delegate to the League of Nations.

The *Archivio Centrale dello Stato*, Rome, has thirty-five files, one box, and eighteen volumes of papers, covering Schanzer's ministerial activities and his work as delegate to the League of Nations. The collection covers the years 1912–50. (Source: *Guida Generale.*)

SCHIESS, Franz Ritter (later Freiherr) von Perstorff (1844–1932)

Austrian diplomat. Embassy attaché, St Petersburg 1870; legation secretary, Tehran 1872, St Petersburg 1874, Athens 1875, Constantinople 1878, Belgrade 1882, Constantinople 1887, Berlin 1891; Ambassador, Tehran 1894; Belgrade 1895; Cabinet Director 1899.

The *Haus-, Hof- und Staatsarchiv*, Vienna, has a collection of his papers. The material includes notes from the years 1901–15; and correspondence and other documents from the years 1882–1916.

SCHIESSL, Johann Ulrich (1813–88)

Swiss politician. Federal Chancellor 1848–81.

His diaries for the years 1850–75 are at the State Archive of Berne Canton (0.2m).

SCHIRMER, Kurt (1877–1930)

German Consul-General in China.

A collection of his papers is held at the Political Archive of the Federal German Foreign Office in Bonn. It comprises one packet of documents, including material on China. (Source: Mommsen, *op. cit.*)

SCHLEICHER, Kurt von (1882–1934)

German officer and last Chancellor of the Weimar Republic. After exerting pressure on President Hindenburg he was appointed to replace Papen following the election of November 1932. His attempt to rely on the army, win support from the Left and split the Nazis failed. He was succeeded by Hitler after barely two months in office, and murdered in 1934 in the 'night of the long knives'.

The German Federal Military Archive, Freiburg im Breisgau, has a small collection of Schleicher's papers, relating above all to his work in the Defence Ministry, and to domestic, foreign and economic policy (1m). Other papers were confiscated by the Gestapo, and have since been lost. (Source: Mommsen, *op. cit.*)

SCHLEIDEN, Rudolf (1815–95)

German diplomat and Liberal politician. Hanseatic Minister in Washington and London.

The University Library in Kiel has fifty-one bundles of Schleiden's papers, and a further collection is at the City Archive in Hamburg. (Source: Mommsen, *op. cit.*)

SCHLÖZER, Kurt von (1822–94)

German diplomat. Consul-General of the North German League in Mexico; German Ambassador to Washington; Prussian Ambassador to the Vatican.

A collection of his papers is held at the Political Archive of the Federal German Foreign Office in Bonn. It comprises one packet of correspondence from 1873–1903. His correspondents included Bismarck. Further collections of his letters are at the *Deutsches Zentralarchiv*, Potsdam. Copies of the Bonn collection are available on microfilm at the US National Archives, Washington, DC (T-291, reel 3). (Source: Mommsen, *op. cit.*)

SCHMERLING, Anton Ritter von (1805–93)

Austrian diplomat and politician. Interior and Foreign Minister. Later Prime Minister and President of Supreme Court. Member of the National Assembly in Frankfurt 1848.

A collection of eleven boxes of his papers is held at the *Haus-, Hof- und Staatsarchiv*, Vienna. Copies from this collection, mainly correspondence from the years 1848–86, are held by the German Federal Archive at its depot in Frankfurt. (Source: Mommsen, *op. cit.*)

SCHMITZ, Richard (fl. 1930s)

Austrian politician.

The *Haus-, Hof- und Staatsarchiv*, Vienna, has a collection of his papers, including material on foreign policy in 1932 and 1933. However, most of the material is concerned with Austrian domestic politics and the Austrian political parties, above all the Christian Social Party and the National Socialists.

SCHNEE, Heinrich (1871–1949)

German colonial administrator. Governor of German East Africa.

A collection of his papers is at the *Geheimes Staatsarchiv*, Berlin. It covers the years 1880–1944, and contains personal papers; his diary from the First World War; manuscripts; and notes and reports relating to the colonial service. (Source: Mommsen, *op. cit.*)

SCHOEN, Albrecht Wilhelm Freiherr von (1886–1960)

German diplomat. Served in Addis Ababa 1932–34. Ambassador to Chile 1936–43.

A copy of his memoirs is held by the Political Archive of the Federal German Foreign Office in Bonn. His papers are privately owned. (Source: Mommsen, *op. cit.*)

SCHOEN, Hans von (1876–1969)

German diplomat. Ambassador to Greece 1922–26, and to Hungary 1926–33.

His papers are privately owned. Copies of documents, correspondence and extracts from his memoirs are held at the Political Archive of the Federal German Foreign Office in Bonn. (Source: Mommsen, *op. cit.*)

SCHÖNMEYER, Alfred Carl (1868–1953)

Colonel of the Chilean Army and diplomat.

The *Krigsarkiv*, Stockholm, has a collection of two bundles and two volumes consisting of letters, speeches and documents as well as photographs of the Russo-Japanese War of 1904.

SCHROETTER, Erich (1875–1946)

German diplomat. Ambassador in Kovno, Lithuania 1924–26; Consul-General in Barcelona 1926–28; Ambassador in Reval 1928–32, and in Dublin 1936–37.

A very small collection of his papers (0.3m) is held at the Political Archive of the Federal German Foreign Office in Bonn, covering the years 1920–42. The collection contains personal papers, press cuttings and correspondence with diplomats and foreign office officials. (Source: Mommsen, *op. cit.*)

SCHUBERT, Carl Theodor von (b. 1882)

German diplomat. Embassy counsellor London 1920; State Secretary in the Foreign Office 1924–30; Ambassador, Rome 1930–32.

A collection of his papers is held at the Political Archive of the Federal German Foreign Office in Bonn.

SCHUBERT, Miroslav G. (b. 1895)

Czechoslovak diplomat. Chargé d'Affaires, Brazil 1921–25 and Iran 1927–32. Subsequently Counsellor and Deputy Envoy to Germany 1934–38. Consul-General in Munich 1945–48.

Two boxes of his papers (in Czech and English, covering the years 1936–77) were given by Schubert in 1978 to the Hoover Institution, Stanford University, California. The correspondence and papers include material on the Second World War, the Russian occupation of Czechoslovakia in 1945, inter-war diplomacy and communism in Czechoslovakia (including the 1948 *coup*).

SCHÜCKING, Walther (1875–1935)

German diplomat. Member of the German peace delegation to Versailles 1919; judge at the International Court of Justice, The Hague 1932; Deputy President of the German *Liga für Völkerbund*, a pro-League of Nations organisation; president of the German branch of the Inter-Parliamentary Union.

The German Federal Archive, Koblenz, has a collection of his papers which includes documents on international law, pacifism, the armistice and peace negotiations at Versailles, the war debt and the treatment of prisoners of war in Germany. It also contains material relating to the League of Nations, and the International Court of Justice, and Schücking's own political papers, covering his career in the Progressive Party and the Liberal DDP (German Democratic Party). (Source: Mommsen, *op. cit.*)

SCHUCKMANN, Bruno von (1857–1919)

German colonial administrator. Governor of South West Africa.

A collection of his papers is at the *Deutsches Zentralarchiv*, Potsdam. (Source: Mommsen, *op. cit.*)

SCHULENBERG, Friedrich-Werner von (1875–1944)

German diplomat. Minister, Tehran 1922–31; Bucharest 1931–34; Ambassador, Moscow 1934–41.

A collection of his papers is at the *Deutsches Zentralarchiv*, Potsdam. It comprises four boxes and contains material from the years 1923–41.

SCHÜLER, Edmund (1873–1952)

German public servant. Legation counsellor and later head of the personnel department in the Foreign Office.

A collection of his papers is held at the Political Archive of the Federal German Foreign Office in Bonn. It contains memoirs and literary works. (Source: Mommsen, *op. cit.*)

SCHULTESS, Edmund (1868–1944)

Swiss politician. Federal counsellor 1912–35; President of the Confederation 1917, 1921 and 1928.

The Zürich Central Library has a collection of private papers, including correspondence, diary notes, files of documents and lectures. Access to the collection is restricted. In addition three files are available at the State Archive of the Canton Aargau, Aarau.

SCHWIMMER, Rosika (1877–1948)

Hungarian pacifist and feminist. Minister to Switzerland 1918–19.

A collection of her papers is held at the Hoover Institution, Stanford University, California. The collection, in part typewritten transcripts, covers the period 1914–33, and includes correspondence, monographs and newspaper cuttings, relating to such matters as her affiliation with the Henry Ford Peace Expedition 1915–16; her participation in the Neutral Conference for Continuous Mediation 1916 and her subsequent career, both in Hungary and the United States.

SEHESTED, Hannibal de (1842–1924)

Danish politician. Prime Minister and Foreign Minister 1900–01.

A collection of forty-six packets of his papers is held at the *Rigsarkiv*, Copenhagen. The material covers the years 1848–1924 and includes letters and ministerial memoranda (ref. 6321).

SEIPEL, Ignaz (1876–1932)

Austrian politician. Prelate. Christian Social Chancellor 1921–24. Chancellor and Foreign Minister 1926–29.

The Diocesan Archive, Vienna, has two boxes of Seipel's papers. The collection contains his diary, in thirteen handwritten volumes, from 1916–32; three travel diaries; personal and family documents; copies of correspondence from 1917 to 1933; correspondence 1922–25; press cuttings; manuscripts; miscellaneous papers; and printed material. Seipel's correspondents included Lammasch, Mataja, and Eduard von Pappy, Austrian Ambassador in Berne.

SEITZ, Karl (1869–1950)

Austrian Social Democrat. President of the National Assembly and effectively head of state 1918–20.

Most of his papers are at the AVA, Vienna. Eighteen boxes are described as *Nachlass*, and six more have the title 'National Assembly, 1918–20. Office of the President, Karl Seitz'. The collection comprises those papers that were seized in 1934. The *Nachlass* contains five boxes of correspondence from the years 1907–34; material relating to the SDAP; and papers relating to industry during the First World War. There is also material on the period after 1920, and a collection of printed material and speeches from the years 1924–30 (ref. 27/24). The WSLA, Vienna, has eight boxes (seventy-three files) of his papers, with a detailed inventory, and the Vienna City Library (WSLB) has twenty-five letters. In addition, the VGA, Vienna, has seven files containing personal documents; press cuttings; a cartoon collection; photographs; and condolences on his death.

SEITZ, Theodor (1863–1949)

German colonial administrator. Governor of Cameroon 1907 and German South-West Africa 1910.

Most of his papers have been lost. His diaries for 1907–08 and 1935–36 are at the German Federal Archive in Koblenz, and material relating to his service in Africa is at the municipal archive in Mannheim. (Source: Mommsen, *op. cit.*)

SETÄLÄ, Eemil Nestor (fl. 1920s)

Finnish Professor and Foreign Minister 1926.

The *Valtionsarkisto*, Helsinki, has a large collection of papers totalling 423 files. These files include documents on Setälä's political and academic career as well as draft memoirs and manuscripts related to his academic work. Also included is his correspondence for the years 1881 to 1935. Access is restricted. Further papers can be found at the *Finlands Ortodoxa Kyrkostyrelses Arkiv*, Kuopio and at the *Finska Litteratursällskap*, Helsinki.

SEVENSMA, Tietse Pieter (fl. 1930s)

International public servant. Librarian of the League of Nations 1927–39.

The League of Nations Archives have one file of his papers covering the years 1927–38.

SFORZA, Carlo (1872–1952)

Italian diplomat and politician. Under-Secretary of State at the Foreign Ministry 1919–20 and 1920 (in the Nitti governments); Foreign Minister 1920–21, under Giolitti. Ambassador to France 1922. Foreign Minister 1947–51.

The *Archivio Centrale dello Stato*, Rome, has ten boxes of correspondence and miscellaneous documents from the years 1913–52. The collection includes documents from the period immediately following the Second World War, and material on the Atlantic Pact. (Source: *Guida Generale*.)

SHEBEKO, N.N. (fl. 1910–30s)

Russian diplomat. Ambassador to Vienna.

A collection of his papers is at the Bakmeteff Archive, Columbia University, New York, where it forms part of the collection of Irina Petrovna and A.A. Shebeko (ref. no. 586). The material includes his typed reminiscences about the origins of the First World War, published in French as *Souvenirs*; personal correspondence 1914–37; official reports on the Balkan situation in 1913–14; notes on events in 1918–19 and the activities of former Russian officials in the West. There are restrictions on the use of the material.

SHISHKIN, Nikolai Pavlovič (fl. 1890s)

Russian diplomat. Ambassador to Greece 1880–84. Subsequently Ambassador to Sweden and Norway 1884–91. Deputy Foreign Minister 1891–97.

A collection of correspondence and papers has been acquired by Birmingham University Library. The collection which is particularly concerned with Serbia and the Balkans, includes documents, official reports, letters and books. There is material on the 'Cassini Convention' with China and letters on political questions from Nikolai Giers. There is extensive material on diplomacy for the period 1876 to 1902.

SIEFVERT, Sigurd Victor (1875–1953)

Swedish Lieutenant-Colonel.

The *Krigsarkiv*, Stockholm, has a collection of papers (four bundles) which includes documents on his period of service as delegate to the Bulgarian government 1926–28.

SIEGFRIED, André (1875–1959)

French diplomat. Interpreter, British Army 1914–17; Secretary-General of the French Mission to Australia, New Zealand and Canada 1918–19; head of the Economic Section of the French delegation to the League of Nations 1920–21; expert at the international conferences of Brussels 1920, Barcelona 1921, Genoa 1922, Geneva 1927, San Francisco 1955.

The FNSP has ninety-four boxes of his papers, divided into seven sections. Material on foreign countries is contained in the first section. Section two contains documents, correspondence, and press cuttings from the years 1904 to 1950. Sections three and five include papers on French politics and Section four contains material relating to conferences during the period 1906 to 1958. Sections six and seven contain material on contagious diseases and the centenary of his birth respectively.

SIKORSKI, General Władiysław (1881–1943)

Polish soldier and statesman. Prime Minister of the Polish government in exile and Commander-in-Chief of the Polish Armed Forces 1939–43.

The Sikorski Museum Archive at the Polish Institute, London, has a collection of his papers covering the years 1932–69 (4.5m). The collection is divided into two parts. The first part consists of the official diary of the Commander-in-Chief of the Armed Forces and Prime Minister. The second part contains official and private documents; correspondence; notes; press cuttings; articles; material relating to his death in an aeroplane crash at Gibraltar; material from the years after his death and papers of his widow, Helena Sikorska. (Source: Milewski *et al.* (eds) *op. cit.*)

SIMONS, Walther (1861–1937)

German public servant and politician. Commissioner General of the German peace delegation to Versailles, April–June 1919. Foreign Minister 1920–21. President of the Reich Court 1922–29.

A collection of papers relating to his career is reported by Kimmich to be at the Political Archive of the Federal German Foreign Office in Bonn. Some correspondence from the years 1919–33 is at the German Federal Archive in Koblenz.

SKIRMUNT, Konstanty (fl. 1920s)

Polish Minister in London 1920s.

Copies of his memoirs are available at the library of the *Katolicki Uniwersytet Lubelski* (Lublin) and the *Biblioteka Jagiellońska, Uniwersytet Jagielloński*, Cracow.

SLAVIK, Juraj (1880–1969)

Czechoslovak diplomat and statesman. Ambassador to Poland 1936–39; Minister of the Interior 1940–45; Minister of Foreign Affairs 1945–46; Ambassador to Washington 1946–48.

A large collection of his papers (forty-four boxes, covering the period 1934–66) was given to the Hoover Institution, Stanford University, California, by Gita Slavik in 1976. There is material on relations with Poland, political developments in Czechoslovakia, communist and émigré politics, etc.

SMIDT, H.J. (1831–1917)

Dutch Governor of Surinam.

The *Algemeen Rijksarchief*, The Hague, has a collection of Smidt papers (1.1m) covering the period 1851–1921 (Inventory 2.21.26: Coll. 189). For further details, see *Inventarissen van D. Bos ... H.J. Smidt, B.D.H. Tellegen* (The Hague: 1970).

SMUTNY, Jaromir (fl. 1930s–40s)

Czech politician. Chancellor to President Eduard Beneš of Czechoslovakia 1938–48; emigrated to London in 1948 and founded Eduard Beneš Institute.

The Bakhmeteff Archive, Columbia University, New York, has twenty-two boxes of his papers. The collection contains published volumes of the Beneš Institute; notes and lectures by Smutny; typed manuscripts on Czech politics and diplomacy 1915–65, the February Revolution 1948, the death of Masaryk, the London government in exile in the Second World War, the Munich crisis of 1938, Beneš's visits to Moscow in 1943 and 1945, and the Sudeten Germans in 1945; reports of the London government in exile; and other material on, among others, Masaryk and Hodža.

SNELLMAN, Teo Kaarlo (1894–1977)

Finnish Legation Counsellor.

The *Valtionsarkisto*, Helsinki, has a collection of twenty-one boxes of papers related to Snellman's diplomatic career.

SNOILSKY, Greve Carl Johan Gustaf (fl. 1870s)

Head of the Political Department of the Swedish Foreign Ministry 1876–79.

A collection of Snoilsky's papers can be found in the Royal Library, Stockholm.

SNOUCK HURGRONJE, Christiaan (1857–1936)

Dutch Colonial Adviser.

The *Universiteitsbibliotheek*, Leiden, has a collection of letters to which access was restricted until 1986. Other material can be found at the Oosterse Instituut, Leiden, and in the A.W.F. Idenburg collection at the *Abraham Kuyperstichting*, Free University, Amsterdam. There may also be some items of interest in the Adriaanse private archive. For further details, contact the Central Register of Private Archives, The Hague.

SODEN, Julius Freiherr von (1846–1921)

German colonial administrator and politician. Governor of Cameroon and German East Africa. Foreign Minister of Württemberg.

A small collection of his papers is at the *Hauptstaatsarchiv*, Stuttgart (0.8m). It contains documents from the years 1864–74, largely on relations between the German states and international treaties and law. (Source: Mommsen, *op. cit.*)

SÖDERHJELM, Jarl Werner (1859–1931)

Finnish Professor and diplomat. Ambassador to Stockholm 1919–28.

The *Valtionsarkisto*, Helsinki, has four boxes of documents, letters and other papers related to Söderhjelm's career as Ambassador to Stockholm 1919–28. Söderhjelm's other correspondence and literary legacy is held by the University of Helsinki Library.

SOHLMAN, Rolf (fl. 1939–45)

Head of Commercial Affairs at the Swedish Foreign Ministry.

The Archives of the Swedish Foreign Ministry, housed at the *Riksarkiv*, Stockholm, have a collection of papers from the years 1939, 1943 and 1944. This includes documentation on Swedish-British-American wartime commercial treaties.

SOKOLNICKI, Michał (1880–1967)

Polish historian and diplomat. Minister to Denmark 1931–36. Ambassador to Turkey 1936–45.

His papers, in part transcripts, have been placed on permanent deposit at the Pilsudski Institute of America Library, New York City. The collection, c. 4ft, covering the period 1908–45, comprises correspondence and documents relating to the Polish independence movement (Polish Legions 1914–18), the Polish Legation in Copenhagen, and the Polish embassy in Ankara 1923–45. A further collection (fourteen boxes, 1931–68) has been purchased by the Hoover Institution, Stanford University, California, from his widow.

SOLA, Ugo (fl. 1920s–40s)

Italian diplomat. First Secretary and Chargé d'Affaires, legation, Belgrade 1923–25; First Secretary, London embassy 1925–26; Minister, Bucharest 1933–38; Ambassador, Rio de Janeiro 1939–42.

A collection of his papers is held at the Italian Foreign Ministry. (Source: Cassels, *op. cit.*)

SOLERI, Marcello (1882–1945)

Italian politician. Minister of War 1922.

The Provincial Archive at Cuneo has forty-seven files of his papers covering the period 1896 to his death.

SOLF, Wilhelm (1862–1936)

German diplomat, colonial administrator and politician. Governor of Samoa. Foreign Secretary, October–December 1918; Ambassador to Tokyo 1920–28.

A substantial collection of his papers is at the German Federal Archive, Koblenz (3.6m). It includes correspondence, speeches and publications; official and political material from his governorship of Samoa and service at the Colonial Office (1911–18) and Foreign Office (1918). There are also documents relating to his diplomatic service in Japan during the 1920s and correspondence from the 1930s. A film of this material is available at the *Deutsches Zentralarchiv* in Potsdam, and the US National Archives has a small amount of material on microfilm. (Source: Mommsen, *op. cit.*)

SONNINO, Sidney (1847–1922)

Italian politician. Foreign Minister under Salandra 1914–16, Boselli 1916–17 and Orlando 1917–19.

The *Archivio Sonnino*, Montespertoli, Florence, has a collection of his papers comprising about a quarter of a million separate documents and covering his entire career as Foreign Minister during and immediately after the First World War. The collection also contains his diary up to 1922. Important parts of the collection are on microfilm and available as *The Sonnino Papers* (fifty-four reels), from University Microfilms, Ann Arbor, Michigan. The microfilms contain approximately 100 000 documents relating to the First World War. A second collection is held at the Historical Archive of the Italian Ministry of Foreign Affairs. It contains a selection of important papers removed from the general collection on his death. The *Archivio Centrale dello Stato* in Rome has one box of papers from the years 1914–19, which came from his secretary De Morcier. (Source: Cassels, *op. cit.*)

SOULIÉ, Michel (1916–71)

French politician and diplomat.

Soulié's papers are in private ownership. (Source: AN, *Guide des Papiers*.)

SPAAK, Paul Henri (1899–1972)

Belgian socialist politician. Minister of Foreign Affairs 1936–39. Prime Minister 1938–39; Minister of Foreign Affairs, 3 September 1939 to 10 May 1940, and in London from 31 October 1940.

Spaak's archives are apparently still in the possession of his widow (1989), and are not accessible. The *Archief en Museum voor het Vlaamse Cultuurleven*, Antwerp, has a collection on Spaak (S.762) which includes letters and documents. The extent and nature of the collection is not known. Permission is needed for consultation.

SPARRE, Christian (1859–1941)

Norwegian Admiral and Minister of Defence 1900–01.

The *Riksarkiv*, Oslo, has a collection of documents (0.3m) consisting of correspondence, notes and printed matter covering the years 1876 to 1958 (Pa. 199).

SPIERENBURG, Dirk Pieter (1909–   )

High official of the European Community.

A collection of his papers is in the General Archives of the EEC Commission, Brussels.

STAAFF, Karl Albert (fl. 1905–14)

Swedish Minister of State 1905–06 and 1911–14.

A collection of Staaff's papers can be found at the University Library, Uppsala.

STÅHLBERG, Kaarlo Juho (1865–1952)

President of the Finnish Republic, 1919–25.

The *Valtionsarkisto*, Helsinki, has a collection comprising 224 boxes which includes Ståhlberg's correspondence for the years 1881–1951, notes and manuscripts of articles and documents on his career in the parliament and Senate. There are also papers related to his period as President, together with some newspaper cuttings and printed material. The papers of his wife, Ester, which consist of 124 files, can also be found at the *Valtionsarkisto*. Most of these contain correspondence from the years 1892 to 1950.

STAUNING, Thorvald (1873–1942)

Danish Prime Minister 1924–26 and 1929–42.

A collection of his papers is held at the *Rigsarkiv*, Copenhagen (ref. 1965). Further collections are held at the State Ministry and the ABA. The papers in the ABA consist of some sixty-six boxes, covering the period *c.* 1900–42. These include speeches, manuscripts and correspondence (including many letters from rank and file members). A printed inventory is available.

STEEN, Johannes Wilhelm Christian (1827–1906)

Norwegian member of parliament. Prime Minister 1891–93 and 1898–1902.

The *Riksarkiv*, Oslo, has a collection of documents (0.7m) consisting of correspondence and printed papers from the years 1864–1905 (Pa. 174).

STEIN ZU NORD- UND OSTHEIM, Otto Freiherr von (b. 1886)

German diplomat. Embassy counsellor in Vienna until the German invasion of 1938.

His papers are in private hands. The Political Archive of the Federal German Foreign Office has a very small collection (0.03m) of copies of extracts from his diaries.

STEINACHER, Hans (fl. 1915–47)

Austrian diplomat. Consul general in Milan. Director of the Popular League for Germandom Abroad 1933–37.

An extensive collection of his papers is at the German Federal Archive, Koblenz (6m). It contains diaries (1915–47); memoirs; documents and correspondence, including material relating to the plebiscites in Upper Silesia and Carinthia. (Source: Mommsen, *op. cit.*)

STELZER, Gerhard (1896–1965)

German diplomat. Embassy counsellor, Bucharest 1938–44. Consul-General, Amsterdam to 1961.

A very small collection of his papers (0.07m) is held at the Political Archive of the Federal German Foreign Office in Bonn. It contains material relating to his diplomatic service in Romania. (Source: Mommsen, *op. cit.*)

STENBECK, John Erland René (1898–1944)

Swedish Major-General. Delegate to Geneva Disarmament Conference.

The *Krigsarkiv*, Stockholm, has a collection of papers (two bundles) which includes material on Stenbeck's work as delegate to the Geneva disarmament conference in 1932 and his role in the Swedish defence commission 1933–35.

STENIUS, Emil Wilhelm (1851–1918)

Finnish Colonel. Governor of Kuopio, 1905–11.

The *Valtionsarkisto*, Helsinki, has two boxes of material which includes letters, telegrams and other papers related to Stenius' career as governor of Kuopio, 1905–11, together with some printed material. Other documents may be found in the Military Archives, Helsinki.

STIKKER, Dirk Uipko (1897–1979)

Dutch diplomat and Secretary-General of NATO. Previously Ambassador to London.

The *Algemeen Rijksarchief*, The Hague, has an extensive collection of Stikker's personal papers (30m) which cover his entire career as Minister for Foreign Affairs and as Ambassador to London. Items in the collection cover the years 1897 to 1980 although access to the papers is still restricted (Summary Inventories 2.21.156 and 2.21.183: Coll. 194). Some other papers may exist in private archives. For further details, contact the Central Register of Private Archives, The Hague. In addition, there is a volume of published memoirs, D.U. Stikker, *Memoires, herinneringen uit de lange jaren, waarin ik betrokken was bij de voortdurende wereldcrisis* (Rotterdam/The Hague: 1966).

STOHRER, Eberhard von (1883–1953)

German diplomat. Minister in Cairo 1927–35 and Bucharest 1935–37; Ambassador to Madrid 1937–43.

A collection of his papers is at the Political Archive of the Federal German Foreign Office in Bonn. It comprises one packet of manuscripts on German-Spanish relations during the First World War. Most of his papers have been lost.

STOLBERG-WERNIGERODE, Wilhelm Prinz zu (1870–1931)

German diplomat in Rome and Vienna.

His papers are at the state archive in Oranienbaum, Anhalt, East Germany. (Source: Mommsen, *op. cit.*)

STRANDES, Justus (1859–1930)

German politician and businessman. Civil governor of Antwerp.

A collection of his papers is at the Political Archive of the Federal German Foreign Office in Bonn. It comprises one packet of manuscripts relating to East Africa, where Strandes was in business.

STRAUCH, Maximilien (fl. 1880s)

Belgian public servant. Replaced Greindl as the Secretary-General of the *Association Internationale de l'Afrique*; later administrator-general of the interior, *Etat Indépendent du Congo*, until 1888.

The Belgian Foreign Ministry has half his papers, and the *Musée de la Dynastie*, Brussels, has the other half.

STRESEMANN, Gustav (1878–1929)

German politician. Chancellor 1923; Foreign Minister 1923–29. As Foreign Minister architect of the Locarno treaties of October 1925 and the Treaty of Berlin with the Soviet Union, April 1926.

A substantial collection of his papers (6m) is held at the Political Archive of the Federal German Foreign Office in Bonn. It covers the years 1887–1929 and contains mainly service documents. This collection is also available on microfilm at the German Federal Archive in Koblenz, and at the US National Archives in Washington, DC. There is an English translation of the published edition of the Stresemann papers.

STRÖMFELT, greve Carl Haraldsson (fl. 1900s)

Swedish Cabinet Secretary 1905–06.

The Archives of the Swedish Foreign Ministry, housed at the *Riksarkiv*, has a collection of papers related to the year 1905.

STRUYCKEN, A.A.H. (fl. 1910–20)

Adviser to Dutch Foreign Minister van Karnebeek at the Paris Peace Conference in 1919.

Struycken's personal papers do not appear to have survived, but cognisance should be taken of the following publications; A.A.H. Struycken, *Holland, Belgium and the Powers* (The Hague 1919) and *De Hoofdtrekken van Nederland's Buitenlandsche Betrekkingen* (Arnhem 1923). Reference might also be made to J. Oppenheim, A.C. Josephus Jitta *et al. Verzamelde Werken* (Arnhem 1928).

STUDNICKI, Władysław (Gizbert) (1867–1953)

Polish writer and historian. Member, Provisional Council of State, 1917.

A collection of his papers (fourteen folders) has been placed on permanent deposit in the Pilsudski Institute of America, New York. The collection includes correspondence; notes; manuscripts of memoirs, dealing with international affairs, especially Polish-German relations.

STUERS, A.L.E. Ridder de (fl. 1914–18)

Dutch Minister to Paris during the First World War.

The *Ministerie van Buitenlandse Zaken* has a file of correspondence from Stuers in the J. Loudon collection, and there is also a family archive with papers up to 1860 at the *Gemeentearchief*, Maastricht.

STÜRGKH, Carl Graf von (1859–1916)

Austrian politician. Minister President 1911–16.

According to Rutkowski, Stürgkh's papers were lost during the plundering of Schloss Halbenrein, shortly after the end of the First World War in 1918.

SUMANS, Villis (1887–1948)

Latvian diplomat. Minister to Italy 1924–26; Minister to France 1926–34; delegate to the League of Nations Assembly 1922–30.

A small collection of his papers (c. one and a half boxes) is now in the Hoover Institution, Stanford University, California. The collection covers the period 1925–38 and relates mainly to Latvian foreign policy. It was given by Lilija Brante-Parupe.

SUNDSTRÖM, Carl-Johan (Cay) (1902–59)

Finnish ambassador and diplomat.

There are three boxes of Sundström's papers housed at the *Valtionsarkisto*, Helsinki. The collection consists of diary notes concerning his career as ambassador in Moscow, Bucharest, Sofia and Peking 1945–59. Access to this collection was restricted until March 1984.

SVERDRUP, Johan (1816–92)

Norwegian lawyer. Member of Parliament and Prime Minister 1884–89.

The *Riksarkiv*, Oslo, has an extensive collection of documents (17m) consisting of Sverdrup's personal and political papers covering the years 1817 to 1902 (Pa. 167).

SVINHUFVUD, Pehr Evind (1861–1944)

President of the Finnish Republic 1925–31.

The *Valtionsarkisto*, Helsinki, has four boxes of documents which include letters to Svinhufvud 1902–03, and a series of congratulatory telegrams. There is also a translation into German by C. von Horschelmans of E. Räikkönen's *Svinhufvud Siperiasse*. The archive of E. Paldani (1858–1917) also contains a collection of letters from Svinhufvud from the years 1902–03.

SWARTZ, Carl Johan Gustaf (fl. 1914–18)

Swedish Minister of State 1917.

There is a collection of Swartz's papers in the City Library, Norrköping.

SWITALSKI, Kazimierz (fl. 1920s)

Polish Prime Minister, April–December 1929.

His journals are in the *Archiwum Akt Nowych*, Warsaw.

SYPERSTEYN, Cornelis Ascanius jhr. van (1823–92)

Dutch Artillery Officer in Surinam 1846–55, and later Governor 1873–82.

The *Gemeentearchief*, Haarlem, has a collection of van Sypersteyn papers.

SZÉLL, Kálmán (1843–1915)

Hungarian landowner and politician. Prime Minister and Minister of the Interior, February 1899 to June 1903.

The Hungarian National Archives, Budapest, have a collection of papers (0.21m) which covers the years 1899 and 1902–03.

SZEMBEK, Jan (1881–1945)

Polish diplomat. Minister in Brussels 1921–24; Minister in Bucharest 1927–32; Under-Secretary of State for Foreign Affairs 1932–39.

The Sikorski Museum Archive at the Polish Institute, London, has a small collection (0.7m) of his papers for the years 1912–55. The collection includes his diaries 1935–39; correspondence; lectures and articles; typescripts in French concerning Soviet affairs and press cuttings. (Source: Milewski *et al.* (eds) *op. cit.*)

SZTÓJAY, Döme (1883–1946)

Hungarian army officer. Military attaché in Berlin 1927–33 and then Minister to Germany from 1935. Became Prime Minister after the German occupation, March–August 1944. After the war, tried, sentenced and executed as a war criminal.

The Hungarian National Archives, Budapest, hold a collection of papers (0.01m) relating to the year of his premiership in 1944.

SZYDŁOWSKI, Stanisłav (1907–78)

Polish diplomat.

The Sikorski Museum Archive at the Polish Institute, London, has a small collection (0.74m) of Szydłowski's papers covering the years 1928–74. The material includes documents relating to his diplomatic and military service; correspondence; documents relating to his activities in Polish émigré institutions and personal papers, documents, notebooks and diaries. (Source: Milewski *et al.* (eds) *op. cit.*)

T

TALAS (GRATSCHOFF), Onni Eugen Alexander (1877–1958)

Finnish professor, diplomat and statesman.

The *Valtionsarkisto*, Helsinki, has a collection of twelve boxes of correspondence, 1905 to 1949 together with manuscript memoirs. Access to this collection is restricted.

TANNER*, Väinö Alfred (1881–1966)

Finnish Social Democratic Leader. Numerous ministerial posts. Prime Minister 1926–28 and Foreign Minister 1939–40.

The *Valtionsarkisto*, Helsinki, has the major collection of Tanner's ministerial papers consisting of sixty-eight boxes. This includes correspondence, drafts and notes of documents on his career, the Peace Conference at Dorpat, and various international organisations. There is also a collection of newspaper cuttings and the whole archive covers the years 1907 to 1965. Further material can be found in the Finnish Labour Archive in Helsinki. (For details of this see *Sources in European Political History*, vol. I, p. 204.)

*Known as Thomasson until 1895.

TARDIEU, André (1876–1945)

French politician and diplomat. Prime Minister and Interior Minister 1929–30; War Minister 1932; Prime Minister and Foreign Minister 1932; Minister of State 1934. High Commissioner to the United States 1917; Commissioner General for Franco-American matters of war 1918–19.

The *Service historique de l'Armée de Terre*, Vincennes, has 130 boxes of papers of the Commissariat-General for Franco-American matters of war, covering the period 1916–21 (ref. 13 N 1 to 130. See Devos *et al.*, *op. cit.*). The *Archives Nationales* has a further collection, comprising 128 boxes of material, including letters received by Tardieu; manuscript notes and documents on the First World War and covers the period 1904–57 (ref. 324 AP 1 to 128). The Foreign Ministry archive at the Quai d'Orsay, Paris, has 122 boxes including files on Morocco between 1906 and 1912; the peace conference and peace treaty; disarmament; the League of Nations; and the economic mission of Tardieu to the United States. The collection covers the period 1906–39. (Source: AN, *Guide des Papiers*.)

TAUBE, greve Arvid Fredrik (fl. 1890–1914)

Swedish diplomat and Foreign Minister 1909–11. Previously Head of the Political Department of the Foreign Ministry 1892–95 and Secretary to the Cabinet 1895–1900.

A collection of Taube's papers can be found in the Royal Library, Stockholm. Further papers can be found at the *Riksarkiv* and in the Archives of the Swedish Foreign Ministry where there are papers relating to some of his years in office, 1895–99 and 1909.

TEISSERENC DE BORT, Pierre (1814–92)

French politician and diplomat. Ambassador to Vienna 1879–80.

Vicomte Edmond de Sèze, Haute-Vienne, has a small collection of non-official correspondence and printed material. (Source: AN, *Guide des Papiers*.)

TELEKI, Count Pál (1879–1941)

Hungarian landowner and counter-revolutionary politician. Prime Minister from July 1920 to April 1921 and again from February 1939 until April 1941.

The Hungarian National Archives, Budapest, have a collection of papers (0.4m) relating to his second period in office between 1939 and 1941.

TETS van GOUDRIAAN, jhr. Dirk Arnold Willem van (1844–1930)

Dutch diplomat. Ambassador in Berlin 1879–94 and Minister for Foreign Affairs 1905–08.

The *Algemeen Rijksarchief*, The Hague, has an extensive collection (4m) of van Tets van Goudriaan family papers covering the years 1600 to 1908 (Inventories 2.21.158 and 2.21.159: Collns 85, 106 and 112). There is also another family archive at the *Universiteitsbibliotheek*, Utrecht.

THEDIECK, Franz (b. 1900)

German public servant attached to division of Interior Ministry responsible for combatting separatism in the Rhineland; adviser to military administration in Brussels 1940–43; State Secretary in Ministry for Inner German Questions 1949–56; Director of *Deutschlandsfunk* 1966–72.

The German Federal Archive, Koblenz, has a large collection of his papers (9m), covering the years 1925–66. It contains material relating to anti-separatism, Eupen and Malmédy and the *Deutschlandsfunk*. There is also correspondence with, among others, Konrad Adenauer, Ernst Lemmer and Jakob Kaiser (1.1m). A further collection, including speeches and essays from the years 1951–63, and correspondence with Heinrich Brüning (1946–53), is at the Konrad Adenauer Foundation. A collection of material, including papers relating to the Saar question in the early 1950s and further correspondence with Adenauer (1954–58), is with the papers of Jakob Kaiser at Koblenz (0.1m). (Source: Mommsen, *op. cit.*)

THEMPTANDER, Oscar Robert (fl. 1880s)

Swedish Minister of State 1884–88.

There are two collections of Themptander's papers, at the University Library, Uppsala and at the *Riksarkiv*, Stockholm.

THIERS, Adolphe (1797–1877)

French politician. Prime Minister and Foreign Minister 1836–40; Head of the executive power of the French Republic 1871; President of the Republic 1871–73.

The manuscripts department of the *Bibliothèque Nationale* has eighty-four in-folio volumes of papers, including twenty-eight volumes of correspondence. Much of the material, which dates from the period 1870 to 1874, relates to military matters, the defence and siege of Paris, and the occupation, evacuation and liberation of French territory (ref. *Nouvelles acquisitions françaises* 20601 to 20684). (See H. Omont, *op. cit.*) The Foreign Ministry archive has a bound volume of documents relating to the negotiations at Frankfurt in 1871, to the German army of occupation; and ten boxes of copies of official political correspondence (ref. *Fonds nominatifs*, no. 170). (Source: AN, *Guide des Papiers*.)

THOMAS, Albert (1878-1932)

French socialist politician and diplomat. Minister of Armaments and War Manufactures 1916–17; Extraordinary Ambassador to Moscow 1917–18; Member of the Peace Conference 1918–19; Director of the International Labour Organisation (ILO) 1920–32.

The *Archives Nationales*, Paris, has a very large collection of material (484 boxes), relating to all aspects of Albert Thomas's career (ref. 94 AP 1–484). The collection includes correspondence addressed to him as President of the *Bureau international du Travail* (ref. 94 AP 378–394), material on colonial questions and on international economic relations (ref. 94 AP 338–343). Other papers are reported in the ILO archive.

THOMSEN, C.A. (1827-96)

Danish politician. War Minister 1872–74 and 1894–96.

A collection of his papers is held at the *Rigsarkiv*, Copenhagen (ref. 2050), which is also believed to have details of other collections.

THUN UND HOHENSTEIN, Franz Prince (fl. 1890s)

Austrian politician. Minister President of Austria 1898–99.

His papers are at the Děčín branch of the state regional archive, Litoměřích, Czechoslovakia.

THYS, General Albert (fl. 1886-1909)

Belgian public servant. Equerry to Leopold II; replaced Strauch as Administrator-General of the Interior, *Etat Indépendent du Congo*, in 1888.

The *Musée Royal de l'Afrique Centrale*, Tervuren, has a small collection of Thys' notes and correspondence 1886–1909, with among others Leopold II, Strauch, Stanley, E. Laurent and A.J. Wauters, also some later biographical material, held in the collection *Papiers Jules Cornet*. An inventory has been published: Marcel Luwel (ed.), *Inventaire des papiers Jules Cornet, géologue (1865–1929)* (MRAC, *Inventaires des Archives Historiques*, no. 1, 1961).

THYSELIUS, Carl Johan (fl. 1880s)

Swedish Minister of State 1883–84.

There is a collection of Thyselius' papers in the *Riksarkiv*, Stockholm.

TIENHOVEN, Gijsbert van (1841-1914)

Chairman of the Dutch Cabinet and Minister for Foreign Affairs 1891–94.

The *Gemeentearchief*, Amsterdam has a collection of his papers and diaries, although there is still some material which remains in family hands. In addition, the *Abraham Kuyperstichting* has seven letters written to A. Kuyper by van Tienhoven in the years 1884 to 1905.

TILLON, Charles (b. 1897)

French politician. Air Minister 1944–45; Armaments Minister 1945–46; Minister of Reconstruction and Town Planning 1947.

The *Service Historique de l'Armée de l'Air*, Vincennes, has one spool of film containing an interview with Tillon from 28 October 1976. There is no transcript. (Source: AN, *Guide des Papiers*.)

TISO, Stefan (1897–1949)

Premier of Slovakia 1944–45.

A diary (in Slovak) for 1944–45 relating to political and military conditions in Slovakia, was purchased by the Hoover Institution, Stanford University, California, from Vladimir Kovalik in 1952.

TISZA, Count István (1861–1918)

Hungarian politician and Prime Minister from November 1903 to June 1905, and again from June 1913 to June 1917. After his resignation, he was active at the front and was killed by soldiers at the outbreak of the Hungarian revolution.

The Hungarian National Archives, Budapest, have a collection of papers relating to his two periods in office (0.32m). These cover the years 1903–05 and 1913–18.

TISZA, Kálmán (1830–1902)

Hungarian landowner and politician. Exiled after the Hungarian War of Independence, he returned in 1861, becoming Minister of the Interior in March 1875 and Prime Minister in October of the same year. He held this position until March 1890 but continued to play an active part in politics during the remainder of his life.

The Hungarian National Archives, Budapest, have a small collection of papers (0.03m) which cover the years 1867 to 1890.

TITULESCU, Nicolas (fl. 1920s–30s)

Romanian politician. Minister of Finance 1920–22; Minister of Foreign Affairs 1927–28 and 1932–34.

A large collection of his papers (c. fifteen and a half boxes) is in the Hoover Institution, Stanford University, California. The collection covers the period 1923–38.

TJARDA van STARKENBORGH STACHOUWER, jhr. A.W.L. (1888–1979)

Dutch diplomat. Minister to Belgium 1935–36 and later Governor-General of the Dutch East Indies.

The *Rijksinstituut voor Oorlogsdocumentatie*, Amsterdam has a collection of papers, copies of which can be found at the *Algemeen Rijksarchief*, The Hague. The papers cover the period from 1925 to 1978 (Summary Inventory 2.21.183: Coll. 264). Some letters written to P.S. Gerbrandy also exist. For further details, contact the Central Register of Private Archives, The Hague.

TOMASI DELLA TORRETTA, Pietro dei principi di Lampedusa (1873–1962)

Italian politician.

The *Archivio Centrale dello Stato*, Rome, has one box of papers dating from the years 1922 to 1927. The material concerns Italian foreign policy during this period, primarily Anglo-Italian relations. (Source: *Guida Generale*.)

TORNAQUINCI, Aldobrando Medici

Italian politician. Under-Secretary of State for Occupied Territories after the armistice.

The *Istituto per la storia della Resistenza in Toscana*, Florence, has a collection of his papers.

TORP, Oscar (1893–1958)

Norwegian Minister of Defence 1935–36 and again in the Government in Exile in London 1942–45. Prime Minister 1951–55.

The *Riksarkiv*, Oslo, has a collection of papers (1m) consisting of correspondence covering the years 1930 to 1950. Other papers can be found in the ABA, Oslo.

TRAUTMANN, Oskar (1877–1950)

German public servant and diplomat. Departmental head and Director of Eastern Division of the Foreign Office 1928–31; Ambassador to China 1931–38.

His papers are privately owned but copies are available at the Political Archive of the Federal German Foreign Office in Bonn. The collection is very small (0.8m) and consists of diaries (1915–16 and 1944), diary notes (1937–38), and material on peace negotiations in the Far East. It is possible that there are papers at the *Deutsches Zentralarchiv* in Potsdam. (Source: Mommsen, *op. cit.*)

TREUTLER, Karl Georg von (1858–1933)

Prussian diplomat. Ambassador in Rio, Oslo and Munich.

His papers are reported by Cecil to be in the possession of Baroness Anne-Katrin von Ledebur at Schwenningdorf in Westphalia. They contain a manuscript of an autobiography written in the 1920s.

TROLLE, Eric Birger (fl. 1900s)

Swedish Foreign Minister 1905–09. Previously Secretary to the Cabinet 1903–05.

The Archives of the Swedish Foreign Ministry has a collection of Trolle's papers related to his years of government service, 1905–08. Other papers can be found at the *Riksarkiv*, Stockholm.

TRYGGER, Ernst (fl. 1920s–30s)

Swedish Minister of State 1923–24 and Foreign Minister 1928–30.

The Archives of the Swedish Foreign Ministry have a collection of correspondence related to Trygger's period of service as Foreign Minister 1928–30. Further papers can be found at the *Riksarkiv*, Stockholm.

TSCHIRSKY UND BÖGENDORF, Heinrich von (1858–1916)

German diplomat. State Secretary in Foreign Office 1906–07; Ambassador to Vienna 1907–16.

The Political Archive of the Federal German Foreign Office has a collection of his correspondence as State Secretary, particularly with Bernhard von Bülow. (Source: Mommsen, *op. cit.*)

TSOUDEROS, Emmanuel (fl. 1939–45)

Greek statesman. Prime Minister of the Greek Government in Exile during the Second World War.

The Tsouderos papers are in the General State Archives, Athens. The collection is particularly strong on foreign relations 1941–44; on relations with the Greek resistance; and on the post-war political and military situation 1947–49. Access is only rarely granted. There are other papers at the Gennadeion Library, Athens. These are available.

TUCHER VON SIMMELSDORF, Heinrich Freiherr (1853–1925)

Bavarian Ambassador to Vienna 1896–1918.

A substantial collection (6m) of his correspondence is held at the *Stadtarchiv*, Nürnberg. (Source: Mommsen, *op. cit.*)

TUKHOLKA, S. (fl. 1890s–1900s)

Russian diplomat.

The Bakhmeteff Archive has a typescript entitled *Ancient Turkey; Memoirs of a Russian Consul General* and six typescript essays on the Russian diplomatic service in the Balkans after 1890.

TURAUSKAS, Eduardas (fl. 1934–58)

Lithuanian diplomat and journalist.

A collection of his papers is held at the Hoover Institution, Stanford University, California. There are nine boxes of material covering the period 1934–58.

TWARDOWSKI, Friedrich von (1890–1970)

German diplomat. Embassy counsellor, Moscow 1929–35; in Foreign Office 1935–43; Consul-General, Istanbul 1943–45; Ambassador, Mexico 1952–56.

The Political Archive of the Federal German Foreign Office has a small collection of his papers relating to the peace initiative of the Pope in 1917 and the internment of Germans in Turkey at the end of the Second World War. (Source: Mommsen, *op. cit.*)

U

UGHET, Sergei (fl. 1900–33)

Russian diplomat. Financial Attaché, Washington embassy.

An extensive collection of his papers is held at the Hoover Institution, Stanford University, California. There are fifty boxes of material covering the period 1900–33.

UNDÉN, Bo Östen (fl. 1920s–60s)

Swedish Foreign Minister 1924–26 and 1945–62.

There is a collection of Undén's papers at the Royal Library, Stockholm.

UNDÉN, Torsten (fl. 1914–18)

Swedish diplomat and Consul-General in Hamburg and the United States.

The Archives of the Swedish Foreign Ministry have two volumes of correspondence from the years 1914–18 and a manuscript copy of his autobiography, *'Minnen och meningar'* written between 1943 and 1951.

URUSOV, Prince Lev Pavlovič (fl. 1900s)

Russian diplomat. Ambassador or diplomat in Paris, Rome, Vienna and Romania.

His papers are at the Bakhmeteff Archive, Columbia University, New York, in the collection under the name of his son, Aleksandr L'vovič Urusov. The collection also includes the latter's own papers and notes of the Budapest Consul-General A. L'vov about Hungary and the events of 1905.

V

VALTERS, Mikelis (b. 1874)

Latvian diplomat and politician. Deputy Premier. Successively Ambassador to Italy, Poland and Belgium.

A small collection of papers for the period 1923–40 is in the Hoover Institution, Stanford University, California. It includes reports to Janis Balodis, Minister of War 1938–40, and minutes of the Riga meetings of Latvian envoys abroad in 1923 and 1935.

VÁMBÉRY, Arminius (1832–1913)

Turkish scholar and journalist. Professor, University of Budapest. Reported on Turkish affairs, secretly, to the British Government.

His papers, covering the period 1889 to 1911 are in the Public Record Office, London (ref. FO 800/3233).

VÁMBÉRY, Rusztem (1872–1948)

Hungarian politician. Ambassador to Washington 1946–48.

Nine boxes of his papers, relating to Hungarian domestic politics and foreign policy, were purchased by the Hoover Institution, Stanford University, California, from Robert Vámbéry in 1975. There are restrictions on access.

VANDEN HEUVEL, Jules (1854–1926)

Belgian Catholic politician. Minister of Justice 1899–1907. Belgian Ambassador to the Vatican 1914–18. Representative at the peace conferences 1919–20.

The *Archives Générales du Royaume*, Brussels, has Vanden Heuvel's archive 1884–1925, containing notes and documents on Belgian foreign policy; the Congo; occupied Belgium; the Vatican in the First World War; and the peace conferences; it includes correspondence with, among others, Carton de Wiart, Davignon, de Favereau, Cardinal Mercier, P. Poullet and Jules Renkin. The *Archief en Museum voor het Vlaamse Cultuurleven*, Antwerp, has a collection pertaining to Vanden Heuvel (H.5911) which includes letters and documents. The extent and nature of the collection is not known. Permission is needed for consultation.

VAN DER ELST, Baron Léon (1856–1933)

Belgian civil servant and diplomat. Jules de Burlet's *chef de cabinet* at the Ministry of the Interior 1889–95, then followed him to the Foreign Ministry, becoming Director-General in 1897 and succeeding Lambermont as Secretary-General of Foreign Affairs 1905. Involved in examination of, and negotiations concerning the transfer of the Congo from Leopold II to the

Belgian state; also followed Leopold's enterprises in China, which were a source of occasional conflict between the King and the Foreign Ministry. Adviser to Leopold II and Albert, and especially powerful under Jules Davignon as Foreign Minister. Was also closely identified with the 'moderate' policy of Davignon's successor Baron Beyens, so that when Beyens resigned following a split in the cabinet in 1917, Van der Elst was soon replaced. Appointed Ambassador to Madrid, but resigned 1919.

The *Archives Générales du Royaume*, Brussels, has Van der Elst's papers 1879–1933, among them notes on matters of foreign and colonial policy and considerable correspondence with Leopold II, Albert and many Belgian politicians and diplomats, notably Beyens, Cartier de Marchienne (then Ambassador in Peking) and Vanden Heuvel. They are of particular interest in relation to the Congo, China and the First World War. An inventory has been published: E Vandewoude, *Papiers du Baron Léon Van der Elst* (Brussels: AGR, 1978), 47 pp. The Belgian foreign ministry has his *dossier personnel*.

VANDERVELDE, Emile (1866–1938)

Belgian socialist leader. Joined the Belgian Workers Party in 1889. Influenced by Hector Denis. Member of Parliament 1894. Prominent in the suffrage movement. From 1900 played a leading role in the congresses of the Second International. Visited the Congo before 1907 and, unusually, favoured Belgian national control over it as a means of putting an end to abuses. Minister throughout the 1914–18 War; appointed joint Minister of Defence August 1917 to November 1918. Secured clauses favouring labour 1919–20 (including one advocating eight-hour day) at the Paris Peace Conference. Minister of Foreign Affairs in the Socialist–Catholic coalition government 1925 to 1927; Minister without Portfolio March 1935 to May 1936, Minister of Public Health 1936–37. Resigned over the government's policy of non-intervention in the Spanish civil war.

The *Institut Emile Vandervelde*, Brussels, has what remains of Vandervelde's archive, which is extensive but very incomplete and consists almost entirely of correspondence covering his range of activities as a national and international socialist leader and statesman. The correspondence is mostly from the period between the wars – among others with E. de Gouffin (Ambassador in Paris), Baron Beyens, Berthelot, Briand, Filippo Turati, Ramsay MacDonald, Thomas Masaryk, as well as Hendrik De Man, Spaak and Jaspar. There are also some notes, press cuttings and correspondence on Spain, and dossiers on defence (1927). The Vandervelde collections have been exhaustively itemised in three published inventories by Robert Abs, *Institut Vandervelde Catalogues* II (1969), III (1972) and IV (1974). (See also Robert Flagothier, *Inventaire d'archives inédites d'Emile Vandervelde, 1925–1927*, Fondation Louis de Brouckère, Catalogue no. 4, 1984.) The *Archief en Museum voor het Vlaamse Cultuurleven*, Antwerp, also has a collection on Vandervelde (V.15557), which includes letters and documents. The extent and nature of the collection is not known. Permission is needed for consultation.

VAN EETVELDE, Baron Edmond (1852–1925)

Belgian civil servant in the central administration of the *Etat Indépendant du Congo* (EIC), Brussels. Appointed Administrator-General for Foreign Affairs 1885; made Head of Department of the Interior, EIC, with the rank of secretary of state 1891; appointed head of the Department of Finance. Left the service of the EIC in 1906.

The *Archives Générales du Royaume*, Brussels, has Van Eetvelde's *'archives de cabinet'* – correspondence and dossiers connected with his work 1884–1914, including correspondence with Leopold II, the governors-general and secretaries-general of the Congo, and correspondence between Leopold II and H.M. Stanley (1886). They also include dossiers on the administration, finances and army of the Congo; its commercial exploitation; the missions; relations with other colonial powers; territorial expansion; and the transfer of sovereignty to Belgium. In addition, the *Archief en Museum voor het Vlaamse Cultuurleven*, Antwerp, has a collection on Van Eetvelde (E.165), including letters. The extent and nature of the collection is not known. Permission is needed for consultation.

VAN ZEELAND, Paul (1893–1973)

Belgian politician. Prime Minister 1935–37, and Foreign Minister until May 1936. Foreign Minister again 1949–52. Involved in European reconstruction. Atlanticist.

The *Archives Générales du Royaume* (AGR), Brussels, has Van Zeeland's archive, which has not yet been fully classified. However, parts of it may be accessible by arrangement with the AGR. The *Archief en Museum voor het Vlaamse Cultuurleven*, Antwerp, has a collection on Van Zeeland (Z.209), which includes documents and letters. The extent and nature of the collection is not known. Permission is needed for consultation.

VARNBÜLER VON UND ZU HEMMINGEN, Axel Freiherr (fl. 1894–1918)

German diplomat. Privy counsellor and chargé d'affaires, St Petersburg; Ambassador of Württemberg to Vienna and Berlin, and Wüttemberg plenipotentiary on the Federal Council (*Bundesrat*) 1894–1918.

The *Hauptstaatsarchiv*, Stuttgart has a collection of material relating to his work and some correspondence. (Source: Mommsen, *op. cit.*)

VENIZELOS, Eleutherios (1864–1936)

Greek statesman. Prime Minister 1910–15, 1917–20, 1924, 1928–32 and 1933. Exiled in 1935.

The papers were acquired in 1962 by the Benaki Museum, Athens. The extensive collection includes state papers 1891–1935, with also much material on Crete as well as his private political and diplomatic correspondence.

VENNOLA, Juho Heikki (1872–1938)

Finnish Prime Minister 1919–20 and 1921–22. Foreign Minister 1922–24.

The *Valtionsarkisto*, Helsinki, has an extensive collection of Vennola's papers comprising a total of seventy-nine boxes. These include material on his parliamentary career and his involvement with many government commissions. Access to this collection is restricted.

VERAART, J.A. (1886–1955)

Adviser to the Dutch Government in Exile in London 1940–45.

The *Algemeen Rijksarchief*, The Hague, has a collection of papers (12.2m) covering the period 1919–55. At present there is no inventory (Coll. 207). Other Veraart material can be found at the *Rijksinstituut voor Oorlogsdocumentatie*, Amsterdam.

VERDY DU VERNOIS, Freidrich von (fl. 1873–1949)

German diplomat. Legation counsellor in Stockholm; resident minister in Cuba 1913–17; and Foreign Office representative to the military government of Lithuania 1918.

The Political Archive of the Federal German Foreign Office has a very small collection of his memoirs covering the years 1873–1949. (Source: Mommsen, *op. cit.*)

VIOLLETTE, Maurice (1870–1960)

French radical-socialist politician and public servant. Minister for General Provisioning and Marine Transport 1917; Minister of State 1936–38; Governor General of Algeria 1925–28.

The Departmental Archive of Eure-et-Loire, which Viollette represented as deputy and senator, has fifteen bundles of papers. These include material relating to colonial matters (Congo, New Hebrides, Ivory Coast, Indo-China, Morocco, Wallis and Futuna and Senegal); the First World War; the defence of North Africa; and Shanghai. The collection also contains some letters received by Viollette (ref. J 798–818). The Maison de Maurice Viollette, Dreux, Eure-et-Loire, has personal papers, papers relating to his career – particularly his governorship of Algeria – and the manuscript of his memoirs. (Source: AN, *Guide des Papiers.*)

VIRGIN, Otto Wilhelm (1852–1922)

Swedish Major-General and Secretary of State.

The *Krigsarkiv*, Stockholm, has a small collection of documents on military affairs contained within the Virgin family archive.

VISCONTI VENOSTA, Emilio (1829–1914)

Italian politician. Under-Secretary of State, then Minister for Foreign Affairs under Farini and Minghetti 1863–64; under Ricasoli 1866–67; under Lanza 1869–73; under Minghetti 1873–76; under Rudini 1896–97 and 1897–98; under Pelloux 1899–1900; and under Saracco 1900–01.

The *Archivio Centrale dello Stato*, Rome, has seven files of his papers. These cover the years 1859–1906, and deal mostly with Italian foreign policy during that period. (Source: *Guida Generale.*)

VISOIANU, Constantin (b. 1897)

Romanian Minister of Foreign Affairs 1945–46. President, Romanian National Committee, Washington.

Five boxes of his papers, covering the period 1937–60, were given to the Hoover Institution, Stanford University, California, by him in 1976 and 1977. There are restrictions and closures on the material, which relates to political developments in Romania, Romanian foreign policy and émigré politics.

VISSER, P.H. (1882–1955)

Dutch diplomat who served in Moscow, Ankara, Copenhagen and Pretoria.

There exists a collection of Visser papers in private hands which consists of letters and lectures from 1925 onward. For further details, contact the Central Register of Private Archives, The Hague.

VITETTI, Leonardo (fl. 1920s–40s)

Italian diplomat. Washington embassy 1925–29; delegate to the League of Nations 1931, and Secretary-General of the Italian delegation 1932; delegate to the disarmament conference 1932–33; Director General of the Department of European and Mediterranean affairs 1942–43.

A collection of his papers is held at the Italian Foreign Ministry. (Source: Cassels, *op. cit.*)

VOGELS, Werner (1888–1942)

German public servant. Assistant head of the office of the Reich Commissar for occupied areas of the Rhineland between the wars.

A collection of his papers is held at the German Federal Archive, Koblenz. Covering the years 1918–32, it includes material relating to his responsibility for occupied areas of the Rhineland. (Source: Mommsen, *op. cit.*)

VOIONMAA, Kaarlo Väinö (1869–1947)

Finnish Professor and Foreign Minister 1926–27. Acting Foreign Minister 1938; member of Moscow Peace Treaty Delegation 1940 and 1944.

The *Valtionsarkisto*, Helsinki, has a collection of six boxes of letters sent to Voionmaa, together with other diaries, notes and academic manuscripts from the years 1906 to 1946. A second large collection from *c.* 1910–50 is in the Finnish Labour Archives, Helsinki. This comprises correspondence (both personal and political), manuscripts, printed material (including some from the international temperance movement), and a few photographs. Perhaps the main content of this collection is concerned with his own academic work.

VÖLCKERS, Hans Hermann (1886–1977)

German diplomat. Embassy counsellor, Madrid 1933–37; Ambassador to Cuba 1937–39; Assistant Head of Reich Protector's office in Prague from 1940.

The Political Archive of the Federal German Foreign Office has copies of a few extracts from his papers, which are in private hands. (Source: Mommsen, *op. cit.*)

VOLLENHOVEN, Maurits Willem Raedinck van, heer van Cleverskerke (1882–1976)

Dutch diplomat. Embassy Counsellor in Brussels 1914–17, and then Minister Resident. During the First World War he acted as protector for the import and distribution of goods, in conjunction with the US and Spanish Ministers. Appointed Ambassador to Madrid in 1921.

The *Ministerie van Buitenlandse Zaken*, has a collection of letters, comprising one file, in the J. Loudon archive which covers the years 1914–17. Other letters can be found in the Beerlaerts van Blokland collection.

VOLPI DI MISURATA, Signor (fl. 1920s–40s)

Italian politician and administrator. Governor of Tripolitania 1922–25; Finance Minister 1925–28; head of Italian war debt commissions in London and Washington 1925–26; president of the Italo-Croatian economic commission 1941–43.

A collection of his papers is at the *Archivio Centrale dello Stato*, Rome, and a further collection is at the Italian Foreign Ministry. Other papers are in private hands in Rome and Venice. (Source: Cassels, *op. cit.*)

VREDENBURCH, jhr. dr. C.G.W.F. van (fl. 1930s–60s)

Dutch diplomat and Minister to Belgium.

A van Vredenburch family archive, comprising two files and two boxes, exists in the *Rijksarchief*, Zuid-Holland, and covers the years 1934 to 1981. Other items of van Vredenburch correspondence can be found in thé Beerlaerts van Blokland collection at the *Ministerie van Buitenlandse Zaken*.

W

WAAL, E. de (1821–1905)

Dutch civil servant in Batavia and later Minister for the Colonies.

The *Algemeen Rijksarchief*, The Hague has a collection of de Waal family papers (0.4m) which covers the period 1821–1913 (Inventory 2.21.173: Coll. 211). For other documents, reference should be made to the A.J. Duymaer van Twist archive.

WACHTMEISTER, greve Axel Fredrik Claësson (1855–1919)

Swedish Foreign Minister 1905.

Wachtmeister's papers are still in private hands, but there is a collection of documents related to Wachtmeister's period of office in 1905 at the Archives of the Swedish Foreign Ministry, *Riksarkiv*, Stockholm.

WADDINGTON, William (1826–94)

French politician and diplomat. Foreign Minister 1877–79; Prime Minister and Foreign Minister 1879; Ambassador to London 1883–93.

The Foreign Ministry archive has a collection in thirteen volumes, two boxes and a microfilm. The collection contains material on foreign policy (ref. *Fonds nominatifs*, no. 176). (Source: AN, *Guide des Papiers*.)

WALDECK-ROUSSEAU, Réné (1846–1904)

French politician. Prime Minister 1899–1902.

The Library of the *Institut de France* has sixty-two volumes or files of papers. The collection includes material on the colonial programme and the China expedition (ref. Manuscrits 4560 to 4620). (See Tremblot de la Croix, *Catalogue General*.) (Source: AN, *Guide des Papiers*.)

WALLENBERG, G.O. (fl. 1900s)

Swedish diplomat and envoy.

The Archives of the Swedish Foreign Ministry have a collection of papers related to the years 1905–07.

WALLENBERG, Knut Agathon (fl. 1914–18)

Swedish Foreign Minister 1914–17.

A collection of Wallenberg's papers can be found in the *Riksarkiv*, Stockholm. The Archives of the Swedish Foreign Ministry also have a collection of papers related to his period of service as Foreign Minister 1914–17.

WALLROTH, Erich (b. 1876)

German diplomat. Minister, Riga 1921–23 and Oslo 1928–29.

A collection of his papers is at the Political Archive of the Federal German Foreign Office in Bonn. (Source: Kimmich, *op. cit.*)

WASSILKO, Nikolaj Ritter von (1868–1924)

Austro-Ukrainian politician and diplomat. Born in Czernowitz, in the Austrian province Bukovina; *Reichsrat* and provincial diet deputy; Chairman of the Ukrainian group in the Bukovina diet; Vice-President of the Ukrainian National Assembly; Ambassador of the West Ukrainian Republic. Noted Austro-Hungarian politician, famous for his role in the peace talks and treaty of Brest-Litovsk.

Most of his personal papers were accidentally destroyed, but what remains is at the AVA, Vienna. There are four boxes, which contain material on the Bukovina; on the Ukrainian question; papers relating to the Ukrainian assembly 1915; proposals of the Ukrainian assembly regarding the occupied area of Russia; political information, correspondence and propaganda activity; the proclamation of the Ukrainian Republic; diplomatic papers relating to his term as Ambassador and on relations between the Ukraine and the League of Nations; and a number of miscellaneous items.

WASSMUSS, Wilhelm (1880–1931)

German Consul in Persia.

The Political Archive of the Federal German Foreign Office has a small collection of his papers (0.6m). The material includes diaries 1916–31; correspondence; private papers and correspondence with the Tehran embassy, the Foreign Office, and the Persian authorities. (Source: Mommsen, *op. cit.*)

WECK, René de (1887–1950)

Swiss diplomat and writer. Legation counsellor, Paris, from 1924.

The Canton and University Library, Fribourg, Switzerland, has a collection of his papers (1m).

WEDEL, Botho Graf (1862–1943)

German diplomat. Privy Counsellor in Foreign Office and Ambassador in Vienna 1914–19.

The Political Archive of the Federal German Foreign Office has a packet of his papers covering the years 1914–19. It contains copies of telegrams, reports and other documents from his diplomatic service in Vienna. (Source: Mommsen, *op. cit.*)

WEDEL, Karl Graf von* (fl. 1877–1914)

German diplomat. Military attaché, Vienna 1877–88; Ambassador, Stockholm 1892–94, Rome 1899–1902, Vienna 1903–07; Governor of Alsace-Lorraine 1907–14.

The Political Archive of the Federal German Foreign Office has a very small collection of his papers covering the years 1878–87. It contains correspondence from his time as military attaché in Austria. (Source: Mommsen, *op. cit.*)

*From 1914 Fürst von.

WEEDE, jhr. Mark Willem van (fl. 1939–45)

Dutch diplomat who served in Berlin and Rome before becoming Chief of the Cabinet at the Foreign Affairs Ministry. Later appointed as Envoy Extraordinary and Minister Plenipotentiary to the Vatican in 1944.

The *Ministerie van Buitenlandse Zaken* has one file of correspondence between van Weede and J. Loudon. In addition, the *Rijksarchief*, Utrecht, has a collection of van Weede family papers dating from the end of the nineteenth century, and the *Rijksarchief*, Gelderland, also has some van Weede items in the van Haersma de With family archive.

WEHBERG, Hans (1885–1962)

German internationalist. Director of International Law Department of the German *Liga für Völkerbund*, an organisation supporting the League of Nations. Professor of International Law at Geneva.

The German Federal Archive in Koblenz has a collection of his papers which includes correspondence relating to the German peace movement. (Source: Mommsen, *op. cit.*)

WEINSTEIN, Jan (1903–74)

Polish diplomat and collector.

Some sixty folders of papers constitute the Weinstein collection in the Pilsudski Institute of America, New York. The papers, on permanent deposit, include correspondence, memoirs, copies of documents from other European archives concerning Polish foreign policy 1918–39, and material on the Polish government in exile.

WEIZSÄCKER, Ernst Freiherr von (1882–1951)

German diplomat. Minister in Oslo 1931–33 and Berne 1933–37; Director of the Political Department of the Foreign Office 1936–38; State Secretary 1938–43; Ambassador to the Vatican 1943–45. Defendant at Nuremberg.

His papers are privately owned, but a microfilm copy is available at the German Federal Archive, Koblenz. It contains diaries and notes relating to foreign policy and material on the Wilhelmstrasse trial, and correspondence and other material relating to the Vatican. The Hellmut Becker collection at the Political Archive of the Federal German Foreign Office in Bonn has a collection of material on his Nuremberg trial. See also L.E. Hill, *Die Weizsäcker-Papiere 1933–50*, (Frankfurt/Berlin: 1974).

WEKERLE, Sandor (1848–1921)

Hungarian politician who served as Minister of Finance 1889–95, 1906 and 1917–18. He also held the post of Prime Minister between November 1892 and January 1895, and again between August 1917 and October 1918. His other period in office was as head of the coalition government of 1906–10.

The Hungarian National Archives, Budapest, have a collection of material (0.55m) which relates to the years 1892–94 and 1919.

WELSCH, Heinrich (1888–1976)

German public servant and diplomat. German representative on Supreme Electoral Court for the Saar 1935–36; Chief Public Prosecutor, Metz, responsible for justice in Lorraine 1940–44; Minister-President of the Saarland 1955–56.

The provincial archive in Saarbrücken has a collection of his papers relating to the Saar and Lorraine (0.5m). (Source: Mommsen, *op. cit.*)

WELTER, Charles Joseph Ignace Marie (1880–1972)

Dutch Minister for the Colonies 1925–26 and 1937–40.

The *Algemeen Rijksarchief*, The Hague, has a collection of Welter papers (0.5m) which consists of one packet of memoirs covering the years 1880 to 1973, and papers in three boxes from the years 1925 to 1956 (Inventory 2.21.175: Coll. 195).

WELTI, Emil (1825–99)

Swiss politician. Federal counsellor 1866–91; President of the Confederation 1869, 1872, 1876, 1880. His project for the reorganisation of the military was voted by the Federal Assembly in 1874 and came into force in 1875.

Collections of Welti's papers and correspondence are to be found both in the State Archive of the Canton Aargau, Aarau, and in the Swiss Federal Archive in Berne.

WENNERBERG, Folke Sunesson (1892–1971)

Swedish Captain, diplomat and minister-plenipotentiary.

The *Krigsarkiv*, Stockholm, has a collection of thirty bundles of diverse documents related to Wennerberg and his career.

WERKMEISTER, Karl (b. 1898)

German diplomat. Foreign Office representative to the military commands in the Netherlands, Belgium and northern France during the Second World War; Deputy Director of Central Economic Office in the British Zone after the end of the war; leader of German group on the European Economic Council, Paris 1950–60.

The German Federal Military Archive, Freiburg im Breisgau, has a small collection of documents and correspondence relating mainly to his service in the occupied West during the Second World War. A further collection, containing documents relating to his work with the Central Economic Office of the British Zone is held at the German Federal Archive, Koblenz. (Source: Mommsen, *op. cit.*)

WERTHER, Karl Freiherr von (1809–94)

Prussian diplomat. Ambassador to St Petersburg 1854, Vienna 1859, Paris 1869–70 and Constantinople 1874–77. Son of Heinrich Freiherr von Werther, Prussian Ambassador to Paris 1824–37 and Foreign Minister 1837–41.

Karl von Werther's papers are held at the *Geheimes Staatsarchiv Preuss.-Kulturbesitz*, Berlin. They include reports from Vienna, and a memorandum on his behaviour in Paris 1870. His father's papers are also held at the *Geheimes Staatsarchiv*. (Source: Mommsen, *op. cit.*)

WESTMAN, Claës Gustaf (1878–1932)

Swedish Cabinet Secretary 1917, statesman and diplomat.

There is a collection of Westman's papers at the University Library, Uppsala. This includes an extensive amount of correspondence with Swedish and foreign personalities and institutions. There are also twenty-two other files related to various international matters including conferences, Anglo-Swedish relations 1915–17 and Swedish diplomatic relations 1910–30. The material also covers his period of service as Legation Secretary in Kristiania 1909–13 and as Swedish Minister in Helsingfors 1918–21, as well as personal papers, newspaper cuttings and biographical material.

WESTMAN, Karl Gustaf (1876–1944)

Swedish Foreign Minister 1936, diplomat and statesman.

The University Library, Uppsala, has a collection of Westman's papers which includes six files related to Anglo-Swedish relations 1915–17; documents on Aland and Finland 1915–39; diplomatic questions 1915–43 and relations with Germany. In addition there is other biographical and family material. The Archives of the Swedish Foreign Ministry have a collection of his official correspondence for the years 1936–38 and his diaries have been published.

WESTMAN, Karl Ivan (fl. 1925–47)

Head of the Political Section of the Swedish Foreign Ministry 1925–28 and Secretary to the Cabinet 1945–47.

There is a collection of Westman's papers at the *Riksarkiv*, Stockholm, and also at the Archives of the Swedish Foreign Ministry for the years 1945–47.

WETTERHOFF, Adolf Fredrik (1878–1922)

Finnish jurist responsible for obtaining German support for an independent Finland during the First World War.

The *Valtionsarkisto*, Helsinki, has a collection of papers consisting of two boxes containing documents, letters and diaries from the years 1915–22 together with material on infantry manoeuvres. Access to this collection is restricted. Further papers may be found in the Military Archives, Helsinki.

WEYGAND, Maxime (1867–1965)

French General. Defence Minister, June to September 1940.

The *Service Historique de l'Armée de Terre*, Vincennes, has thirteen boxes of papers, including material relating to Marshal Foch, the latter's correspondence, and Weygand's mission to Poland (ref. 1 K 130). The *Service Historique* also has twenty-eight dossiers of unclassified material, including documents relating to Foch's career, the peace treaty of 1919, Poland in 1920, operations in the Eastern Mediterranean 1939–40, the battle of June 1940, North Africa 1940–41, and the Supreme War Council 1932–35. The collection also includes correspondence, memoirs, and sixteen note-books containing notes taken between 1915 and 1942. (Source: AN, *Guide des Papiers*.)

WIEDEMANN, Fritz (b. 1891)

German 'adjutant to the Führer'; Consul General.

The Hoover Institution, Stanford University, California, has two files on his work as Hitler's adjutant. The Library of Congress, Washington, has a collection of documents, including papers relating to a mission to London in 1938. (Source: Mommsen, *op. cit.*)

WIEHL, Emil Karl Josef (b. 1886)

German diplomat. Consul General 1933–34 and Minister 1933–37, Pretoria. Director of Commercial Department of the German Foreign Office 1937–44.

A collection of his papers is at the Political Archive of the Federal German Foreign Office in Bonn. (Source: Kimmich, *op. cit.*)

WIJCK, jhr. C.H.A. van der (1840–1914)

Dutch Governor-General of the Netherlands Indies.

The *Algemeen Rijksarchief*, The Hague, has a small collection of papers (0.1m) covering the period 1842–99 (Summary Inventory 2.21.183: Coll. 318).

WIMPFFEN, Felix Graf (1827–82)

Austrian diplomat. Legation Secretary, Naples 1854–59; Legation Counsellor, London 1859–66; Ambassador, Copenhagen 1866; Political Commissar, Verona 1866; Ambassador, Berlin 1866–71, Rome 1871–76, Paris 1876–78, Rome 1880–82. One of the most important diplomats of the Francis-Joseph period.

There are three collections of Wimpffen's papers. The first, in the *Haus-, Hof- und Staatsarchiv*, Vienna, contains correspondence with Roger, Freiherr von Aldenburg between 1861 and 1863, and with Lord Russell in 1862 and 1863; it also contains drafts of Wimpffen's letters from London to Mennsdorf-Pouilly in 1865, from Berlin to Beust, and from Rome and Turin to Andrássy (1872–74). The second collection is in the War Archive, also in Vienna; and the third is in private ownership, at the Wimpffen family home, Schloss Krainberg, near Graz, Styria.

WITTE, Sergei Yul'evič (1849–1915)

Russian politician. Prime Minister 1905–06. Head of Russian delegation to the Portsmouth Peace Conference 1905.

Thirteen boxes of his papers are at the Bakhmeteff Archive, Columbia University, New York, and consist mainly of the original typescripts of Witte's memoirs (now published), and his correspondence. There are also essays, including a two volume work on the origins of the Russo-Japanese war; his direct reports to the Tsar as Prime Minister; telegrams and diplomatic correspondence 1905; letters of Prince Nicholas of Herzegovina; reports on the Finnish Question; material on relations with Kaiser Wilhelm II and negotiations for a commercial treaty with Germany; and documents on the taking of Port Arthur.

WODAK, Walter (fl. 1940s–50s)

Austrian social democrat and diplomat.

Nineteen boxes of his papers are at the *Haus-, Hof- und Staatsarchiv*, Vienna. The collection includes a variety of material relating to his emigration in London and the London Bureau of Austrian Socialists; a file entitled 'Allied Commission Papers/British Element', including memoranda to the British section of the Allied Council; papers relating to Renner's control commission and the Renner administration; political papers and memoranda from his diplomatic career after the war, including memoranda on British foreign policy; the Austrian state treaty of 1955; Yugoslav-Soviet relations 1959; foreign aid; economic cooperation with Hungary, Poland, India and Indonesia; embassy reports to the Foreign Ministry; copies of telegrams concerning the negotiations over the South Tyrol in the United Nations, and material on the EEC and its relations with Austria. There is a great deal of correspondence, and Wodak's correspondents included Friedrich Adler, Renner, Adolf Schärf, Figl, Kreisky, Oskar Pollack, Waldheim, Raab, Gratz, Klenner, Androsch, Leichter, and Kirchschläger. The DÖW, Vienna, has a collection of papers from Wodak's emigration, including correspondence, memoranda, protocols and resolutions, relating to the London Bureau.

WOERMANN, Ernst (b. 1888)

German diplomat. He occupied various minor diplomatic postings and positions in the German Foreign Office between 1928 and 1938, when he became Director of the Political Department 1938–43. Ambassador, Nanking 1943–45.

A collection of his papers is at the Political Archive of the Federal German Foreign Office in Bonn.

WOLFF METTERNICH ZUR GRACHT, Paul Graf (1853–1934)

German Ambassador in London.

Some of his papers are in private hands, others are at the *Deutsches Zentralarchiv* in Potsdam. (Source: Mommsen, *op. cit.*)

WRANGEL, Greve Anton Magnus Herman (fl. 1920s)

Swedish Foreign Minister 1920–21 and diplomat.

The Archives of the Swedish Foreign Ministry have a collection of three volumes of his official correspondence 1914–21 and a further collection can be found in the *Riksarkiv*, Stockholm.

WSZELAKI, Jan (b. 1894)

Polish diplomat. Specialist in Anglo-American affairs and representative of the Polish Government in Exile to the USA 1948–50.

The Sikorski Museum Archive at the Polish Institute, London, has a small collection (0.8m) of his papers covering the years 1940–65. It includes notes and political correspondence with the Polish government 1940–49; diplomatic correspondence 1948–50; correspondence with the Polish embassies in the Vatican 1940–42, and Washington 1940–43; notes of cabinet meetings, October 1939; documents relating to the Polish eastern frontier and Central Europe 1941–50 and correspondence. (Source: Milewski *et al.* (eds) *op. cit.*)

WUORI, Eero Aarre (1900–66)

Finnish politician and diplomat.

The *Valtionsarkisto*, Helsinki, has a collection of fifteen boxes of documents and other printed matter largely related to Wuori's diplomatic service between 1944 and 1946. Access to this collection is restricted. Other material is to be found in the *Ammattiyhdistysarkistossa*, Helsinki.

WYSOCKI, Alfred (fl. 1930s)

Polish diplomat. Ambassador to Berlin 1931–33. Ambassador to Rome 1933–38.

His Polish typescript memoirs are in the Ossolineum Library, Wrocław.

Y

YLÖNEN, Kaarlo (1878–1955)

Finnish State Counsellor.

The *Valtionsarkisto*, Helsinki, has five boxes of papers related to Ylönen's work as an archivist with the State Secretariat, and to his work as a delegate to the commission on archival matters between Finland and the Soviet Union from 1924 to 1929. The collection also includes some of his academic work.

YRJÖ-KOSKINEN, Aarno Armas Sakari (fl. 1922–51)

Finnish politician, diplomat and statesman.

The *Valtionsarkisto*, Helsinki, has twenty-one boxes of documents and diaries related to Yrjö-Koskinen's career as a diplomat from 1922 to 1951.

Z

ZAHLE, Carl Theodor (1866–1946)

Danish Prime Minister 1909–10 and 1913–20.

A collection of his papers comprising three volumes and twenty-one packets is held at the *Rigsarkiv*, Copenhagen. It covers the years 1872–1946 and includes letters, personal papers, diary notes, manuscripts and political papers (ref. 6545).

ZECH, Julius, Graf von (1885–1945)

German Ambassador in Helsinki and The Hague.

His papers are at the *Deutsches Zentralarchiv*, Potsdam. (Source: Mommsen, *op. cit.*)

ZECHLIN, Erich (1883–1954)

German diplomat. Consul-General, Leningrad 1928–33; Ambassador, Kovno, Lithuania 1933–41; Ambassador, Helsinki 1941–44.

The Political Archive of the Federal German Foreign Office has a very small collection (0.25m) of his papers covering the years 1943–45. It includes notes, documents, reports, and correspondence relating to eastern Europe 1914–45. (Source: Mommsen, *op. cit.*)

ZECHLIN, Walter (1879–1962)

German diplomat. Foreign Office 1924–32; Ambassador to Mexico 1932–33; attached to Madrid Embassy during the Second World War.

The Political Archive of the Federal German Foreign Office has a small collection of his papers (0.4m). It includes notes, correspondence, lecture manuscripts, and personal papers. (Source: Mommsen, *op. cit.*)

ZEITSCHEL, C.T. (fl. 1939–45)

Adviser at the German embassy in Paris *c.* 1941.

A collection of his papers is held at the *Centre de documentation juive contemporaine*, Paris. (Source: Mommsen, *op. cit.*)

ZELIGOWSKI, Lucjan (fl. 1920s)

Polish general.

Some papers are at the Pilsudski Institute of America Library, New York. The collection comprises records of the commission, of which Zeligowski was chairman, which investigated the coup led by Pilsudski in 1926. Certain records (*c.* 120 items, 1920–22) of Alexander Prystor are also at the Pilsudski Institute of America Library. The collection comprises reports of all departments of a government comprised of Wilno and the surrounding Lithuanian territory, established and headed by Zeligowski. It includes documents concerning Polish-Byelorussian and Polish-Ukrainian relations; and posters relating to the Polish Diet elections (1922).

ZIMMER, Max (b. 1872)

German diplomat in Constantinople.

The *Deutsches Zentralarchiv*, Potsdam, has three files and three envelopes containing political reports from Asia Minor, memoirs, lectures and personal correspondence. (Source: Mommsen, *op. cit.*)

ZOELCH, Josef (1893–1935)

German public servant in the Foreign Office 1929–33. Diplomat in Tehran 1933–35.

The Political Archive of the Federal German Foreign Office has a collection of his papers, including correspondence, covering the years 1932–35. (Source: Mommsen, *op. cit.*)

ZUYLEN van NIJVELT, Julius Philip Jacob Adriaan, Graaf van (1819–94)

Dutch Minister for Foreign Affairs and Ambassador to Belgium, Britain, Turkey, Prussia, Russia, and Austria.

The *Algemeen Rijksarchief*, The Hague, has an extensive collection of van Zuylen van Nijvelt papers (12m) covering the years 1352 to 1945 (Inventories 2.21.05, 2.21.179–181: Colls. 26, 102, 105, 109, 110, 191 and 262).

APPENDIX

Select Bibliographical Note

Alsberg, P. A. *A Guide to the State Archives in Israel* (1973).

Bauer, George W. *International Organisations 1918–1945* (Wilmington, Delaware, 1981).

Bittner, L. *Das Gesamtinventar des Haus-, Hof-, und Staatsarchiv*, 5 vols (Vienna, 1936–1940).

Boijen, Richard and Paridaens, Anne-Marie. *Aperçu des fonds d'archives du musée royal de l'armée, Liste des inventaires disponibles* (Brussels, 1980).

Cassels, A. *Italian Foreign Policy 1918–1945* (Wilmington, Delaware, 1981).

Grant, S. A. and Brown, J. H. *The Russian Empire and the Soviet Union: A Guide to Manuscripts and Archival Materials in the United States* (Boston, Mass., 1981).

Haegendorn, M. van. *Les archives générales du Royaume à Bruxelles, Aperçu des fonds et des inventaires* (Brussels, 1955).

Kimmich, Christopher, M. *German Foreign Policy 1918–1945* (Wilmington, Delaware, 1981).

Milewski, Waclaw, Suchcitz, Andrzej and Gorcyzcki, Andrzej (eds) *Guide to the Archives of the Polish Institute and Sikorski Museum* (London, 1985).

Mommsen, Wolfgang A. *Die Nachlässe in den deutschen Archiven (mit Ergänzungen aus anderen Beständen) Teil I* (Boppard am Rhein, 1971), *Teil II* (Boppard am Rhein, 1983).

Oberleitner, Wolfgang E. *Politisches Handbuch Österreichs 1945–1980* (Vienna [österr, Bundesverlag], 1981).

Palm, Charles and Reed, Dale. *Guide to the Hoover Institution Archives, Stanford, California* (Hoover Institution Press, 1980).

Schmutz-Pfister, *Repertorium der handschriftlichen Nachlässe in den Bibliotheken und Archiven der schweiz/Répertoire des fonds manuscrits conservées dans les bibliothèques et archives de la Suisse/Repertorio sommario dei fondi manoscritti nelle biblioteche e negli archive della Svizzera* (Berne, 1967); *Zuwachsliste/liste complémentaire/lista complementare, 1968–1978* (Berne, 1980).

Swietochowski, Tadeusz, *Guide to the Collections of the Pilsudski Institute of America*.

Toustier Bonazzi, Chantal de, and Pourcelet, François (eds) *Guides des Papiers des Ministres et secrétaires d'état de 1871 à 1974* (Paris, 1978).

Vandewoude, Emile, *Inventaire des archives relatives au développement extérieur de la Belgique sous la règne de Léopold II* (Archives générales du Royaume, Brussels, 1965).

Young, Robert J. *French Foreign Policy 1918–1945* (Wilmington, Delaware, 1981).